Ian Fleming

A Personal Memoir
of the Man Who
Created James Bond

Robert Harling

Biteback Publishing

This paperback edition published in Great Britain in 2020 by
Biteback Publishing Ltd
Westminster Tower
3 Albert Embankment
London SE1 7SP
Copyright © Robert Harling 2015, 2020

ISBN is 978-1-78590-547-6

10 9 8 7 6 5 4 3 2 1

A CIP catalogue record for this book is available from the British Library.

Set in Fournier MT Std

Printed and bound in Great Britain by
CPI Group (UK) Ltd, Croydon CR0 4YY

CONTENTS

ACKNOWLEDGEMENTS

As a family, we would like to express our gratitude to literary agent Jonathan Conway for his unremitting and, as Robert would say, 'zestful' commitment to the project, and for steering the manuscript towards the Robson Press. Jeremy Robson's enthusiasm has been boundless, as has Melissa Bond's patience and expertise throughout the editing process.

War artist John Worsley's (1919–2000) pen and ink drawings were originally commissioned by Robert Harling for *Amateur Sailor* and *The Steep Atlantick Stream*, his wartime account of life as an RNVR officer on corvettes escorting the North Atlantic convoys. More examples of Worsley's drawings and paintings are held by the Imperial War Museum.

The writing of these memoirs occupied Robert Harling during the years following, at the age of eighty-three, his reluctant retirement from editing *House & Garden*. It could have been a difficult period – time on his hands, and the fact that his home had been burgled on three successive occasions in as many weeks, with the loss of many of the items he had collected over the years – but he was philosophical, saying that, having seen men drown, possessions were irrelevant. What was important was life. Once the house was rearranged to his satisfaction, he immediately got to work on the manuscript, recording his friendship with Ian Fleming. An intermittent diary he'd written during the war no doubt proved useful, as did the journal he kept during the Condé Nast years.

He wrote the first draft in longhand, and, after each successive draft was re-typed, he would go through, changing a sentence or two here, a paragraph there – literally cutting and pasting as he went. As a typographical designer trained long before computers were introduced, he was handy with scissors and Cow gum. The manuscript remained a work in progress until he died. We feel sure that Robert would have been as thrilled as we are to see the final draft published.

Nicholas, Simon and Amanda Harling
September 2015

ROBERT HARLING,
MAN OF MYSTERY

Who was Robert Harling? The author of this wonderfully candid memoir of his great friend Ian Fleming was well known in his day as a typographer and type designer, architectural critic, advertising executive and a notably long-serving editor of *House & Garden* back in the great era of the glossy magazines. Harling, a handsome and rather raffish character, who stalked around Mayfair in a black fedora, was a key figure in mid-twentieth-century graphic design. He makes an appearance in *The Spy Who Loved Me* as the expert compositor on the *Chelsea Clarion*. There are elements of Harling that are clearly recognisable in Fleming's creation of the character of Bond. Through two decades of close male camaraderie, which started in wartime naval intelligence, Harling and Fleming shared a multitude of esoteric interests, including an intrepid fascination with sex.

Harling was a master of obfuscation. No one knew where he had come from. He romanticised his past. So much so that even I – a friend of his for forty years, veteran of countless intimate lunches at the Causerie in Claridge's (Robert's favourite place for entertaining female friends) – swallowed the tale he told about his parents dying young and Robert, as a boy, being brought up in Brighton by a family friend, whose husband was a dairyman. This was the account he gave in his semi-autobiographical novel *Amateur Sailor*, published (typically) under a pseudonym, Nicholas Drew.

It only emerged later, after Robert's death in 2008 at the age of ninety-eight, when I came to write his entry for the *Oxford Dictionary of National Biography*, that both his parents had survived until well into their seventies. His father had been a taxi driver living in north London. This was where the young 'Robbie' was brought up and went to school. He had also drawn a veil over the fact of his first marriage to a young drapery saleswoman named Mary Adelaide. Harling later became an accomplished thriller writer, but his towering achievement was to fictionalise himself.

When Harling first met Fleming in late summer 1939, just before the outbreak of the Second World War, he was already well established both as a designer and a typographic entrepreneur. With his friend James Shand, Harling conceived and published an innovative specialist graphics magazine. Instead of simply covering conventional fine printing, *Typography* included lettering on every level. The first issues, for instance, featured Kardomah tea labels; the second contained an analysis of train ticket typography. Harling's eclectic tastes in typographical ephemera anticipated 1960s pop culture in a fascinating way.

Typography formed an immediate bond between the two men, when it emerged that Ian Fleming had subscribed to the magazine right from the beginning. Fleming was, by then, already working surreptitiously in naval intelligence. He had been impressed by Harling's 'News-Reel Maps' for the *News Chronicle*, a series of data maps and captions containing information for the general public on likely

German invasion points in the coming war. Fleming recruited Robert to redesign the admiralty's then lamentably dowdy *Weekly Intelligence Report* over the first of what developed into a long series of convivial and confidential male-to-male lunch meetings, first at Scott's and later on at the Etoile.

What I love about this memoir is the vivid sense it gives us of the burgeoning friendship between two witty, clever, sophisticated men, very different in background: Fleming, with his establishment values derived from Eton, Sandhurst, the City and the admiralty; Harling, working-class in origin, a self-invented man of charm, ambition and professional finesse. The two men shared a certain inner loneliness. War suited both of them. They both had a taste for action, an almost boyish longing for adventure and escapade.

Harling, always a keen sailor, had volunteered for the navy in the early days of war. In May 1940, in charge of a whaler, he took part in the evacuation of Dunkirk. Promoted to a sub-lieutenant, he then became the navigator of a Corvette, on convoy duty in the Western Approaches. In 1941, conscious of his special talents, Fleming extracted Robert from the navy, recruiting him to work in the Inter-Services Topographical Division (ISTD). This department interacted closely with intelligence in collecting information on ports, beaches and other potential enemy targets. It was something of a cloak-and-dagger operation.

Harling's far-flung foreign forays, travelling under cover, often to exotic places, gave scope for unlimited sexual liaisons. One of these was with Andrée, Parisienne mistress of a 'Turkish bigwig', encountered, Harling tells us, through eye-to-eye contact in an Istanbul café. Harling's ISTD travels and diversions, reported back to Fleming in such novelistic detail, have obvious parallels in Fleming's fictional James Bond. Remember, it was Harling to whom Fleming first confided, over a wartime picnic of Calvados and rations in 1944, his intention to write 'the spy novel to end all spy novels'. James Bond bears a distinct resemblance to Robert in his sardonic elegance of manner and his cool sexual expertise.

Robert talked of Fleming often, with affection and admiration. But, more than I had realised, Fleming played an increasingly influential role in Harling's professional career. After ISTD, Fleming summoned him to join 30 Assault Unit (30AU), the outfit referred to by Robert as 'Fleming's Secret Navy', formed to operate on the front line at the end of the war to capture German codebooks, wireless equipment and security documents before these could be destroyed by the retreating enemy. Harling became the unit's expert on mines and minefields.

It was also Ian Fleming who used his influence as foreign manager of the *Sunday Times* to get Robert appointed typographical consultant to the paper – a weekend job he doted on, adoring the dramas of the ever-changing Saturday night front pages. The journalistic world of power politics enthralled him, and Robert's Fleet Street thriller, *The Paper Palace* (published in 1951), is the best of all his fiction, chillingly observant of the journalistic mores of the time.

Another Fleming introduction brought Harling to *House & Garden*, the Condé Nast magazine based in Vogue House, which he ruled as a wonderfully autocratic editor from 1957 until 1993. It was here, as his so-called merchandise editor in the 1960s, that I first got to know Robert, who ran his small staff of mini-skirted young assistants like an amiable harem, extracting us one by one for lunch or coffee and a rundown on our sex lives. He never got the hang of feminism.

Reading this memoir brings Robert Harling back to me in his gloriously risqué, idiosyncratic wit. Whether the subject of discussion is gussetless knickers (a favourite of Harling's) or sadomasochistic sex (Fleming seems to have liked it, Harling certainly does not), their recreated dialogue discussions, as Harling recollects them, are immensely entertaining. But more valuable still is Harling's view of Fleming as the 'deeply ingrained melancholic', who never quite recovered from the death of his glamorous, devoted (although endlessly put-upon), chestnut-blonde girlfriend Muriel Wright. Muriel – Wren despatch-rider, crack polo-player, James Bond girl personified – was killed in one of the final doodlebug raids on London by a bomb descending on her elegant mews house.

Harling shows all his novelist's acumen in his account of Ian Fleming's eventual marriage to 'Annie', the socialite ex-wife of Lord Rothermere. He watches with dismay and a growing fascination 'the gradual dissolution of their early passion into their tragically querulous relationship'. Fleming's miseries stand in stark contrast to Harling's own demonstrably happy marriage to Phoebe Konstam, a well-known Harley Street psychiatrist's assistant, whom he spotted in Regent Street and later on accosted with his usual sexual aplomb in Leicester Square.

Phoebe was a beautiful woman with a penchant for gold shoes. They lived in an exquisite eighteenth-century Gothic house in Surrey, hung with paintings by Eric Ravilious and Edward Bawden – Robert Harling's friends. The Harlings had three children, Nicholas, Simon and Amanda, all of whom became writers. Robert carried on 'scribbling', as he liked to call it, into his great old age.

This memoir of Ian Fleming, Harling's last substantial work, throws new light on the creator of 007, but I think it reveals just as much of Robert Harling himself – that debonair and dashing, multi-talented, enchanting and extremely private man.

CHAPTER I

WEEKLY INTELLIGENCE REPORT

I first met Ian Lancaster Fleming a month or so before the outbreak of the Second World War. I was a guest at a publisher's scrum masquerading as a book launch party in Bedford Square, doubtless one of the last of those publicity-prodding ventures before Hitler vanquished their viability.

A brief and seemingly carefree introduction by bibliographer John Carter implied that Fleming and I shared interests in typography and bibliography, and should become acquainted. Fleming was about 6ft tall, of athletic build with strong features, dark-haired and conventionally attired in a dark blue double-breasted suit.

Carter then left us to our own exchanges, which soon established that his implications had been well founded: Fleming, a book collector – of a somewhat dilettante order, as I learned later – and myself, a graphic designer and typographer on behalf of book, magazine and newspaper publishers, printers and others. The encounter seemed to sponsor immediate mutual interest and we were soon well away, talking much the same lingo within our first ten minutes.

Inevitably, we began to discuss the monograph written jointly by Carter and another eminent bibliographer Graham Pollard concerning a group of literary forgeries by a would-be literary scholar. The publication had prompted quite a flutter of esoteric fame for the authors among book collectors, scholars and dealers. We were both clearly admirers of the work. 'A superb piece of detective work,' Fleming opined, following my comment that the title of the slim volume – *An Enquiry into the Nature of Certain Nineteenth-Century Pamphlets* – was the most covetable title I had come across in recent years. Fleming admitted sharing my view, adding, smiling: 'But you scarcely seem to practise these titular extravaganzas yourself. I've been a subscriber to your magazine with its singular title from its very first number.'

I admitted that he had a point. *Typography* was the simple but comprehensive title of a somewhat spasmodic quarterly I edited, having co-founded its publication three years previously with James Shand, owner of the Shenval Press. As printers of the experimental, expensively produced journal, we were concerned exclusively with recondite typographical matters – from early type designers to modern newspaper presentation. Eight issues had been published at 2 shillings a copy. War was to end publication. Occasionally, I see sets listed at vastly enhanced prices in catalogues of rare books: I recently noticed a set on offer by an East Anglian bookseller for well over £100.

In the course of our ensuing conversation, Fleming confessed that he had asked Carter to set up the evening's introduction, as he had been considering asking my advice on what he thought might prove an unusual typographical task. And certainly unprofitable, he added. His Majesty's Government would doubtless prove, as usual, a miserly paymaster. Intrigued, I said I would be interested, despite the bureaucratic shortcomings.

A few days later, Fleming telephoned and suggested meeting. We agreed on lunching at Scott's, then in Coventry Street, overlooking Haymarket, apparently a long-favoured base for both of us. We duly met. He seemed somewhat surprised when I opted for mineral water to match his choice of a somewhat stronger concoction; I was also somewhat surprised by his relentless cigarette-smoking. My zest for playing squash and sailing had kept me a confirmed non-smoker. Happily, however, we agreed on the virtues of grilled plaice, a speciality of the house.

After opening generalities, Fleming outlined his typographical request: unusual but simple. Would I be willing to make suggestions for improving the presentation of an admiralty journal that had come his way? He thought I would find the task interesting, but, he repeated, formidably unremunerative.

On my ready acceptance of the task, he said he would ask Charles Morgan – the theatrical critic and playwright, who, by some remote circumstance, was also involved in the publication – to give me a call. Understandably, I queried the nature of the eminent critic's involvement in these naval matters.

'Well, he was a Dartmouth type once upon a time – in what we call the Great War, although I think a greater may be on the way. He slips into the admiralty from time to time as a kind of communications mandarin – and probably to keep in touch with one or two of his long-ago naval contemporaries. He also takes a keen interest in the journal I've just mentioned.'

'A journal with a covetable title, no doubt.'

'Highly doubtful. The *Weekly Intelligence Report*, more generally known as the *WIR*. Morgan will bring a copy.'

I was curious to meet the critic, reputedly one of the most affectedly mannered Fleet Street practitioners, and certainly one of the most influential commentators on the worth or otherwise of new plays. I was also even more curious about Fleming's own connection with the admiralty and casually sought enlightenment. After all, he was again sporting a dark blue suit, this time single-breasted, far removed from naval provenance.

'Oh, I also slip into the admiralty from time to time,' he said smoothly, as if this were a daily stint for most Londoners.

'I see,' I said, seeing nothing at all.

We then returned to our respective interests in the publishing world. His own were perhaps somewhat odd, he admitted, for he was far more concerned with book collecting than book design. Indeed, he had commissioned Percy Muir, the eminent bookseller and bibliographer – a mutual friend, we discovered – to collect what he jocularly termed – although not in public, he hastened to add – 'milestones of original thought'.

'Starting with what or with whom? Genesis?'

'Not quite that far back,' he said, grinning. 'Mainly first editions. Darwin's *Origin of Species*, which Muir got for a tenner; Lenin's 'Communist Manifesto', which cost a good deal more; Einstein's *Relativity*. That kind of thing.'

'That kind of thing,' I repeated dimly, as if we had been discussing a somewhat esoteric story in the front page of that morning's copy of *The Times*.

He grinned. 'And your own?'

'Designing anything that needs to be printed: from tea labels to timetables; from dust wrappers to maps concerning the coming war – these, rather a recent venture.'

He was, suddenly, quite clearly interested: 'Maps for whom or what?'

I mentioned these recent additions to my graphic endeavours: so-called 'News-Reel Maps' for the *News Chronicle*. The maps also carried panelled captions – for which I was also responsible – listing details of population, industrial output, military strength and/or weakness in those areas susceptible to likely German and/or Italian expansion. 'Simple data maps for the coming war. Made-to-measure info for the newspaper public,' I concluded.

He nodded. He'd seen them. Was I also responsible for those other regular and up-to-the minute maps and captions in the *News Chronicle*: the so-called 'Strategy Tests'? They seemed to be by the same hand.

'The very same,' I agreed.

4

'Quite unusual and imaginative journalistic innovations,' Fleming declared, continuing: Did I see much of Gerald Barry?

Occasionally, I said, but I dealt mainly with Philip Jordan, the foreign editor, or with Paul Reilly, features editor. I had, however, begun to see the editor during recent weeks. 'Strategy Tests' had aroused a good deal of interest among readers, prompting numerous letters and suggestions. More space was now being given to the maps and texts. Occasionally they were even featured on the leader page.

How did I get and check my facts?

'The London Library, mainly. Or the press offices of the various embassies. Or the *News Chronicle*'s own library people. All very helpful. Most knowledgeable characters when the subject is the coming war.'

Fleming nodded and confessed himself an avid reader of newspapers. He was amused to learn that I was both cartographer and captioneer, and interested to learn that I was also discussing with Gerald Barry the possibility of a fresh typographical design for the paper. This item of news seemed of particular interest to Fleming.

'Interesting,' he mused. 'Any major interests outside typography?'

'Not many. Historic smaller houses, skipping most of the stately homes. Winter sailing, racing a national 12-footer with the Ranelagh Club at weekends on the Thames; crewing in various off-shore races in the summer. Plus a lively interest in the opposite sex. Not necessarily in that order, of course,' I concluded.

And his own? He grinned and obliged. 'Golf. Bridge. Dining out. And, yes,' he added, 'I also share your third choice. Also not in that order.'

Our main interests thus established, we drifted back to newspapers. I gathered that he occasionally played bridge with Lord Kemsley, owner of the *Sunday Times*. Hence, no doubt, his interest in all aspects of my *News Chronicle* connection. And, along with Sefton Delmer of the *Daily Express*, he had covered for Reuters the fairly recent trial in Moscow of the Vickers engineers accused of spying. Currently, however, he was spending a good deal of his time at the admiralty.

Although still curious, I forbore to probe deeper.

Our meal proved to be a lengthy and pleasurable indulgence with exchanges of views, prejudices and so forth. We seemed to have a good deal in common. By three o'clock we agreed that we would soon meet again.

Our exchanges had included our respective addresses: 'to guarantee answers to future requests for typographical data' in Fleming's words. I thus learned that he lived in Ebury Street in what I had hitherto assumed, *en passant*, to be a Nonconformist chapel with an impressively pedimented columned façade. Not so, Fleming affirmed. The building was now divided into four flats, one of which he rented. He was equally interested to learn that I lived in one of a score of recently built flats skilfully infiltrated into a mainly Georgian cul-de-sac off Fleet Street. We were amused to learn that we both resided in fairly unusual quarters in central London.

We parted at the top of Haymarket. I had enjoyed our meeting. Fleming had proved a lively companion. I suspected that his interest in the opposite sex was unlikely to be one-sided. He was ready-made for depiction by any lively portraitist as a successful yet fairly care-free man-about-town. And clearly very English.

During the following week I lunched with Percy Muir, one of the most enlivening and agreeable worldlings I have known: bookseller in the West End, bibliographer of wide renown and loyal subscriber to *Typography*. He was interested to learn of my current typographical endeavours and amused by my confession to puzzlement concerning Fleming's hobby. Years later, I noticed that Muir was referred to as 'cockney' by one of Fleming's biographers, a woefully erroneous reference to this quietly spoken, agreeably articulated raconteur and most urbane and erudite of bibliographers. Concerning Fleming's bibliographical interests, Muir admitted: 'He gives me a free hand to seek out these volumes to add to his library, which must already be worth quite a packet.'

'A customer worth having.'

'True enough, if only he didn't want each volume he acquires for his collection to be boxed in a black, board case and with his coat of arms on the side. I hadn't even known he had one.'

'Most of us have. Look into the history of the Muirs. You'll find one.'

'I think I'll concentrate on the Flemings – or this one, anyway, for the moment.'

'Is he loaded?'

'Somehow I don't think so, but I'm told his mother is. Anyway, he always seems able to buy the books I suggest, although he invariably tries beating down the price of most of them.'

'Even though he picks your brains for finding the bargains?'

'He's a Scot. I'm a Scot. We understand these side issues.'

'God help the rest of us.'

Muir laughed. 'You seem to get along well with Shand – another total Scot.'

'True enough,' I agreed.

'I think Ian's on to something really worthwhile with his unusual hobby. He's only thirty or so. If he lives to be sixty, I reckon his collection will be worth a modest fortune.'

'D'you know what he does at the admiralty?'

'Not the foggiest. I gather he's in some intelligence outfit there.'

We left the subject of Fleming at that and moved on to more wide-ranging gossip, concerning the bookish world, for Muir was not only the leading expert on all aspects of children's books but also a bibliographer of rare percipience in wider fields, especially in that division of the bookish world he was beginning to corner on Fleming's behalf. Decades later, well after the deaths of both men, the collection assembled for Fleming was to be sold at a lofty price to a university library in the United States.

A day or so later, following a languid introductory telephone call, the elegant and affectedly Byronic Charles Morgan came to the office-atelier on the top floor of a magnificent Adam house in Hertford Street, Mayfair, owned by Lord Delamere, director of an up-and-coming

7

advertising agency that retained my supposedly relevant talents as semi-resident art director.

Morgan was above middle height, bony, grey-faced, slow-moving, somewhat self-consciously portentous, I thought, and seemingly under-fed and over-worried. His comments were uttered very quietly, almost deferentially, more in the manner of a bypassed bishop than a lionised literator with an impressive renown as novelist, playwright and critic. I decided I was probably one of the few of my generation who had read both *The Fountain*, his recent novel and bestseller, and his long-ago first book, *The Gun Room*, in which he had given the Royal Navy a rough handling, recording the savage treatment meted out to mid-shipmen before, during and after the First World War.

The admiralty journal which Morgan tabled for discussion that afternoon – the *WIR* – was issued to naval officers in ships and stations at home and abroad. The publication, an 8-by-5-inch green-paper-covered stapled booklet, was an extremely dull example of a typical current house magazine. From my comments I imagine Morgan thought he might be in for shocks. My first thought was that the doubtless intriguing contents deserved a more lively pres-entation than that used for the contents of the booklet I retained for consideration and restyling.

My first submission, made to Morgan a week later – after dis-covering that the *WIR* was engrossingly readable throughout – demonstrated how the *WIR* could (and, I hoped, should) become a serious tabloid news sheet, which, I contended, would be more readily welcomed in ward rooms than the currently dull-looking booklet, more akin to a church magazine or bureaucratic report than a lively up-to-the-minute naval news sheet with unusually interest-ing reports and features. Why should such interesting narrations be so dolefully hidden within such a dreary format?

I could see that Morgan was quite horrified by my suggestions and the dummy I put before him. He shook his head despondently, clearly convinced that Fleming had sent him to a zombie and quite certain that their lordships would be horrified by my outrageous suggestions which, presumably, he was determined they should never see, lest he was associated with so outlandish a project.

I accepted this would-be gentlemanly thumbs down and, a few days later, submitted a revised dummy along relevant but trad lines, which, I hoped, might still manage to provide naval officers with a more readable journal. Morgan telephoned to say that everyone concerned had agreed to these suggestions and he wished to pass on their commendations. He was clearly relieved. An appreciative note from Fleming followed from Ebury Street, with a postscript to say that he hoped that we would meet again and that he was still keeping in touch with the oncoming war via my continuing *News Chronicle* 'News-Reel Maps' and 'Strategy Tests'. Meanwhile, he had passed the OK to the admiralty pay-bobs for what proved to be the modest fee he had predicted.

I sent a note to Ebury Street mentioning my amusement and not a little confusion in my sessions with Morgan, adding that I would doubtless see my simple amendments to the *WIR* somewhere distant on active service, which seemed to be imminent.

Apart from a couple of amatory missives, that casual note proved one of the more significant messages I have penned in what has, against various odds, proved quite a long life.

CHAPTER 2

RECALL FROM WESTERN
APPROACHES

I volunteered for the Royal Navy on Monday, the second day of the second great war of the twentieth century. My gesture was neither gallant nor zestful, for I was (and remain) more inclined to seek accord rather than discord in most controversies that come my way. Yet this seemed the logical and doubtless inevitable action for anyone in a situation similar to my own.

I was in my late twenties. I was fit. I sailed. I swam. I climbed. I was keen on travel. More to the point, perhaps, I was free of dependents. Indeed, my responsibilities were probably as minimal as a man could have, living in the heart of London. Hence my shaky belief that I might be of that material from which the admiralty affirmed in various public notices a wartime naval officer could possibly be fashioned. The details I proffered were noted: I was informed that I would be interviewed in due course.

Meanwhile, in company with a score of other aspirants, I was swotting for a first mate's ticket, then deemed a 'must' for any aspirant hopeful for a commission and soon to be facing a naval interviewing board. We were under twice-weekly instruction from an ex-Merchant Marine officer, one Captain O. M. Watts, in an office-turned-seminary above the yacht equipment showroom he had founded just off Piccadilly.

An unscheduled and certainly unexpected spin-off from this course was an invitation, during one of our afternoon sessions, to take part in what was already proving to be a major naval evacuation of our defeated army driven back to the French coast and now 'assembling' – if that was the word – on the beaches outside the port of Dunkirk. The evacuation was likely to continue through the following days and nights, possibly over the rest of the week. This side of the invitation seemed somewhat vague, Captain Watts admitted. Nobody knew anything for certain. Who was game to go? Almost everyone present – a score or so – said 'Snap.' Three hours later, we foregathered opposite Green Park and were transported to Greenwich in Royal Navy vans.

I thus found myself a naval volunteer given a temporary wartime ranking – termed T124, I seem to recall. As I had had experience of seagoing craft, I was put in charge of one of the several somewhat antique Royal Navy (RN) whalers resuscitated from heaven knows where. These were to be towed by Thames tugs cross-channel until the Dunkirk beaches were reached under cover of darkness. The whalers would then be cast off to be rowed ashore to help rescue our troops on the beaches now under continuous bombardment from the German forces encircling the port. The exercise was given high marks in the semi-official figures of our rescued army forces, published much later. So, rather earlier than expected, I experienced the sharper end of modern war at fairly close quarters.

Within a week of those historic events – which I duly recorded in the *News Chronicle* and over the BBC – I was summoned to a fairly bleak office in Grosvenor Gardens to be interviewed by three senior officers in the Royal Navy: two captains and a commander, clearly plucked from retirement. Dutifully, I answered their questions concerning schooling, sailing, craft, career. Inevitably Dunkirk, headline of the hour, cropped up. My inquisitors suddenly switched from their Q&A routine to requests for first-hand reportage. The interview lengthened until the senior of the trio said: 'Well, Harling, many thanks. Very interesting indeed. We must let you go now, but I think you can take it from here that you are in!'

The others, smiling, nodded heartily.

Two mornings later I received instructions to report for training to HMS *King Alfred*, a so-called stone frigate, but more accurately and prosaically, an intended public recreational centre recently built on the esplanade at Hove in Sussex.

In this manner I became an Acting Temporary Probationary Sub-Lieutenant Royal Navy Volunteer Reserve. No man gets much above himself with that prelude to his identity. The Royal Navy defines its echelons most clearly.

Further experiences of the sharper end of war soon followed. Despite the admiralty's deprecatory touch denoting my rank as a naval officer, I was appointed to navigating duties in a corvette engaged in North Atlantic convoy escort duties.

Without overmuch conceit, I might have expected in due course to gain command of a corvette, as did Nicholas Monserrat and other contemporaries in *King Alfred*. In time of war, sea lords have always been prepared to lower their impeccable standards for those untouched by Dartmouth tutelage. With consummate authority they cast their nets more widely to enmesh likely hopefuls for advancement, especially those possessed of commendation from a senior officer concerning officer-like qualities and so forth. I knew that I was regarded by my commander as a fairly efficient navigating officer and that sooner rather than later I would be enmeshed.

Thanks, however, to the lack of justice in this uncertain world – in which I have long had substantial faith – that casual meeting with Fleming in the immediate pre-war period sponsored evasion of this seemingly inevitable nautical net.

Hence a modest but necessary divergence to my narrative.

In Oxford, around the same time, late 1941, Colonel Sam Bassett of the Royal Marines, head of the fledgling Inter-Services Topographical Department (ISTD) decided that he needed to add to his staff of geographers, hydrographers and academics, mostly drawn from a variety of donnish disciplines, an officer for peripatetic but scarcely specific duties. This officer would probably be Royal Navy Volunteer Reserve (RNVR), would probably have been a one-time amateur sailor with some knowledge of charts, maps, plans and the rest of the cartographical miscellany, and, preferably, one who had possibly been a pre-war journalist with some investigative experience and able to present his findings in a no-nonsense prose.

In his search for the officer with these simple, but, to the service mind, somewhat otherworldly and obscure qualifications, Colonel Bassett turned (more or less inevitably, I later learned) for advice to Fleming, by then Commander I. L. Fleming RNVR, and personal assistant to Rear Admiral John Godfrey, RN, director of naval intelligence (DNI).

I write 'more or less inevitably' because Fleming, I also learned later, had acquired, in peacetime, an unusually wide range of contacts well outside the conventional naval round – from the City and Reuters to motor-racing and skiing. Fortunately for me, Fleming also had a retentive memory. He recalled my name and my typographic, cartographic and journalistic interests, and also my last note to him. If still alive, he decided, I should currently be serving somewhere in the service. He consulted the navy list and set about enquiries concerning my whereabouts and duties, soon learning that I was a seagoing officer within the notoriously iron grip of the admiral commanding Western Approaches. Fortunately, I had been put ashore temporarily with a severe bout of gastric flu after an especially hectic spell of Atlantic convoy duties. My temporary base was a pensioned-off First War cruiser, HMS *Caroline*, HQ of Atlantic escort craft, moored alongside a sombre Belfast quay.

Having recovered from the flu, I was awaiting a fresh appointment – doubtless a return to convoy duties.

An obliging RN commander, however, took Fleming's enquiries seriously and managed the virtually impossible task of loosening me from the legendary grip of the admiral commanding the Atlantic Approaches. Twenty-four hours later, I was in London. I telephoned Fleming and was instructed to report to him at the admiralty the following morning. Thus, almost two years after our earlier meetings, we met in a fairly scruffy waiting room adjacent to what I was later to learn was the legendary Room 39.

This time, I wasn't surprised to see him in the uniform of a commander RNVR. 'Almost two years since your *WIR* contributions to the pre-war effort. Since then, you've presumably seen evidence of those efforts,' he said, genially.

I nodded, adding a few words of gratitude for his recollection of that long-ago commission and his consideration in bringing me to this new way of naval life, whatever it was likely to be.

'The chance of directing round pegs into round holes in the Royal Navy, Harling, is an extremely rare but agreeable experience, especially in wartime,' was Fleming's dry reply. 'One must take these occasional chances when they come one's way. In any case, between these solid bulwarks I can tell you that the director of naval intelligence made an especially convincing case for your transfer. I merely gave things a little extra push. Best of luck.'

For 'director of naval intelligence' read 'Fleming' in this instance, I thought, and thanked those lucky stars that must have been hovering above Bedford Square months before.

He asked whether I had enjoyed my seagoing life.

'Reasonably, but too boring and repetitive. And too few landfalls,' was my verdict.

He laughed. 'You may well find the job on offer – in the ISTD – not typographical, by the way,' he emphasised, smiling, 'a bit too land-based, although there may well be the occasional seagoing interlude.

But nobody knows. The job's as shadowy as that. But I recalled your activities in civil life and they seemed pretty well what was needed for this sketchy job.'

He then briefly informed me that as a personal assistant to the DNI he had continuous contacts with various inter-service intelligence outfits. He briefly outlined the job awaiting me, admitting that his words could scarcely tot up even to an elementary outline of what was and would be involved.

'Frankly, it's a brand-new job. Everybody professes to know what's needed yet nobody knows how or even if it will work. That's why Colonel Bassett roped me in. I recalled your cartographical interests and newspaper background and thought you might be interested in these dim, dark prospects. Are you?'

'Very.'

'Well, the colonel's due here tomorrow. Drop in about this time. Just send your name through to me from the Whitehall entrance. I'll introduce you and then leave you to sort things out between yourselves.'

He did just that. I was interested to note that despite the colonel's superior rank he was clearly impressed or, at least, influenced, by Fleming's authoritative air and probably his daily proximity to Admiral Godfrey, head of all naval intelligence, including the colonel's own specialist topographical department.

Colonel Bassett would have proved the perfect prototype for a senior regular officer of Royal Marines in any Noël Coward film or Gilbert and Sullivan opera: small, wiry, ramrod spine, weathered face, quizzical grey eyes, impeccably uniformed plus First War ribbons with a trio of exotics I couldn't place. His manner was precise, even staccato. 'If Ian thinks you could be the man for the job, that's good enough for me. I can't give you much information about your likely duties. My researchers and geographers tell me we need someone more operational. If you're interested, why not have a shot?'

'Why not?' I echoed.

'My chaps are mainly university research types: geographers, geologists, academics, plus a couple of naval hydrographers. Their main job is to prepare handbooks and up-to-date operational appreciations of terrain, beaches and so on. They get stuck on some of the details needed today or by tomorrow at latest. The slope of a beach. Plans of a fishing port. Exact location of certain oil tanks. Number of bridges on a particular railway line and so on. These things crop up all the time. They can't always find the answers. They tell me they want someone who can dig 'em out. That'll be you. What d'you think?'

'Sounds interesting.'

'I'm glad you think so and hope you'll find it so. Meanwhile, I've brought along these notes about the division. Signed by me but compiled by someone you'll meet: a don, Freddie Wells. I think you'll find the notes useful, and Wells extremely helpful. I realise it's all a bit different from what you've been doing so far but Fleming thinks your peacetime activities could prove very useful. And, by the way, he tells me you're due for a spot of leave.'

'So I was told in Belfast.'

'Good. See you in a week's time then. Your digs will be arranged in one of the colleges. Hertford, I believe. Get your travel warrants here and count on Oxford as your base – for the time being, anyway. After that, I think you'll be in for a good deal of movement. Meanwhile, enjoy your leave!' he concluded genially, although the words sounded more akin to a command than benediction.

I was fairly confident that I would enjoy my leave, as a few months before the war I had bought from a Welsh corn merchant a small cottage in the village of Beddgelert in Snowdonia. I recall that the price asked in those jittery days for this two-up and one-down, perched above a lively stream and looking across to the mountains, was £150 freehold. I had furnished the place sparsely but snugly so that it was a ready-made retreat for anyone seeking a recuperative week. I had also encountered an elderly neighbour willing to keep her caring eyes on the place. I spent my few days rambling rather than climbing, reflecting rather than reading, but mainly sleeping, and dipping occasionally into those notes on topographical intelligence the colonel had loaned me.

A week later I duly reported to the colonel at the headquarters of ISTD in the School of Geography in Mansfield Road, Oxford. Here two hydrographers, a captain and a commander RN, who clearly saw themselves as operational elitists among a gaggle of academics, worked in their vast, well-lit chart room. Most of the other researchers were scattered around in nearby collegiate buildings and Nissen pre-fabs.

The colonel's first introduction was to his indispensable confidant and advisor, Freddie Wells, a Classics don at University College, who was to become a congenial colleague. He had already arranged with Colonel Kenneth Mason, professor of geography and a noted Himalayan explorer, that, whenever necessary, I should have rooms in Hertford College, of which the professor was also a fellow.

In later days, returning from distant places at short notice, the resilient one-time mountaineer and explorer usually managed to get me into a set of college rooms. The contrast between a cramped warship cabin and the luxury of two rooms that stayed upright, plus the services of an attentive college servant, was heady stuff, although I found the rooms as cold as anything the Atlantic could inflict in winter months. If by some remote chance Hertford College was full up, Wells would slot me into Professor Arthur Goodhart's rooms in the master's lodge at University College. On two occasions I even occupied the rooms of Lord Beveridge, master of the college, doubtless far away on one or other of his welfare fact-finding missions.

Wells and I soon established an agreeably casual friendship. His was as distant a personality from Fleming's as I could have met in a decade. He was around thirty, of middle height, with an ingenious, cherubic face and wavy fair hair. I thought he looked more like an undergraduate who had just come up than one of the university's foremost academics. I was also occasionally astonished by his worldly innocence. He, in turn, no doubt, was probably equally surprised by remarks and views deriving from my own markedly more raffish pre-war world of journalism and advertising. Yet despite the extreme limits of his experience, he was a sound judge of men, working long and loyally with and for the colonel, who unashamedly confessed that he was utterly out of his depth with any kind of intellectual problem or person.

Within a crowded week of enquiries, meetings, introductions and so on, Wells had partly clarified my job. Although the RAF photographic reconnaissance unit at Medmenham was steadily producing interpretations of enemy strengths and weaknesses from aerial photographs taken from high-flying Mosquitoes, the navy and army were woefully short of shore and ground-level photographs of beaches, hinterland and inland terrains. As an example of the paucity of our official topographical knowledge, Wells mentioned that the total visual data available concerning the Norwegian coastline before the German invasion was a clutch of Raphael Tuck scenic postcards.

Wells's words and needs were to prove a guarantee of almost two years of inquisitive and near and distant travels and meetings with some very odd birds indeed. I was occasionally in Oxford, but more frequently abroad, seeking answers to the longer-term queries of the geographical boffins in Oxford. I could go anywhere, ask anyone, do virtually anything so long as I got the topographical data they needed, and my cover remained unbreakable and my true purpose unsuspected. And if I could bring back photographs of the required beach, plans of the required port, or data concerning unlikely bases, so much the better.

When, for example, a small, German-occupied Mediterranean island was a possible target, pre-war Greek importers of sponges seemed likely to be useful contacts. They took some tracking down but proved responsive. But no sooner had I returned to the admiralty than Lord Rothschild of MI5 was on the blower, for this particular sponge importer was on their bugged list. On another occasion, Sacheverell Sitwell had sizeable photographic archives concerning Mauritania, then occupying the attention of the geographers. And when the possibilities of the under-belly of Germany was discussed, a well-known poet with a pre-war passion for the Danube and its villages was mentioned as possessor of a weighty portfolio of well-captioned photographs. He queried whether, apart from his photographs, his specialised knowledge of the Balkans would make him useful as a recruit to one or other of the services. I passed on his CV to Fleming who forwarded the record to MI5. Two days later Fleming's covering note: 'Pray break the enclosed news as gently as you can to your patriotic but somewhat over-ambitious poet.' The succinct report was: 'Communist and known bugger – important points omitted from CV.'

Engineering firms and architectural practices which had engaged on pre-war contracts abroad were forthcoming with photographs and drawings: invaluable data, casually acquired in peacetime discussion and business encounters, now proved even more useful in warfare. Demand by the boffins for less accessible topographical data took me from the Middle East (including Turkey in mufti) to Iceland, which the Germans were always rumoured to be on the verge of invading to gain the supreme Atlantic U-boat base; and even to the Pacific for a share of the topographical know-how acquired by the US Navy. And so on and on.

I was doubly fortunate in my two bosses: one official, the other somewhat less so throughout these tasks.

The first, my official boss, was the 'mysterious Colonel Bassett', as he has been termed. Although a strict disciplinarian in the tough tradition of the Royal Marines, he was an unusually understanding chief for someone occasionally needing to act outside formal regulations. Above all, he was far from mysterious.

Secondly, as I was frequently moving between Oxford, the admiralty and distant places, I was continuously in contact with Fleming, and gradually came to know him from our somewhat casual official exchanges conducted in seemingly mutually agreeable fashion. He began to use my foreign trips for the occasional unofficial letter or message to deliver to Naval Intelligence Division (NID) officers abroad or requesting odd enquiries to be made. Above all, he was invariably keen to have first-hand reports concerning NID officers in distant outposts. As I had, he contended, 'an unholy and inquisitive interest in the background and behaviour of mankind and, of course, womankind, and no axe to grind', I was invariably thoroughly quizzed on my return from distant travels, usually at Scott's or the Etoile – my most favoured pre-war restaurant – to which I introduced Fleming as an alternative to Scott's or Kettner's.

A tentative friendship was casually established in these meetings, quizzes and exchanges. I was intrigued and occasionally amused by his adherence to establishment values, probably inevitable in one who had lived and worked within a series of immutably conventional institutions: Eton, Sandhurst, the City and now the admiralty. He was a made-to-measure personal assistant to the tough and ruthless DNI, for he was efficient, sophisticated, energetic, dutiful, unable to suffer fools even ungladly, even for a split second, and clearly ambitious to make his mark in the service. His elder brother, Peter, had established himself pre-war in the army. Their mother, I gathered, was not averse to pointing out this disparity in the respective pre-war achievements of her two elder sons. Having missed out on these clamping maternal experiences, I was deeply curious concerning their effects on character and conduct in others.

An instance of these contrasts cropped up after my return from an early trip to the Middle East. A typical Fleming quiz at Scott's would be fired off at an odd and unexpected moment during the meal. 'I gather you enjoyed this so-called Turkish stint, including Istanbul. Why and how?'

'I was parked in the Pera Palace. Very agreeably, thanks to the consideration and advice of Commander Vladimir Wolfson.'

'What d'you think of him?'

Vladimir Wolfson, a White Russian, had escaped from Moscow to Britain while in his early teens. After Cambridge and the City, he had been recruited to naval intelligence and stationed in wartime Istanbul.

He was well suited and well placed there, as linguist and questor. Above all, as one who was more English than any Englishman he was clearly determined to do everything possible for his adopted homeland. He had proved a notable help to me.

Fleming grinned as I gave full value to the commander's identity, tenacity and worldly wisdom.

'Made for the job, you think?'

'Absolutely.'

'Roughly my own view. I gather you brought back the required charts and maps. I gather you also enjoyed Istanbul. Why?'

'Basically because, as a born perambulator, there was so much to see between naval researches. Wolfson took care of that. I saw a good deal of the Bosphorus. I also met a far-from-home Parisienne. Very relaxing and attentive, and also trying her best to enjoy Istanbul during her enforced stay.'

'How did she get from France to Turkey? Probably a spy.'

'Possibly, but she said she was one of several Parisiennes who had found Istanbul a profitable pre-war parking lot, and that she was now the mistress of a Turkish bigwig who was busy making his ambitious way up the diplomatic ladder and not an unduly over-frequent visitor to her flat, despite the fact that he handsomely underpinned her monthly money-bag.'

'I take it you kept your lips fully sealed.'

'My lips were fully engaged elsewhere. We didn't discuss typography, topography or even oceanography even once.'

'Trust Harling!' Fleming said, grinning.

'Duty first! Isn't that the great naval tradition?' I claimed. 'Here I am, awaiting my next task. Yearning for it.'

He grinned. 'Then what? How d'you get back from Istanbul after you left Wolfson?'

'Asked him to OK my due leave. He gave me a week's freedom to make my own way back to Alex. Not even leave. Naval duties.'

'How was your return achieved?'

'Train from Istanbul to Ankara. Having seen those lunar landscapes from the plane, I wanted to see them more closely. I also wanted to look around Ankara, ancient and modern. Spent a couple of days there. Even bought a Kelim prayer rug from a dealer with no English, and myself no Turkish. A bargain in pigeon French.'

'And then?'

'I've always wanted to see Aleppo, so I dropped in.'

'Still not in uniform?'

'I was by then. After Aleppo, I spent a couple of days in Beirut. I know an army medico base there. Very entertaining. Paris on the Med.'

'And then?'

'Cadged a lift from a French courier going down to Haifa. From there an Israeli courier down to Gaza. Finally, a lift in a British Army truck back to Alex. You should try it sometime. Wartime hitch-hiking. The art of movement-without-effort. But, then, your travels are sponsored from on high with the ambassadorial limo awaiting your whims outside the hotel.'

'Very funny!' he said, but, then, to my surprise, added that he doubted he would prove to be any good at the practices I'd outlined.

'No need to be a shrink to see that,' I said. 'You're far too busy giving orders than proffering requests. Anyway, dropping in on an army staging post with the certainty of a lift scarcely comes under the heading of hitch-hiking. All laid on.'

'How d'you set about your requests?'

'The usual drill for all and sundry. Just turn up and say where you need to get to. That's all – and always enough. Come back in an hour's time or six, tomorrow morning's the usual drill.'

He nodded, as if in understanding, which I doubted. 'I'm either not that arrogant or not that suppliant,' he mused.

'As an amateur shrink I'd say this snippet of self-analysis concerning arrogance is 100 per cent correct. Any hint of suppliance in your make-up is sheer blarney.'

He hooted with laughter, his usual dismissal of any subject taking too personal or untoward a turn. But this was not to be his last word on my Middle Eastern travels.

Somewhat over-casually, he queried: 'You mentioned this French tart. How d'you meet her?'

'You're talking about my friend, Andrée, in Istanbul, I gather. We met via the ancient device of eye contact in a local café.'

'What followed the eye contact?'

'Queries concerning her arrival in that remote area. Hints concerning her lifestyle. A few further drinks – mine non-alcoholic, of course. Responsibility for both bills, of course. Invited back. Age-old stuff.'

'What about her abode?'

'Quite pleasant. Couple of rooms quite near the Pera. She'd gone out there pre-war, tempted by tales of Turkish millionaires. Didn't find any, but soon found the war's well-heeled executives in the Pera. Quite profitable. Why not? Frogs, Krauts, Brits, the lot. Then met her local bigwig and opted for comfort – apart from the odd encounter. She's one of the fortunates of her trade. As I was too, I daresay, in meeting her.'

He laughed. Heartily.

'I'll take your word and memory for your belief. Describe your Andrée in thirty words.'

'Is this an official request or an addendum to my official notes on my journey of enquiry?'

'As it comes. It won't appear in the *WIR*, that's for sure.'

I laughed. 'As it comes then. Late thirties or early forties. Well dressed. Slim. Dark. Beautiful legs. Good features. Halting English. Sense of humour. Merry acceptance of her set-up so far from home. Alas, I've no snapshot. "Well geared for her lifestyle" is probably the simple caption I'm hunting for.'

'Probably,' he agreed, laughing. '"A well-matched randy pair far from home" is the caption I wouldn't have to hunt for. I take it that apart from your silence on nautical matters she provided a lively late-night entertainment.'

'To the matter born and burnished,' I said, grinning.

'Did you see her again?'

'The following evening.'

'Same routine?'

'Shorter supper session. Longer domestic session.'

More laughter from Fleming. 'And no spilled secrets with any spilled sperm?'

'Not a chance!'

'So be it,' he said with a grin. 'Let's get moving.'

We moved.

Years later, well into the Bond years, Fleming also visited Istanbul, but, true to what had become the established routine in his rounds of thrilling cities, he was invariably the guest of a local celeb with Rolls-Royce ... and so on and on thrown in.

'Plus an ideal guide to all the local showplaces, no doubt,' I suggested at that later date.

'What a hope! No exiled Parisienne tart came my way, if that's what you're implying,' he affirmed gloomily, acknowledging his remembrance of my erstwhile self-indulgence.

CHAPTER 3

TRAVELS AND TRAVAILS

T he somewhat hazy-seeming tasks for which Fleming had trawled me from Western Approaches grew phenomenally, due mainly to demands from all three services.

There were early requests – a Fleming move – for photographs of beaches, ports, bridges and other potential targets in enemy territories, and a search for contacts who might be aware of the salient features of other potential targets in now-enemy territories. These developments, however, entailed a vast and valuable increase in the receipt, registry and return of photographs and other data. Fortunately, this work, in its early stages, was in the care of three unusual but extremely capable wartime volunteers. By far the senior of this trio was Miss Cicely Stanhope, a character guaranteed to delight any foreigner studying the oddities and eccentricities of the English upper crust. She was well into her fifties and, in appearance, mildly reminiscent of the actress, Margaret Rutherford, and possessed of several similar mannerisms. Above all, she was an unashamed social snob, vastly prideful of her Stanhope pedigree but deeply saddened by the inescapable fact that she and Lord

Stanhope were the last of their line. Her pride extended to the family's stately home at Chevening in Kent and she expressed pleasure that I had visited and been impressed by the architectural merits of the house. Her wartime duties in the admiralty had hitherto been closely concerned with matters relating to codes, but she made no demur when seconded to fresh and vastly different duties in the ISTD. This staid and seemingly olde-worlde grande dame was shrewd, dedicated and sceptically selective in her handling of the enormous barrage of topographical material which virtually – but never quite – engulfed her.

I soon learned, when introducing her to her new labours, that she was an ever-ready social gossip, despite her sealed lips concerning her work in ISTD. I also learned that she had a somewhat scornful view of Fleming's moma, Mrs (Evelyn) Valentine Fleming, deeming her a highly successful arriviste and activiste in the world of the would-be aristocrat. To my surprise, she was well acquainted with Ian Fleming's amatory record and, strangest discovery of all, was fond of his devoted long-term, long-suffering girlfriend, Muriel Wright. Fleming would have been mildly unnerved by the scale of her intimate awareness of his affiliations, including his disastrous relationship with a certain Monique Panchaud de Bottomes from Geneva, and his ongoing liaisons with a couple or so of London lady-loves of more mature years.

The two other assistants were much younger. One, English, in her thirties; the other, French, in her twenties. Both were smart, well dressed, charming and exceptionally able in their manifold duties. They worked long hours without demur or complaint, documenting the vast and ceaseless inflow of photographs, plans, sketches and the rest. By the early months of 1943, the thousands of incoming photographs necessitated considerable storage space. An ISTD photographic library was set up in the New Bodleian in Oxford, with a complementary contact register in London. Admiral Godfrey was delighted by these logical additions to wartime intelligence. Fleming was somewhat less enthusiastic. 'Paperwork never won wars,' was his contribution.

With the encouragement of Colonel Bassett, and Freddie Wells,

I had been energetically involved in all the early stages of these two projects, but their swift growth and my frequent absences abroad soon demanded more continuous care in their development. Fortunately, two unlikely administrators were recruited, supremely adaptable to these onerous responsibilities: Anthony Hippisley-Coxe, RNVR lieutenant commander and one-time Dartmouth type, who had left the Royal Navy to train as an architect – becoming en route an authority on the history of the international circus – took over the contact register; and Rodney Slessor, a tall, suave, grey-haired executive – brother of the RAF high-up – took over the photographic library. After an initial and persuasive BBC national broadcast by Slessor, engineers, geologists, architects, yachtsmen, sportsmen, holiday-makers, as well as overseas wanderers of all kinds, fired in their pictures. Relevant selections from the collections were swiftly copied, catalogued and readied for despatch to needful claimants from all three services.

Fleming kept a watchful eye on all these innovations and activities, for Admiral Godfrey was a notable enthusiast for yet another of what he termed 'elements in basic intelligence', a view well demonstrated in his own naval renown as a pre-war navigator in the Far East.

My final assignment for ISTD was in the company of Colonel Bassett. He had been invited to visit the US service chiefs in Washington to outline the nature and scope of our topographic enquiries. To my surprise he suggested that, as I had been so actively involved in these ISTD developments, I should travel with him.

Lunching with Fleming, I asked whether he had been responsible for my inclusion in this venture.

'Not a chance,' he responded emphatically. 'But after I heard the trip was on and that Bassett was in a determined mood to have you with him, I also spotted a chance of a few oddments of more casual info coming my way from distant sources. And if you get as far as Delhi on your way back, via a route Bassett has in mind, please, don't forget to contact Admiral Godfrey, now chief of the Royal Indian Navy and based in Delhi, somewhat distant from the sea.'

Fleming had recently mentioned this seemingly sudden promotion to DNI and I had heard in Oxford more of the new chief's identity: until recently commodore, now Rear Admiral Edmund Gerard Noel Rushbrooke, awarded DSC in the First War, currently in his early fifties.

I was emboldened to make a few enquiries concerning our new chief. Fleming clearly had a vastly different view of his present boss from that which he had held for Godfrey. 'Decidedly different from our original boss,' he announced after a moment of judicial reflection. 'More a schoolmaster than a pirate, I'd say.'

'Not too dull, I trust.'

'Neither as dynamic nor as demonic as his predecessor.'

'One would probably have to go to Hollywood for that.'

Fleming smiled. 'As the soothsayers contend: time will tell.'

A week later I duly embarked on the *Queen Mary* with Colonel Bassett, but saw little of him during the passage. He had received the rarest of wartime gifts from the gods: a cabin to himself, in a packed-to-the-bows troopship. Junior officers, such as myself, were four to a cabin, but we soon learned that this arrangement verged on the indulgent, for in crossing eastward, carrying US troops to Europe, the liner carried up to 10,000 passengers employing 'the hot berth' routine: half a dozen or even eight to a cabin with three different sets of occupants to each set of bunks during each 24-hour span.

After an extremely busy and seemingly successful week in Washington and a two-day break, part duty, part less-dutiful, I was ready to pack my bag for return. Colonel Bassett, however, said that he was proposing to return to the UK alone. He had decided – on the advice of Fleming and our recent hosts – to direct me to Brisbane to meet the US intelligence types involved in the Japanese campaign. I would travel to San Francisco, then be flown to Pearl Harbor, thence to Brisbane where I would be met by an RN rep. I would make my way home by the best route available, 'east or west'.

'I envy you,' the colonel said, smiling somewhat unconvincingly, 'but we're notoriously weak on Jap intelligence. Give yourself a day or so off in San Francisco. You'll be based in Brisbane for your first week or so.'

My job would be to seek out topographical intelligence which might prove potentially useful for Oxford prior to forthcoming battles in the Pacific. I was given a comprehensive list by the colonel.

I spent three weeks probing in Australia. At one point, early on, I was questioned – as a suspected spy – for the best part of an hour by General Willoughby, MacArthur's intelligence chief. Apparently he had been informed that I might possibly be making untoward topographical enquiries concerning areas likely to be in the American orbit within the next few months. Final clearance came with a limp apology from the general and the offer of boiled sweets, along with the comment: 'Limeys always seem to like boiled sweets.'

'Before or after interrogation?' I asked.

He laughed heartily, showing me the door, adding: 'You leave this office as a proven innocent ally.'

I thought Fleming would be especially interested in the enquiry technique of his US oppo.

Fortunately, I was able to collect a good deal of topographical data, later deemed useful, some even vital, by the mystery men of Oxford, despite the modest time allowed for the task, but perhaps I was too intrigued by the manifold attractions of the cities and femininity of western Australia.

A signal from Fleming decreed that I should make my passage home via Delhi and Alexandria. My round-the-world trip thus continued with a thirty-hour non-stop flight from Perth to Colombo, in a Catalina flying-boat. Our send-off on this inaugural flight had a laconic farewell touch by the station commander:

> This is the first of these flights. We know little enough what to expect. It's essentially a trial run. Hopefully nothing exceptional awaits you. If you have to ditch, I'm afraid nobody will come looking for you. The Japanese have the Cocos Islands and the adjacent seaways. Have a good trip.

From Colombo I flew north to Delhi, reporting to Major-General Lamplough, who, as a colonel of the Royal Marines had been one of the two deputy directors of NID in the admiralty, and for whom I had carried out enquiries alongside topographical quests. By an odd chance, I also had a brief off-the-record glimpse of Lord Mountbatten, head of South East Asia Command (SEAC), at close quarters.

At the head of a posse of pretty Wrens, he had ridden over from the viceroy's lodge to one of the outlying lodges of the vice-regal estates in which I had been offered temporary quarters by a peacetime acquaintance, now a desktop warrior. They all dismounted. Mountbatten chatted with my host, and agreed to stay for drinks. I was absorbed, listening to this beguiling, vainglorious, handsome man, possessed of all those elusive, ageless Peter Pan qualities apt to cling to so many middle-aged, even antique, Dartmouth types. He spoke of his time as a cadet, when he had presented his first cheque to his bank. Told by the cashier that he must endorse the cheque on the reverse, he had hastily scrawled: 'I heartily endorse this cheque, Louis Mountbatten.' His accomplished anecdotage was enjoyed all round.

A further hoped-for but unexpected encounter was with Admiral Godfrey, now Admiral Commanding the Royal Indian Navy. I was invited to tea at the admiral's official residence, a visit enlivened by a local snake-charmer who provided music and displayed the enchantments of his pet in the garden while we watched, sipping our tea as casually as if we had been cheering the antics of a retriever puppy on the Sussex downs.

After carrying out cabled instructions for a couple of jobs to be done for ISTD in Alexandria, I returned to London. I had been away for almost three months. At odd moments en route, I wondered whether a signal I'd received from Fleming might herald some other activity he had in mind. I was restless and not averse to a change from ISTD. I hoped I wasn't reading too much into the signal.

I reported to Room 39 on my return. We duly lunched at Scott's for Fleming's usual relentless quizzing. Travellers from their trips returning, he claimed, were among the most productive sources of useful off-the-record data concerning NID's distant representatives and operations. Not everything could be said in signals. At the end of the inquisition, he said: 'And what will you do now or next?'

'See what the colonel has in mind. But what about your signal?'

'Have you ever heard of 30AU?' he queried, after a distinct pause.

'Never.'

'Well, it's short for Number Thirty Assault Unit. A naval assault unit, that is. Nowadays a particular hobby horse of mine, wished on me by the DNI well before he was booked for India. Glued to me by his successor.'

'Who or what is assaulted?'

'The enemy. Occasionally. Basically, the unit's job is to seize enemy equipment, ciphers, scientific know-how before such material can be destroyed. The unit did very well in north Africa and Sicily. Now, it's getting ready for France. Come back to the admiralty and I'll give you enough relevant bumf to acquaint you with your probable naval future. Guard the file with your life. Study carefully and let me have it back in the morning. Seems a logical enough task for you to be middleman between ISTD and 30AU, anyway. Possibly between 30AU and me.'

'The additions to your job seem never-ending.'

'I get by. Each provides its attractions as well as preoccupations.'

'And rewards?'

'Few and far between.'

'Can you give me an outline of what awaits me?'

'Basically cyclopaedic, but I'll try.'

He began hesitantly and concluded fairly briefly.

'As usual, we borrowed the idea from the Hun, but think we've improved on it. They used an operational intelligence unit in Crete: trained paratroopers and the rest. Captured our ciphers and God knows what else. Set us back some months in the Med.'

'And now we've got our own unit?'

'More or less. Anyway, read the bumf. If you want a truly active life for the last stages of the war, this could be the job.'

'And Colonel Bassett?'

'I'll square him. Actually, he's already aware that I'm after you for a few outings. I've mentioned my intentions and he's in agreement. Meanwhile, by way of an echo of our very first meeting, I've one or two unified topographical, typographical tasks for you. Odd the way I land these jobs in your lap. First, from various surmises and enquiries, I gather that 30AU would probably profit from a set of target guides they could, and would, very willingly carry in their battledress. Leaving things to a university press means one's guaranteed leather-bound volumes suitable for a college library in fifty years' time. 30AU needs something far more practical and ephemeral, something akin to a Fleet Street guide to enemy working whereabouts. Needed very soon, in fact. Immediately, preferably.'

'Sounds more promising than my efforts with the *WIR*.'

Fleming grinned, recalling. 'You'll be given a free hand – up to a point. Nothing elaborate, but something practical and clear-cut. I've also another specifically typographical task for you.'

'Falling like gifts from the gods.'

He grinned and went on. 'This one is somewhat less warlike. The other evening, playing bridge with Lord Kemsley, he asked if I knew someone who could take a fresh look at the design of the *Daily Sketch*, his ailing tabloid. I recalled your antics at the *News Chronicle* and casually mentioned that he might see what you could offer. He seemed rather interested in the notion. If you're also interested, I'll ring the old boy when we get back to the admiralty and fix a date.'

'I look forward to the notion.'

'Good, but first read all the 30AU bumf I'll be loaning you.'

'Can't wait. How soon would his lordship want me to look over his tabloid?'

'Pronto. You can have three days' leave, to include the 30AU stuff, the Kemsley job, as well as any current blonde.'

'I understood from the colonel that I was due for more after my solo travels.'

'Come off it. I'll wager your time away from authority was one long beano. Anyway, I'll sort it out with the colonel as he's still your nominal boss.'

Back in Room 39, Fleming rang through to Kemsley House, spoke to his lordship's secretary and fixed a meeting the following afternoon: Lord Kemsley. Kemsley House. Gray's Inn Road. 4.30.

'Now for the alleged relevant 30AU bumf,' Fleming said, taking a bulging foolscap folder from a lower drawer in his desk. 'Most of it's ancient history by now. But some of it could prove interesting and profitable. Why don't you get to Oxford tomorrow morning, see the colonel, get your leave fixed, see K in the afternoon at Kemsley House and spend this evening and tomorrow night with this bumf?'

'What about the necessities of life? Meals, feminine company and so forth!'

He smiled. 'Anyway, bring it back here Thursday morning. Guard with your life. What a hope!'

'What a homecoming!'

He laughed. 'You once said you were in this war for fresh and, hopefully, novel experiences. Here's another half-dozen brand-new experiences heading your way. Be thankful. Bless your benefactor.'

'I'll reserve any deserved blessings until our next meeting!'

Absorption in Fleming's offerings occupied hours of that evening and a late night in my Fleet Street retreat. I learned that 30 Assault Unit had been formed in September 1942 in order to seize enemy intelligence, ciphers, equipment and so on for NID to despatch to relevant technical outfits, all desperately keen to have such data for inspection and comparison. I vaguely recalled that the Battle of Crete had been fought and lost in the early months of 1941. Had we been all that quick off the mark? The unit had originally been known as 30 Commando, but had recently been renamed 30 Assault Unit, with two wings: naval and Royal Marine. Reading between the official lines, I could sense how the DNI, having been deputed by the First Sea Lord to form such a unit, had passed on the job to Fleming, lock stock and gun barrel. A few months later, following Admiral Godfrey's posting to India, his successor, Rear Admiral Rushbrooke, had undoubtedly found 30AU and its manifold and frequently inexplicable activities a further oddment on his plate. Hence Fleming's current plateful.

The naval wing of the unit comprised a core of half-a-dozen executive officers, to which were added, as requested or needed, specialists – not necessarily naval – in mines, missiles, torpedoes and the rest of mankind's current malevolences. The specialists carried out their specific enquiries within the unit's protection and then returned with their findings, actual and/or theoretical, to normal duties.

To my surprise, I learned that the Royal Marine wing of the unit, totalling around a dozen officers and some 250 fighting men, had been trained with the object of getting these specialists to their specified targets, protecting them, covering their forays and, hopefully, their withdrawals with their findings.

My way through this maze of records of the unit was made clearer by Fleming's succinct comments throughout the many pages, some scribbled, some augmented by signals and notes. I hadn't expected anything as enthralling. Reading on encouraged my own burgeoning interest. Recruitment into what was clearly an extremely active, yet still fairly small naval wing, seemed to offer an entertaining prospect between now and the war's end. Anything else would be an anti-climax compared with these offerings, I decided.

I reported to Colonel Bassett the following morning having caught a fiendishly early train to Oxford. He'd had Fleming on the blower the previous day. I would remain on the strength of ISTD, the colonel explained, but would be seconded to 30AU as 'specialist topographical officer'. Fleming had been insistent that this was an apposite label. After all, the unit would be needing plans, dossiers, and possibly models, relating to likely targets. Hence my logical enrolment.

I thanked the colonel for his generous gesture. 'What Ian provideth, Ian taketh away,' the colonel said, with a wry smile. 'But not quite. You'll still be seeing quite a lot of us. Now, bring me up to date with your movements after we went our respective ways in New York. The alleged experts back here are delighted with what you've sent and brought back. I'm grateful too, by the way. Also, by the way, Fleming, with his usual generosity, has suggested that you should have three days' leave. My greater authority in this particular area allows me to extend three to seven. I gather you'll be seeing him tomorrow. Tell him of my extension. Now, let's adjourn to the canteen.'

We adjourned to an absorbing hour of recollection and forecasts. As usual, I silently saluted the colonel's wide-ranging know-how concerning all aspects of ISTD outside paperwork.

I returned to London in the early afternoon and proceeded to Kemsley House. All wars doubtless provide odd asides for a minority of more fortunate participants.

His lordship was fairly tall, broad-shouldered, moustached and bespectacled. His briefing was brief indeed. Handing me a copy of that morning's *Daily Sketch* and speaking from his desk chair he said: 'I'm extremely keen to see a brand-new format for this newspaper. Above all, I want something fresh, something new to Fleet Street and the world beyond. Ian thinks you might well be able to show me something new and practical. If those elusive qualities can be combined with strength, novelty and a truly competitive punch, I shall be extremely grateful. The problem is both as simple and as complex as that.'

He smiled a thin smile, and went on to say that the full resources of a type-setting and proofing unit in the St Clement's Press would be awaiting my typographical diktat. I should ask for the head printer. He was expecting me. The press did not print the *Daily Sketch*, but was fully equipped to carry out my projected designs. A modicum of secrecy was deemed advisable. 'Not that such a thing as secrecy exists in Fleet Street,' he added, with another small smile. 'When would you care to start on this odd commission for a naval officer? Ian even said possibly tomorrow morning. Is that true?'

'Why not? I'm very keen, and I'm on leave for a day or so.'

He made a note, which allowed me four days with the resources of the press, starting on the morrow. He smiled. 'Ian tells me that I shall be agreeably surprised by your suggestions.'

'Let's hope Ian's a bit of a prophet,' I told myself as I made my way back to the Gray's Inn Road.

For the rest of the week I had as strange and entertaining a leave as any active service naval type possessed of typographical interests could have hoped to enjoy before reporting back for further active service. Mornings in the press room. Afternoon sessions at my drawing board in my flat in Crane Court. Evenings – and, hopefully, nights – with any current heart-throb.

Forty-eight hours later, a dozen copies of my eight-page suggested format had been printed for me to take to Lord Kemsley. I rang Fleming to ask whether he would care to see the proofs, and I made a detour to the admiralty. He studied the pages for some minutes and said prophetically: 'Of course, he ought to do something as revolutionary as what you've suggested here. Otherwise, he'll lose the whole shooting match. My forecast is that he'll love it and leave it. I hope I'm wrong! It's not my particular world, but that's my forecast.'

I left Room 39 and proceeded to Kemsley House.

His lordship studied the pages for a quarter of an hour or so, while I sat on an office chair sideways to his desk, answering an occasional query. Then, looking up, he said: 'Ian was absolutely right. He promised something quite different from anything I might expect. These pages are a revelation – even a revolution – in showing how the *Sketch* might look. There is one insurmountable drawback to that possibility, Harling. I am not a newspaper revolutionary. I never was. I am a newspaper proprietor. My main interests are journalistic integrity and increased annual profits. I find these pages fascinating and instructive, but I fear that you will never see this newspaper on the news stands.' He smiled the thinnest of smiles and went on: 'I have never ventured into dangerous newspaper practices. My apologies, but I'm afraid I must include your suggestions under that heading. Perhaps post-war...'

Following this personal, threadbare conclusion, he opened the top drawer of his desk and placed the dozen copies within. 'Ian was, I fear, all too right. I'm glad to have seen your work. I may even show your suggestions to my board, even the editor of the *Daily Sketch*, but I doubt it. You have demonstrated the possibilities open to a courageous man with a new tabloid in mind and money to burn.' He reached across his desk and took up a small envelope, which he passed to me. 'For your trouble and invaluable suggestions, Harling. I'm very grateful for your submissions. They've made me think along fresh lines. That's something unusual, anyway.'

I took the envelope, made my farewell and left. In the lift I opened the envelope, which contained a cheque for £500, doubtless due to a Fleming suggestion. A generous, helpful and healthy pay-off, I thought, for sheer self-indulgent entertainment on a week's leave.

I socked him lunch at Scott's the following day. He'd already heard the sad news. 'Kemsley was, apparently, vastly interested and impressed by your notions, but he's not made for these Beaverbrook gestures. I think I more or less forecast the result.'

'Too true, but if he's interested, why not have a shot at trying them out?'

'As I promised or foretold, this whole exercise sums up Kemsley's financial strength and journalistic weakness. I suspect his brother, Camrose, would have taken a chance.'

For several years I retained a copy of that blunted effort, which has now, alas, disappeared. Post-war, however, Allen Hutt, the newspaper historian, somehow managed to acquire and reproduce the front page of my unattributed dummy in his book *Newspaper Typography*:

the tail end to an improbable wartime interlude for an active war-time sailor.

Clearly a time for a mildly philosophical acceptance of fate's give-and-take. After all, I had had an entertaining week. I could now forget newspapers and their design until the war's end. At my leave's end, I moved tentatively into 30AU.

CHAPTER 4

RENDEZVOUS WITH 30AU

'We'll go down to The Citadel straightaway,' Fleming announced the following morning, at the admiralty. 'Forget Fleet Street. Now's your chance to get to know the naval catacombs. Curtis is due within the hour. I've suggested you should lunch together. This way!'

Two offices in the capacious basement deep below the Mall and the admiralty had been allotted to 30AU: small, compact cabins, furnished in minimalist manner, their bleakness relieved by the warm tones of the wooden desks and filing cabinets. An allegedly efficient air-conditioning system sought to provide reasonable working conditions. But not for me, I secretly vowed.

As Fleming was explaining some of the office gadgetry, Dunstan Curtis was shown in by an admiralty messenger. He was of middle height, and clearly something of a dandy whether in uniform or (as I learned later) civilian garb. Brief introductions were made; Fleming then announced his departure. 'I have to get back. See you later. From now on, this will be your London base. Both

41

of you. Especially yours, Dunstan. You'll be getting the services of
an Oxbridge blue-stocking. She arrives tomorrow.'

Two hours later, Curtis and I returned from the Officers' Dining
Club in Craig's Court, across Whitehall, having covered the main
aspects of our respective backgrounds and hopes for the future. He
was to become a close friend in war and peace. A year or so older than
I was, his mildly pointed rufus beard, plus a new brass hat following recent promotion to commander RNVR, gave him something of
the air of a Captain Kettle, a literary label also occasionally invoked
by others. An initial Distinguished Service Cross gained in the raid
on St Nazaire was followed by a bar following the success of 30AU's
operations in north Africa.

He had an unusually agreeable voice, soft-toned, unaffected but
effective in discussion, except with Fleming, as I soon saw and heard.
That first meeting established that his seemingly natural charm had
been doubtless polished through the years by persuasive use and theatrical interests. I judged that he could probably prove fairly touchy
and quick-tempered if things went against him. This proved to be
true, but, in the Anglo-Irish tradition, he also proved to be as quick to
calm down and put a sharpish temper aside as he had been to explode.
Such suddenness in returning to friendly chit-chat can prove disconcerting to those unused to such mercurial switches of temperament.
Yet – most of his disputants were swiftly pacified by the succeeding
charm. But again, not Fleming.

From that first meeting and later journeys, I gradually pieced
together Curtis's earlier life. He was the son of an Irish schools' inspec-
tor and a rather Bohemian mother, the founder and head of Langford
Grove, a widely praised girls' school in Essex. After Eton and Trinity,
Oxford, Curtis had taken, somewhat casually, to the law. Although
highly articulate and a natural hair-splitter in discussion and dispu-
tation, his preference was for the theatre and its extrovert ambience.
In due course he had become friends with Michel St Denis, the eminent French stage producer-director, who was at that time running

a small, experimental theatre in Islington. There, Curtis had met a young Anglo-American actress, Monica Forbes, one of the four sisters of that latter-day literary light, Alistair Forbes. She and Curtis had married a year or so before the war.

In common with most Anglo-Irish extroverts, Curtis was a fluent expositor of notions, and also, unlike many of the kind, an attentive listener. His humour was quick, quirky, querying. He liked to know where he stood with contemporaries, to be aware of their principles (if any) and prejudices (if extreme). In service matters, he was quick, occasionally too quick, to resent what he regarded as an encroachment upon his authority. I soon sensed that much of this touchiness derived from a deep sense of insecurity. I sensed that his comparatively modest social background had made him unduly respectful of the wealth and worldly assurance implicit in the Etonian background. I sometimes thought he yearned for those attributes. His father was dead and his mother's achievements, although of the highest order, were scarcely likely to sponsor latter-day, outsized wealth. When I met him, he was currently suffering the prods of a major chip which clearly outweighed all others: Ian Fleming.

The two Etonians were as suspicious of each other's ambitions and intentions as a pair of wary lynxes. Fleming regarded Curtis as something of a lightweight, despite his proven courage and gift for leadership in action. He also clearly envied Curtis his gongs and achievements in action. Curtis regarded Fleming as a typical Eton swell and athlete, now a dictatorial and dogmatic backroom bureaucrat, invariably unaware of the need for on-the-spot decisions concerning ever-changing conditions on land or sea. Above all, he resented Fleming's official, unconditional control of 30AU, contending that the views of the men involved in action were consistently overborne by this desk-based manipulator. He could not accept the basic and decisive factor: that when it came to service in-fighting, he was no match for Fleming, a far stronger character and a consummate politico. Indeed, as I had swiftly learned, Fleming had his own way in

43

every matter of importance. His was the voice of naval authority. Not even the most determined Anglo-Irishman could stand against this implacable establishment figure of solid Scottish stock, anglicised to the steeliest degree.

I soon learned that in their conflicts each man invariably had some degree of reason on his side, but the degrees were usually right angles apart. As one of nature's voyeurs and lacking any ambition in what I sincerely hoped would provide, even after four lively years, an agreeable finale to a temporary naval career, I could not begin to understand the intensity of their ambitions and antipathies.

Although Fleming remained a non-active combatant in the war, I soon realised that his job was of extraordinary range and authority for an RNVR officer. He had earned the respect of two successive directors of naval intelligence, as well as that of many other senior officers. Indeed, one senior US naval type had claimed that Fleming was really the DNI. He was undoubtedly highly regarded by the boffins – civilians and naval officers – with whom he shared Room 39, where all major naval intelligence decisions were discussed and finalised. That respect, not lightly given, was clear to see.

Fleming undoubtedly regretted his lack of seagoing experience. He once affirmed that I had been fortunate in this respect and he clearly envied Curtis his operational successes. His one brief experience of guns fired in anger had been as the DNI's observer in a Hunt class destroyer operating offshore in the Dieppe raid. Scarcely a bold-enough christening for him to be able to rank as a man of action, especially for one with Bond probably already in mind.

Later, I came to sense that Curtis allowed his swashbuckling successes to govern much of his thinking. He could not rid himself of the perhaps forgivable belief that the man on the bridge or in the armoured car knows best. History records that many men of action have suffered from similar convictions, followed by similar conflicts. Unfortunately, these sharp differences of personality and outlook can mount up, rankle and cause trouble at all levels, especially in wartime, as most martial histories copiously document. They can also prove of inordinate interest to an observer.

As I came to know both Fleming and Curtis well, becoming the frequent confidant and sounding board for the explicitly expressed views of each concerning the other, I also developed a lively appreciation of the talents, achievements and foibles of each and increasingly liked them both. Above all, I let them fume and kept their secrets. Fleming once asserted that I was one of only three men he trusted, without request, to keep a secret, whether erotic or erroneous. That implied, I hoped, that he appreciated the corollary that I was also the recipient of Curtis's trustful views along the same lines. The crux was physical chemistry: neither had a pennyworth of understanding or tolerance for the other. An extraordinary but scarcely unique situation in any service in any war. Looking back, I sense that I became a friend to each simply because I was apt to take more lightly those aspects of the war which they took so seriously.

So much so far for my two imminent taskmasters: one directional from the admiralty and the other operational in the field.

My first 30AU task was to list enemy equipment and data which divisional heads in the admiralty and elsewhere wished the unit to acquire and deliver ASAP.

Word had certainly got around that the unit did both acquire *and* deliver. Orders ranged from demands for the latest German ASDIC equipment, hydrophones and mine detector units to data concerning U-boat structure and tactics, the maximum readings marked on any depth gauges uncovered. Details of German underwater beach defences, oil fire defences, scaffolding defences, even scorched earth defences, were further inevitable requirements. So, too, was all data connected with infra-red or ultra-violet rays for signalling or detection. All were beyond me. Happily, I was assured that appropriate specialists would invariably be nearby.

The lists had their oddities. Although the director of gunnery obviously needed data on automatic guns (40mm and below), anti-aircraft

ammunition of all calibres, predictors, sights and RDF equipment associated with ship-borne guns and mountings, a proviso had been added
that, although such equipment might well prove of great value, even
more valuable data might be gained, especially for the future, from
enemy officers' notebooks and recent secret publications. The most
curious request of all, however, was that: 'In view of the approach-
ing completion of the *Graf Zeppelin*, information about tactics, and,
in particular, air torpedo tactics would be of great interest.'

'I suppose we'd be shot down if we do happen to capture the *Graf
Zeppelin* and set out for Hyde Park or the admiralty parade ground,'
Curtis observed, after I mentioned this exotic and/or esoteric requirement. I wondered whether he was already harbouring fancies for yet
another DSC, or even a posthumous VC this time.

My own warped view was that supplying the shopping list would
keep a small combined army, navy and air force unit of battalion
strength busy for a decade. Meanwhile, I settled down to do my limited best for the unit.

Fortunately, work in the depths of The Citadel was leavened by
outside excursions. I frequently travelled to Oxford: by train when
alone, by staff car when with Curtis. He wanted to meet the geographers, hydrographers and, above all, the model-makers, who were
already at work on their first project: the Villa Maurice, the German
naval HQ, at Octeville, the Cherbourg suburb. I also suspected that
he was, understandably, also rather keen to sport his resplendent new
brass hat, while seeing whether he was still on the books at Trinity
and could stay in college overnight. Fortunately, he was. Equally fortunate, accommodation in Hertford College was invariably available
for myself.

I soon discovered that Fleming consistently indulged his talent for
surprise. As a deeply ingrained melancholic, he had probably discovered that depressives need to stage surprises in which to involve
friends as well as themselves. These surprises chiefly depended upon
invitation and movement.

One of the first of his surprises was a descent from Room 39 to The Citadel to ask when I was due in Oxford to check the proofs of the pocket target guides I had been commissioned to design. 'When might we expect to see final proofs?' he demanded.

'I heard this morning that proofs are awaiting me at ISTD. I was reckoning to collect tomorrow.'

'Good. I'm off to Bletchley this afternoon and I'll meet you at Oxford tomorrow and drive you back. We've one or two things to discuss.'

I was driven to Oxford early the following morning in one of the unit's Jeeps by a youthful marine, one Gordon Hudson, who was to prove a sterling aide in future travels. I had arranged to meet Curtis in ISTD to view some models. He was vastly impressed by the presentation by two young pre-war architects, whose models of 30AU's likely targets were being assembled in the large lecture room in the School of Geography. Curtis spent much time in silent contemplation of the model of the Villa Maurice, a complex structure that had so far managed to escape both land and air attacks, and was, hopefully, soon to be the object of closer and fiercer Allied attention. The architects-turned-model-makers were also applying their skilled hands and three-dimensional imaginations to other projected targets.

More concerned with my own two-dimensional tasks, I found proofs of the first group of pocket target guides awaiting me. These eight-page industrial and technical gazetteers, sized to fit any uniform pocket, covered a dozen cities and towns in northern France likely to be holding German-dominated technical and manufacturing resources: Nantes, Lille and so on. On the insistence of Fleming and to the dismissive irritation of Curtis, I had collected from the topographical boffins all available up-to-date data for these new-style target guides covering all likely operations in the near future. I need hardly add that Curtis was, nevertheless, quick to seize a set of the guides as soon as they were off the presses. 'For my own further guidance,' he claimed, smirking.

The only example from these ephemera I still retain is that for Nantes: dusty, dirtied and with its pages scribbled with addenda, more or less doubling the scope of the printed data. The text was set in Gill Sans type in the best university press tradition. I hope a set is still to be found in the Imperial War Museum or some lesser mausoleum, for, in due course, they were accounted of invaluable use by the professional probers attached to 30AU.

Fleming arrived in the DNI's staff car during the morning, returning from his overnight trip to Bletchley and a meeting with Sefton Delmer and Donald McLachlan. Those notable specialists in 'black radio' and subversive broadcasts to the German Navy, had been introduced into naval intelligence by Fleming, who subsequently masterminded many additions and aspects to their activities, thus adding further twists to his ever-widening involvements in naval intelligence.

After a brief session with Colonel Bassett, Fleming had crossed to the model-makers for a view of their achievements. He admitted that he was apt to be unduly impressed by the work of practitioners in these activities as he lacked even the slightest skill in the graphic and modular arts. He was especially impressed by those who could draw. That I had already discovered, for he had swiftly dismissed a recent lunchtime contention on my part that anyone could draw, first firmly closing both eyes and then starting to sketch the image seen in the mind's eye, then pressing on. 'Sheer graphic balderdash!' he had declared.

Fortunately, he was as approving of the target guides as of the models, both projects sponsoring smiling moods that day. Fleming then concluded his decision-making by affirming that he wished to take over the Jeep, which he was keen to try out, having an interest in all motorised novelties. I recalled his earlier stated interest in fast cars. He announced that he had sent his staff car back to London and proposed that I should give Hudson the rest of the day off to return to London 'by warrant or quick wit'. The Jeep could be collected the following morning at the admiralty.

We lunched briefly in the ISTD canteen and then took off. 'I'm proposing a somewhat roundabout return trip,' he said, as we climbed into the Jeep. 'I hope it doesn't sound too prep school, but I'm proposing that we meet my mother.' He glanced at his wristwatch. 'Three o'clock in Nettlebed.'

I was mildly winded by this somewhat unexpected assertion. 'Where's your mother arriving from?' I queried as we moved off. 'And where's Nettlebed?'

'Her current home from home: 20 miles or so from hereabouts. Nettlebed is by way of being a Fleming family outpost and hideout. You'll soon hoist in its topographical positioning.'

We pressed on. He was clearly enjoying his day off.

In Nettlebed we parked the Jeep behind a large limo and I thus met his mother: Mrs Evelyn Beatrice St Croix Fleming, widow of Major Valentine Fleming, peacetime banker, killed in the First War. I had heard of Mrs Fleming via Cicely Stanhope, admittedly not the most simpatico among biographical reporters. My erstwhile admiralty help-mate had dismissed Fleming's mama as a 'lifelong arrogant snob'. And that was that! One snob's dismissal of another.

Fleming introduced his mother and half-sister, Amaryllis, begotten of Mrs Fleming by Augustus John. I was amused, recalling Miss Stanhope's comment on that liaison: 'In common with at least one of her sons, Mama's sex life hasn't been all that above board.'

I found Mrs Fleming a woman of somewhat imperious mien: obviously a one-time beauty, now a fully fledged despot; tall, mildly old-fashioned in attire and appearance but wholly commanding in demeanour.

I was deputed to take care of Amaryllis. We walked to and fro along the high street taking opposite paths to our elders. I decided early on that I was the fortunate one in this somewhat outré familial village rendezvous, for Amaryllis proved to be a lively charmer, attractive, talkative and attentive; characteristics she was to continue to demonstrate in later years when she had become a cellist of international renown; dying, alas, far too soon.

Twenty minutes later, on a round-up call from Fleming, fond farewells were exchanged and we were again on our way.

Yet this encounter was a mere prelude to the afternoon's friend-ship frolic. Within a few minutes of what I had presumed to be the final lap of our onward journey to the admiralty, Fleming suddenly demanded whether I had ever met a duchess.

'Not during the past week or so. Why?'

'Because we're just striking south to meet one.'

'Does she know we're on our way?'

'She does.'

'Is there a duke in the near or distant background?'

'There is – or more accurately, I suppose, there was. He's now very much in the background. She's in her thirties, he in his sixties. A bit of an old war horse. She's his third wife. I imagine they'll divorce post-war. Do these details suffice?'

'I appreciate your answers. You sound as if you think me rather inquisitive. Doesn't most successful intelligence derive from persis-tent questioning?'

'I'll ask the next spy I meet.'

We returned to our light-hearted chit-chat during the ensuing journey to Send Grove near Woking – the country retreat of Loelia Duchess of Westminster, the second extroverted and determinedly forceful woman in Fleming's life I met that afternoon. The fact that the duchess was a close friend was made manifest in no uncertain manner. As Fleming climbed from the Jeep he was virtually encom-passed in an affectionate half-nelson by his clearly well-built hostess and then given extremely leisurely kisses on both cheeks, plus the greeting: 'Ian, darling! How marvellous!'

The duchess was tall, dark and extremely handsome, a sexy-seeming, effervescent woman of the world, clearly accustomed to getting her own way and ways. I wondered whether Fleming was one of those ways, especially after having witnessed that effusive greeting. Watch-ing the greeting, I recalled that en route, Fleming had added a few more details to his sketchy profile of our hostess-to-be. Loelia West-minster had recently parted from her husband, the second duke, and one of the richest men in Britain. She had been unable to cope with his demonic jealousy and bullying wish to keep her more or less under lock and key in the family's London mansion, just off Berkeley Square. After ten years or more she had quit.

From the moment of our arrival I became rather more interested in Send Grove than in its chatelaine. The house was as enchanting a medium-sized period house as any traveller interested in English domestic architecture could hope to find at journey's end. Not only was it beguiling architecturally but its rural setting was equally pleasing. These exterior delights were well matched within: first by a handsome curved stairway, skilfully encompassed within the entrance hall of a house touched by rare and modest grandeur, plus furniture and decorative qualities to match.

Our hostess and I were refreshed by tea, and Fleming by a less conventional afternoon beverage provided without query. Conversation was lively and carefree, mainly concerned with their mutual cronies. As they talked, I sensed that our hostess had probably played a lively part in Fleming's past, a viewpoint emphasised by the warmth of their farewells, even more effusive, if possible, than the warmth of their greetings.

Our journey back – this time uninterrupted – was enlivened by discussions concerning the duchess and the new life and home she had made for herself after quitting the ducal home in Davis Street, Mayfair. Now, as I record that episode, I realise how little we ever know of the future. A decade or so after that first meeting, Loelia Westminster was to prove a close and lively colleague in my post-war journalistic career.

As if to put a final touch to the afternoon's social round, Fleming said he had received from Curtis an invitation to a 30AU dinner/ dance at the Gargoyle Club, doubtless a farewell party preceding the imminent departure of 30AU for France and, hopefully, if somewhat presumptuously, the final stages of the war.

Fleming asked if I was proposing to attend the shindig?

Of course. What of himself?

He didn't know yet, he said, adding the typical touch: 'Curtis is so damned theatrical, and far too keen in making these ostentatious gestures.'

'I think they're equally appreciated by both seagoers and stay-at-homes.'

'Maybe,' Fleming virtually growled.

I pointed out that the forthcoming party was virtually a naval closed shop, and that any theatrical leanings were doubtless due to Curtis's pre-war background. No Royal Marine officers had been invited. I was certainly looking forward to the evening. The Gargoyle Club would, I hoped, prove a splendid opportunity to view the wives, girls and/or women with whom my comrades-to-be were currently consorting.

'Your curiosity would be more acceptable in an eighteen-year-old marine!' was Fleming's view.

I grinned, but the question of his own 'yay-or-nay' attendance was left in limbo. A secret wager with myself was that he would be there on the night. This would be an ideal opportunity to view his Muriel, or her successor. This was also an opportunity, I had decided, to introduce a recent acquaintance of my own: a serious yet merry would-have-been medico, if her Latin had been more learned, and, in view of her unexpected silver coiffure in one so young, re-christened Silvertop.

As a footnote to the occasion, I can add that biographers have attributed the notion for this farewell spree to Fleming, but such touches of normal bonhomie were quite foreign to his nature. The notion was solely a Curtis-sponsored event, typical of the man and his fondness for occasions.

The 30AU shindig at the Gargoyle Club must have presented an eccentric contrast to the normal membership of the club: journalists, artists, executives, film and stage types, and the occasional upper-crust celeb from the gossip columns. Several temporary officers of the three services were members of the club, but I doubted whether so many naval officers in uniform had previously been seen there *en bloc*.

From the opening moment the party went with a swing.

My fairly certain surmise that Fleming would be present was confirmed, but I was surprised on one count. I had been expecting that he would be escorting Muriel Wright, the enchantingly dotty, beautiful numero, virtually a mascot for all naval officers in the unit. From various grapevines, including my Stanhope source, I had learned that she had been Fleming's well-heeled paramour on and off for several years and was now a naval despatch-rider, officially allotted to Naval Intelligence Division duties and messages in order to be in close proximity to her heart-throb. Rumour suggested, with clear-cut supporting evidence, that with the undoubted aid of his previous admiral, Fleming had fixed this convenient arrangement. I had also learned that this beguiling despatch-rider lived in a mews house just off Eaton Square, which had also frequently been Fleming's home from home. I had come to know Muriel quite well fairly quickly, and was on first-name terms, using her authentic 'Muriel', never the gruesome 'Mu' label, which, Curtis informed me, was the moniker used by her closest friends, including Fleming. I also learned that pre-war she had begun to establish herself as a fashion model. I could see why. Once her helmet was doffed and those chestnut tresses gaily shaken out, she was revealed as what she truly was: a delightful, fey, slim enchantress. She was also, Curtis added, something of a crack polo-player.

'Ian Fleming has been dangling her on a string for years,' the doughty Stanhope had declared. 'And she's a darling! I can't see how or why she's stayed with him for so long. He must be a blind brute. Everything one hears about him confirms that.'

'Perhaps she is the blind one,' I had contributed.

Little wonder we all hoped to see her at the Gargoyle.

Dunstan had arranged a very long table, with paired chairs at each end. He proposed to share one end of the table with his attractive American actress-wife, Monica. The other pair would be reserved for Fleming and partner, doubtless the Wren despatch-rider we doted upon. Instead, Fleming arrived with another charmer, introduced as Pamela Tiarks from the U-Boat Room, The Citadel base for the tracking of the German craft. Surprisingly, this latest companion was also possessed of very easy-on-the-eye silvered hair, beautifully coiffured. This rare and striking adornment to her good looks had a special interest for me, for I was escorting my own version of a fashionable Silvertop.

Doubtless due to much of my boyhood having been passed in the care of a still-fairly youthful silver-haired aunt, I had long been responsive to unexpectedly but natural silvery tresses in younger women. My guest was even more naturally besilvered than Fleming's companion. To emphasise what must have been among the rarest of coincidences, his partner was also known, perhaps inevitably, as Silvertop.

At an appropriate moment early in the party, Fleming said: 'Why don't we swap our respective Silvertops for the rest of the evening? I've known mine for ages. Where d'you find yours?'

'Noted her six months ago in Regent Street. Met an old flame and lost sight of her. Spotted her again a month ago in Leicester Square, spoke to her and here she is.'

'D'you do most of your picking-up in that area? Isn't it rather reminiscent of your Istanbul procedure?'

'Part of the job, normally, but this one happens to be PA to a shrink.'

'She little knows the kind or size of the psycho problem she's got on her hands now,' Fleming said, grinning and returning to his partner. 'She should act quickly and introduce her latest coup to her boss. She should have his views. I wouldn't mind seeing his report either.'

Later, dancing with Fleming's Citadel beauty, she asked how well I knew Fleming.

'Superficially, fairly well. Comprehensively, scarcely at all. How well do you?'

'Comprehensively probably, but still not even fairly well.'

'Nevertheless, a sound beginning,' I said soothingly, but she was far too worldly wise to fall for such sop and said: 'It's all you ever get with Ian. At least, all any woman ever gets, I suspect. He's like those handfuls of sea water one grabbed when paddling on the beach as a child. Gone in a second. Right through one's fingers and just as smoothly. Well and truly gone.'

'Not necessarily for keeps. Obviously not. Hasn't he escorted you here this evening?'

Pamela nodded, smiling. 'Well, yes, I give you that. He's a notable re-appearer. Just says, "Hello, where've you been?" as if it's all been one's own fault that one hasn't figured in his recent life. Then everything starts all over again. For another two or three weeks. Never where has *he* been?'

'Why not just relax and let it start all over again?'

'One tried, but it's a pretty lopsided arrangement. The re-appearances are all his. Certainly not recorded on any timetable on my dressing table.'

'Perhaps he's a mildly lopsided character. Probably inevitable in characters who've had life all their own way.'

'He affects not to have had such an easy ride, but you're probably right. How difficult has your own life been?'

'Probably a good deal easier and cosier than most, especially Ian's, but we're discussing *his* emotional, erotical, social make-up not *mine*. Remember?'

She laughed, yet somehow seemed saddened by the set-up in which she found herself. Elsewhere in London, I thought, Muriel was doubtless equally saddened by her absence from a party of which she would undoubtedly hear via admiralty gossip.

The Gargoyle evening proved a memorable jamboree, continuing to a late hour, although Fleming and his guest left early.

Fortunately, my own Silvertop's plans ousted all such extraneous reflections. In the taxi to Fleet Street she commented on the charms of wartime naval officers. 'Temporary naval types, but clearly men of experience in wider worlds. And somehow merrier.' She then moved on to the lengthy odds of two natural Silvertops, both presumably around thirty, attending the same party.

'Further proof of the sagacity of wartime naval types,' I suggested, adding a note that this was irrevocably my favourite shade for coif-fured grandeur.

She laughed. 'More naval blarney. How many natural-tone Silver-tops have you met?'

'Two. But no go. I've spent my life – or at least the past year – seeking the right one. A fascinating quest, especially this current venture, if I may say so.'

She laughed. This time loudly. 'What unmitigated liars, tale-spinners and underminers of womanly willpower these wartime-only naval types really are! But do carry on. Say as much as you like along the same lines.'

On that felicitous note, I paid off our taxi and we turned into my Fleet Street cul-de-sac.

CHAPTER 5

PRELUDES TO D-DAY

Although I had kept myself fairly fit and was vaguely deter-mined to be fitter, I thought I should see what kind of preparation the unit might offer someone mildly wishful to play their part in any untoward happenings, if they were spry enough to get ashore. My secret hope was that we were unlikely to be involved in anything as out of date and barbaric as hand-to-hand encounters.

To further those enquiries, I travelled down to Littlehampton one morning with Curtis in his chauffeured staff car, a latter-day wartime indulgence I was delighted to share.

He swiftly dismissed my qualms concerning lack of battle training. Neither he nor any of the other executive officers and specialists had been called upon for such exertions in north Africa. 'What on earth are those allegedly trained marines for?' he demanded. 'Fighting is their job. At least, that's why they've been recruited.'

I mentioned that in all the most successful westerns and war films, kitchen hands, backroom boys and the occasional chaplain were invariably called upon to do their best in legendary death-and-glory stands. Curtis admitted that our own kitchen hands would probably be far more efficient in an heroic kill-off than preparing a meal in any kitchen, and that happily, so far, the unit had thrived without a chaplain, although intermittent attentions from a roving padre had been promised.

I did, however, take a refresher course in marksmanship with both rifle and revolver. I soon put aside the rifle, for I was an indifferent marksman as I had demonstrated long ago on the school range. I preferred a revolver, although, here again, I demonstrated that I had not been to the weapon born. The petty-officer instructor could not cure what seemed my innate inability to counter the weapon's kick, invariably over-rectifying my sighting line. My aim was always too low. 'You'll never kill a Kraut the way you aim, sir,' he lamented, after our first lengthy session. 'Never!'

'But I'll probably hit him, at least, won't I?' I queried after one such castigation. 'And in a most telling region, surely?'

The instructor nodded, clearly unconvinced. 'He'll never 'ave kids, if that's what you mean. You always seem to get 'em in the goolies.'

'But wouldn't that be fairly disconcerting? Even decisive?'

'Best Krauts are dead Krauts!' was his clear-cut view and repetitive declaration. My display was clearly far short of the expertise he demanded. My fault remained and would doubtless remain. Not only did I lack the killer instinct; I also secretly hoped that no German goolies would be worse for wear post-war due to my wayward marksmanship.

On my return to the admiralty, I learned that to cope with the ever-increasing range of my own travels between the admiralty, Oxford and Littlehampton, I had been granted one of the unit's official Jeeps in the care of Hudson, the Royal Marine driver I had already met. I counted myself extremely fortunate to have been thus provided, especially with my driver to-be: a ruddy-faced cockney with ready grin and merry eyes set within lids half-closed, as if he were seeking to pass himself off as a shy and wary oriental. Marine Hudson was to prove for the remainder of the war as loyal and resilient a support as any officer could hope to find. The sergeant major of the marines had assured me that the young driver was immensely proud of his acceptance by the Royal Marines, and determined to prove his worth. He had quickly made himself into a sound combat-trooper, a parachutist, a first-rate shot and that rarity: a safe, fast and mechanically knowledgeable driver. More to the point I found him a consistently entertaining carrier. Typical were his early extra-martial remarks – or rather shouts – made on our first trip, returning from Oxford at something over 80mph down the Henley Fair Mile.

'80, sir! Marvellous! To think I couldn't even drive a month ago!'

'Marvellous maybe, but 80's far too fast!' I bellowed back. 'Even criminal!'

'Quite safe, sir!' he asserted, dropping smoothly to 70, then to 60.

'I understood that our Jeeps are castrated so they can't do over 60,' I said, as soon as we could talk rather than shout.

'We soup 'em up, sir,' was his cool but misplaced reassurance. I let it pass.

In other spheres of knowledge he was prepared to confess to being less omniscient. Passing St Paul's Cathedral one morning, he asked about the building: what was it?

'St Paul's Cathedral, no less, Hudson.'

'What's it for, sir?'

I explained further.

'But why down here, sir?'

I asked where he would have sited the building.

'Oh, more up west. Somewhere near Leicester Square or Piccadilly. Somewhere in the middle of things.'

Perhaps in view of the nation's declining faith and the generally westward movement of so many lives away from the City, he had a point.

Due, no doubt, to Fleming's quotidian concern with every aspect of his unit's efficiency in all likely missions and manoeuvres, 30AU was extremely well equipped for transport, with a sufficiency of Stag-Daimler scout cars and Jeeps. In these endeavours he was well backed by Colonel Woolley, leader of the marines. The scout cars were armed with Bren guns and could accommodate crews of three, or even four at a pinch, especially on hot summer days. Writing about those Stags now brings back memories of imprisoned limbs in claustrophobic heat. Yet they were sturdy and exceptionally reliable vehicles. When a rare mechanical fault was diagnosed, I was always reassured to see two or three marines peering knowledgably into the depths of the engine. Such mechanical misdemeanours provided irresistible but soluble challenges to them, insoluble mysteries to me. They clearly had all the answers, for the engines invariably re-roared within minimal time-spans.

On two occasions prior to D-Day, the unit was involved in manoeuvres with various elements of the army based in the southern counties. Fleming was absent from these activities, but Curtis enjoyed taking off for the tactical discussions with army chiefs which preceded these exercises. He would return to announce how 30AU had been or would be deployed in this or that play-acting performance below the Downs or along the coast. I was present on a couple of occasions, thoroughly bewildered by the exercises by day, mildly impressed by the skill of the Royal Marine cooks by night. I had long suspected that land-based martial life was not for me. These exercises confirmed the soundness of that self-knowledge. I also suspected that any forthcoming land-based martial experiences would be quite unlike these outings. How right I was!

A further revelation concerning 30AU, which Fleming frequently and fiercely deprecated, was that the two wings – Royal Navy and Royal Marines – were not especially close or communicative. I put this mutual distaste down to two factors: Royal Navy Volunteer Reserve officers were amateurs with a variety of pre-war interests, and wishful to return to their far more absorbing academic or professional careers; Royal Marine officers were mainly regulars and inevitably inclined towards more technical interests. The two wings shared the same mess, but were set miles apart by their vastly disparate interests and humours. A further difference was that officers on the naval side were apt to be flippant and cynical in comment, wartime officers only. Contrarily, the Royal Marine officers were there for life, if preserved, and consistently serious. As if to counter suspicion that he might be on the side of the naval contingent, Fleming was always ready to give serious attention to any subject raised by the unit's Royal Marine colonel.

Some of the marines had been through the north African campaign, but most were new to the enlarged unit – still learning to acquire martial skills they had not previously practised, but now keen to demonstrate those skills as soon as possible. They were prideful of their green berets and their Royal Marine status. Those who had made their parachute jumps took a special pride in the wings on the sleeves of their battledress. Occasionally, in the way of bravados throughout history, members of the unit made themselves mildly assertive in the pubs and dance-halls of Littlehampton and further afield. Behaviour to be deprecated, no doubt, but inescapable. Their officers, fiercely insistent on good behaviour in town and country, made things pretty hot for any marine overstepping the mark.

Typically, Fleming suddenly staged a demi-semi-official visit to the unit, doubtless hoping that the comparatively recently appointed DNI, Rear Admiral Rushbrooke, would wish to be on visiting terms with his very own assault unit. A surprisingly smart parade was staged for this near-regal visit. Later, Fleming expressed the admiral's admiration for the turnout and his gratification to both Commander Curtis and Colonel Woolley for their impressive performances. Perhaps the splendid midday meal put on by the Royal Marine cook was also mildly helpful in this commendation.

As Fleming had intimated, the new DNI was a vastly different character from his predecessor. I rather agreed with Fleming's assessment that he was more akin to a self-deprecating schoolmaster than to the assertive sea-and-land dog he had succeeded. I was amused to note that, in common with Admiral Godfrey, his successor was already clearly wholeheartedly dependent upon Fleming – certainly as far as 30AU was concerned. In other interests too, rumour asserted.

On my next meeting with Fleming, two days later in London, I mentioned, perhaps too casually, the imminence of D-Day and my hoped-for place in the proceedings. He rather dampened matters by saying that I shouldn't bank on being in the overseas party. He would need someone in The Citadel possessed of an adequate wartime background and well acquainted with the unit's needs.

I pointed out that Curtis thought his No. 1, Lieutenant Commander George McFee RNVR, was not all that fit and needed a less onerous spell for a while. He had been with the unit throughout the north African and Sicilian campaigns and was scarcely enjoying a state of health generally deemed needful for active participation in the looming fracas. I knew these facts well enough as I had come to know and appreciate McFee's qualities during my trips to Littlehampton. Curtis had already sounded me out. If a successor to McFee were needed at short notice, would I take over? Willingly, I had affirmed.

'I'm well aware McFee's below par health-wise, but he's irreplaceable in the unit,' Fleming said, succinctly closing the subject with the comment that an erstwhile seagoing officer would be an asset in the admiralty.

I remained silent.

CHAPTER 6

A BRUSH WITH D-DAY

A ny final carefree flings before D-Day were, however, followed by a far-from-carefree decision by Fleming.

Fleming reiterated to Curtis and me that his need for a
reliable officer to man the 30AU base in The Citadel overrode all other
considerations and he had decided that I should be the one. How else
could he be kept in touch with the movements and operations of the
unit? How else would he know all that was to be known at any time
on demand from the DNI? Even more important, the First Sea Lord
was beginning to take a keen interest in 30AU's probable operations
and wished to be kept in touch. He, Fleming, would be that touch-
stone and would, therefore, need someone who could reliably keep him
in touch with the very latest info concerning the unit's movements.

He went on: the unit had been formed to provide cover for the scientists and technical experts likely to be attached to the unit in their
researches. He needed a similar specialist to man The Citadel desk:
that meant an officer with active service experience, some know-how
concerning intelligence requirements, and well versed in evaluating

63

the worth of received data. All detail work would be in the hands of Margaret, the young Cambridge don – the 'blue-stocking' now installed in The Citadel. How the hell could he be expected to cope with the unpredictable activities of the 'cowboys and indians' of 30AU in the field without an experienced aide nearby?

Needless to say, I found this decision highly pertinent two or three weeks before the likely D-Day, but profoundly depressing. Under the toxic influence of excitement and apprehension, I had begun to anticipate the unknown prospects in much the same manner as I had ventured to Dunkirk. I knew, too, that I would miss the agreeable company of those I had come to know so well, so swiftly.

Curtis briefly sought to change this decision, but Fleming cut short those views by the statement that the DNI thought the arrangement the best in the circumstances. Why else had I been brought back from India so decisively? I might catch up with the unit if they suffered any substantial losses on or after D-Day; in the meantime, he needed a level-headed character in the admiralty.

'Sooner, rather than later, we shall need another officer,' Curtis protested. 'The sooner Harling sees how we operate, the better.'

'You've been trained to your job and Harling's been trained to his. Or so alleged. I want a responsible No. 1.' He turned to me: 'Weren't you a seagoing officer, No. 1?' he barked.

'Presumably that's why Curtis thinks I'd be useful in his outfit.'

But Fleming was in no mood for any would-be lighter touches. 'You'd better reconcile yourself to the fact that you are now No. 1 in The Citadel,' he snapped.

'Yes, sir,' I said dutifully, silently cursing his guts.

'Noted,' Curtis added, preparing to quit the room. 'I'll leave now, sir. With your permission.'

'Keep in touch,' was Fleming's terse farewell, ignoring the heavy sarcasm.

Both Curtis and I knew well enough that Fleming had a point. Most of his decisions were realistic. As usual, he softened such blows: 'I'll sock you lunch at Boodles if you're free and seek to discuss less touchy matters,' he said, leaving, five minutes after the departure of Curtis.

Over the meal, however, he had more to say on his decision. First and foremost, I was the only one in the unit who talked more or less the same language. Next: now that I had come to know the officers in both the RN and RM wings, knew their names, knew their likely targets, had even prepared their target dossiers, I was uniquely fitted for The Citadel. Above all, I would be able to keep him in touch with more aspects of the unit's operations more readily and authoritatively than anyone else close to the outfit, including himself.

'What a hope!' I murmured, but went on – would he stand by his semi-promise: that at the first opportunity or unit catastrophe I would be given the chance to join the outfit in their martial endeavours?

'We'll see!' was his simple, even curt response. 'Part of your job will be to see that the unit avoids catastrophes.'

I was no good at miracles, I mentioned, as we moved on to less explosive subjects.

Meanwhile, as the world learned later, the chiefs of staff were engaged in their own fierce discussions and disputations concerning the feasibility or otherwise of an imminent D-Day. Appalling weather conditions dominated the Channel day after day. As we now know, Montgomery and Admiral Ramsay were eager to go while Leigh-Mallory and Tedder of the RAF were hedging their bets.

As I needed to check last-minute details concerning the unit's Stag cars and Margaret was clearly capable of holding the fort, I decided to spend a day at Littlehampton and drove down very early two days later. Soon after my arrival in the early afternoon, Curtis suddenly decided that McFee and I should accompany him in his staff car to Brighton. In the best Gaelic-Celtic tradition he had decided to visit a fortune-teller then practising her soothsaying skills behind a minis-cule, darkened shop-front on the promenade facing the sea. Out of the three of us, only Curtis wished to look into what seemed a possibly dodgy future. McFee and I wandered along the seafront I had come to know so well in boyhood. On our return we encountered a thoroughly reassured Curtis. There would be shadows, he had been told, but he would certainly emerge from the fray to face what appeared a rosy, if hazy future.

'Your appointment as First Sea Lord, no doubt,' McFee hazarded. 'She probably hadn't the nerve to tell you.'

'It's a thought,' Curtis murmured. Promotion appealed to him no end.

I was now included in all Fleming's admiralty discussions with Curtis concerning the coming operations. I could see that I was taking shape as a thorough-going shore-based executive. I didn't fancy the prospect one jot.

Three 30AU parties would disembark. The largest force – mainly marines, plus specialist naval officers, would land with the US forces. Their main objective would be the German Naval HQ, the Villa Maurice outside Cherbourg. Subsidiary objectives would be the naval arsenal and the E- and R-boat pens in the port. A smaller party would land in the British sector with the Douvres radar station as primary objective and what was thought to be the HQ of the German coastal defence batteries between Douvres and Tailleville. Curtis would lead the third party, landing at Arromanches with RNVR officers, specialists in torpedo, explosives and radar technology.

Following what we thought might be our final chat before D-Day, Curtis returned to Littlehampton, having offered a few final words of commiseration. The unit would probably move off to its assembly points outside Southampton within three or four days. He would seek to keep in touch. 'I still think you'll be with us,' he said, more in hopeful compassion than authentic belief, I thought.

My gloomy situation, however, changed suddenly and decisively two mornings later. An official note from Fleming informed me that he had considered Dunstan's 'bleatings' and the DNI had put forward an authentic RN lieutenant pay-bob to work alongside Margaret. I could now make arrangements to join 30AU forthwith. 'Pray consider this as essentially a temporary appointment,' was the postscript. Neither of us could have prophesied how temporary.

I went up to Room 39 to thank him. 'You may soon find you've nothing to thank me for,' he said, bidding farewell. 'All I ask is that you should prove duly grateful when I recall you to more worthy and worthwhile duties in this building, which you seem to regard as a dull, provincial office rather than a wartime centre spot.'

'Noted. So I'm more or less on loan?'

'"Observer" was Dunstan's well-chosen word,' he said dismissively, but grinning.

Years later, lunching at the Etoile having recently scanned a tattered journal I thought I had lost, I asked Fleming whether he recalled that long-ago change of mind.

'More or less,' he said, playing for time. 'Refresh my memory.'

I refreshed.

'I seem to recall that the DNI wanted a place for a youngish RN lieutenant pay-bob he'd encountered in his seagoing career. I interviewed the applicant. He seemed keen on the job, well trained and well married. As you were one of the few unmarried officers in the unit, I decided that you should be straightaway placed in the inevitable shortlist of the expendables. Reasonable?'

'Very. But what about your own unmarried state?'

'Touché, but I saw myself as a proven Room 39 man. You were so keen to join the "cowboys and indians", I decided I'd better let you go. A farcically benevolent gesture, I thought at the time. Fortunately, the pay-bob proved 100 per cent up to the job, until he was in turn replaced by James Fawcett, the best ever for the job. So you weren't missed one tiny whit – as you may also recall.'

I recalled.

I clearly recalled that personally significant day. I had asked Margaret to try to get a signal through to Curtis; duly collected a travel warrant for Southampton; taken a taxi to Fleet Street; changed from blues to battledress and, finally, caught a train. Therein, viewing my kit-bag in the rack and reviewing the new way of life it symbolised, I had wondered how worldly wise or even plain sensible I had been in these would-be martial manoeuvres. Well, I could only wait and see what I had let myself in for. Certainly somewhat different from anything the Atlantic or those solitary, far-flung journeys of enquiry my membership of ISTD had sponsored. And certainly decidedly different from a fairly cosy life in The Citadel more or less guaranteed, I thought, as I had viewed, a few minutes later, over the lip of a coffee cup in the buffet coach, the dreary effects that the appalling weather had had on the fields beyond. I hoped that the opening days of June might prove more clement, especially in France.

Margaret, with her usual skills and persistence, had got a signal through to Curtis, who had also received official word from Fleming. I was met at Southampton.

That evening, sitting in his staff car, affecting omniscient preknowledge of my transition, Curtis outlined the prospects ahead, with a map of the Côte de Nacre spread on his knees. He said he had thought of including me nominally on his strength as 'topographer', one of the three allotted specialist naval officers destined for the Douvres landing. That seemed logical, as he thought the unit had with them the Oxford-made model of the radar station. On the other hand, I would probably become more aware of the nature of my likely job if I went along with himself and the small group of naval officers and marines, mostly drivers, and their mixed bag of vehicles. That particular landing was planned for D-Day. Our objectives would be a number of radar stations in the Arromanches and Port Bassein areas. The rest of 30AU – the major force – under the command of Colonel Woolley, RM, plus the remaining specialist naval officers, would land on D+2 on Utah Beach with the Americans, joining in their hoped-for advance on Cherbourg, which was expected to fall within a week.

British forces were to be across three beaches, codenamed Gold Beach, Juno Beach and Sword Beach. These three areas would take care of the planned western section; a segment of some 30 miles of the 60-mile arc of the Côte de Nacre.

The remaining segments of the arc, designated as Utah Beach and Omaha Beach, would be the responsibility of the US forces, encompassing five beaches, extending from St Laurent in the west to Ouistreham in the east. A comprehensive description of the area was to be found in the relevant guidebooks, Curtis said, grinning and quoting: 'A picturesque stretch of coastal cliff and beach which has sponsored the rise of a succession of small seaside resorts.' In the company of thousands of others, we were soon to learn that the same 'stretch' was about to become one of the more momentous and bloody battlefields in military history.

A section of the 30AU, designated X Troop, was to land in two parties on Juno Beach at forty-five minutes and fifty-five minutes after H-hour, originally planned for 0735 but delayed via signal for ten minutes. Once ashore, X Troop would link up with the main fighting force in this sector of the beach. 'Once we are ashore, that is,' Curtis added for good measure, before making dutiful enquiries concerning my last interview with Fleming.

'I thought I detected a touch of compassion for all of us,' I said.

'What a hope!' said Curtis, as dismissively as expected.

For the rest of the evening we gave our attention to a meal magically conjured by the RM cook, backed conversationally by reminiscences, mainly about Littlehampton, of all places.

Our crossing was to be in what was hopefully termed an LCI (Landing Craft Infantry), designed to carry between sixty or seventy men and three or four officers. My companions were two RM officers I had not met previously. The LCIs were reckoned to be the most efficient seagoing craft among the armada, well able to cope with the manifold problems of heavy seas, getting to the relevant beach and disembarking fighting men on an uncertain shore. Their navigating officers had been trained to the limits of their tricky and demanding jobs. Thanks to our coxswain, clearly a determined and efficient seaman, our passage, although far from comfortable, matched up remarkably well to our revised time of arrival. Although well designed for their task, the craft were extremely buoyant, offering no cosy berth for anyone on board wishful for a nap, especially with the grey night gulping out still more of the relentless rain which had already upset the major plan by a couple of days.

The night was as dark as any the Atlantic had offered to the earlier months of my naval career. The sea became increasingly choppy and the men increasingly and more revoltingly seasick. The three officers had the alleged amenity of a cigar box of a cabin, crushed together in dubious shelter.

A couple of miles offshore, I began to realise that nothing – beach or bunker – would appear as what we had been informed. The vast and increasingly dense smoke-screen which overhung the world would doubtless overhang the beach. These man-made clouds derived from the intensity of the bombardment from the offshore warships, due to cease, we hoped, before our disembarkation. Curtis had been briefed that this planned bombardment would flatten everything and everyone on the enemy side well before we landed.

What a hope!

Meanwhile, noise, noise and more noise dominated the world.

As we closed in, the enemy machine guns took over, directing fire on incoming and disembarking craft. Already the beach was littered with bodies dead or maimed. Other craft around us were more or less upended on the offshore obstacles, tales of which had implanted more fears among us than any other potential horror. Fortunately, rising tide, official delays and the efficiency of our coxswain were on our side. Luck and skill got us ashore. In an unbelievable moment we had grounded. So far I was unscathed, I thought, following another officer down the lowered ramp into the sea and wading ashore, head down, following others across the narrow beach to a cross between sea wall and craggy outcrop which seemed to be offering shelter to earlier arrivals. Why not me, too?

The narrow foreshore was a ghastly mess with dozens of vehicles wrecked and forsaken. Many men were also wrecked but not for-saken: medics were already at work. So, too, were the enemy machine guns. The sea was a mess, too. Craft, going astern, having done their job, had been caught in hidden offshore obstacles: mines, steel cages, barbed wire, oil drums and the rest. Many of these obstacles were also lethally explosive, as we saw. We had been told our landing would be on a thinly manned stretch of the coast and that we would be covered by a protective barrage from Royal Marines in written-off tanks fitted with howitzers. Not a chance! Our promised protectors had proved either too heavy and unwieldy for offloading, or yet more junk for the fiercer seas. Most had sunk, we learned later.

The machine-gun fire from houses, and bunkers set in the dunes, which had, supposedly, been shattered and put out of action by aerial bombing, or fleet bombardment, still controlled the foreshore. Within minutes, however, the North Shore forces were ashore and already into battle. One by one the German outposts were subdued, their defenders killed or, far fewer, captured. The under-cover approaches by the Cana-dians using heavy fire and hand grenades were proving too much for the enemy. We watched as four or five Germans were marched down to one of the prisoner of war pens. Time had no meaning. My watch indicated that we'd been ashore almost an hour, but that hour could have been five or ten or more. Gradually, the Canadian tanks assembled. Later, we learned that several of those had also been lost in the landings.

Yet, in an extraordinarily short time, the shore defences were wholly out of action. Even a brief lull seemed to have taken over, but not for long. A quick countdown confirmed that members of X Troop were all present and correct. The tanks for the North Shore Regiment which had followed the troops ashore rather than vice versa – the official plan – were apparently fully assembled into what I assumed to be a rough-and-ready battle-order for the drive inland. Many of our own vehicles were now also ashore. The invaders of Juno Beach began to ready themselves for the battles ahead.

The forward assault formations of the North Shore Regiment were already bloodily involved. Their first objectives were Courseulles-sur-Mer, a small port noted, Curtis had said, for its oyster fishery, and St Aubin-sur-Mer. Both would fall pretty quickly we had been told. But no objective fell quickly that day. The fight for Courseulles entailed dogged and bloody street battles, as did that for St Aubin. Official optimism had been ill founded. German snipers exacted a heavy toll throughout the day, many of their damnable pockets resisting to the last man. Prisoners were taken but not that many. More than four hours of relentless street battles were needed before St Aubin was reckoned to be clear of resistance, and the afternoon was well on the way towards dusk before the last German came out to surrender. They had clearly followed instructions to delay the invaders to the limit.

Meanwhile, the main North Shore force was moving on, ourselves with them. The Canadian colonel was clearly determined that his shock troops would fight the street battles while the main force advanced towards the major objective, Caen, bypassing the battles being fought by his assault troops. Not for the first time in my life, I wondered whether there had ever been a military genius who had evolved an imaginatively preposterous strategy of bypassing enemy forces *in toto* and taking over towns *behind* the massed forces of the enemy. Stuck in one of our scout cars, theorising in such a manner was inevitable. I was merely a useless cipher. I had decided that very early on.

Occasionally surfacing to look around, protected, I hoped, by the steel hull of the scout car, I could see and hear only chaos. Plus smells, a mix of many, all salubrious. I was certainly the *observer*, the role Curtis had claimed for me. I could not second his additional view that I would prove a potentially useful appendage. Impostor was my own word, with a fond and hopeless wish to be elsewhere, probably that Citadel.

After St Aubin-sur-Mer, the major objective was Tailleville, or rather the important radar station between Tailleville and Douvres. By the evening, our small 30AU advance force had been reinforced by the arrival of Pikeforce, eponymously codenamed after its leader,

Captain Geoffrey Pike RM (althogh often given the code name Wool-force, too).

Fierce opposition was still being encountered every yard of the way, enemy sniping still continuous and accurate. Casualties rose among the Canadians as the ceaseless activities of the medics confirmed.

Tailleville wasn't taken until the evening and then at heavy cost. The Canadians had lost well over 100 men in the hard day's labours. Needless to say, those not dead were conclusively deadbeat. For most this had been their initiation into battle.

Attacking the radar station was out of the question. Heavy artillery shelling had shown how tough were the defences of concrete bunkers and outworks. The attack would take place the following day. Meanwhile, Pikeforce was ordered to dig in. We did the same. Rumour and counter-rumour, commands and counter-commands continued throughout the following morning. Naval warships lying off Arramanches had been requested to shell the radar station prior to the proposed attack, but that plan had been downgraded by higher priority. Postponement to D+2 was ordered. By then the main force would have disembarked on Utah Beach.

To our disbelief and gloom, we soon learned that the main body of the unit under its commanding officer, Colonel Woolley, had landed on time on D+2 at Utah Beach, but, while still in the fields beyond the beach, the unit had come under attack from German planes and had suffered heavily, with over twenty casualties, including an officer and three marines killed. A dozen others had been shipped back to hospital in England. Few were likely to be passed fit for active service again in under three months. A young RNVR sub-lieutenant had been left for dead, but managed to croak to stretcher-bearers that he was still around.

Our gloom was intensified by the news that the North Shore Regiment had been ordered to link up with the main Canadian forces, due to join the attack on Falaise. Their place was taken by a battalion of the Black Watch. They in turn were ordered to press on and the Camerons moved in, followed by the 4th SS Brigade. Inevitably, the radar station became an isolated stronghold in no man's land, the area encompassing the station swiftly becoming a supply dump and encampment. The SS Brigade moved on.

Finally, following fierce artillery shelling, 41 Commando moved in with tanks and took the station. Members of 30AU were clearly chagrined by the 41 Commando performance, especially on being ordered to join up with the main 30AU force on Utah Beach. Curtis deputed two specialist naval officers and myself, with half-a-dozen marines, to stay behind to carry out necessary technical searches. He would push across to the main body of the unit. As a vast quantity of what was already deemed to be extremely valuable material had been uncovered, getting this back to the UK by lorry and sea was declared to be top priority. Signals had already been exchanged.

Somewhat tentatively, Dunstan asked whether I would supervise the transfer of this load (or rather, loads) to the coast and accompany the specialists on the trip. But, he emphasised, I was to make sure that I would be returned to the unit quickly.

Would such a swift return convince Fleming of my usefulness to 30AU in the field? With the perversity of all humanity I was beginning to think that my immediate future was with the unit.

I put this to Curtis. 'Leave that to me!' he insisted. 'I shall probably be in the UK next week. We can discuss everything then. I want you here, or wherever we find ourselves, next week!'

So, with one of the unit's 15cwt vans loaded to the gunwales with papers, equipment and two naval specialists, I crossed the Channel once again, within a week of departing. Four years earlier I had twice been out to Dunkirk and back within three or four days. I was certainly proving a quick-change wartime would-be warrior. Secretly, I realised that such fragmentary occasions were, in modern warfare, the enviable lot of those unattached to regiments or ships.

Back in the UK, our load of German technical know-how was put ashore and forwarded to various admiralty departments in a remarkably short time, due to far more friendly weather conditions at sea. I made my farewells to the scientific boffins, entrained to London, and, after a welcome Fleet Street kip, reported the following morning to The Citadel, to take up formal duties once again. I noted – oddly enough with approval – that the new pay-bob executive RN lieutenant seemed already wholly in charge.

Despite the horrors of D-Day, I already wished impatiently to return to the unit. Could any shrink sort that one out? Perhaps I should request Silvertop to fix a consultation with her highly respected boss. Again, what a hope! I knew well enough that I was suffering from that eternal conflict in millions of men throughout history: a convinced civilian and pacifist discovering, to his vast surprise, that warfare and its picnics and perils exercised an inexcusable, yet inexplicable spell upon his peacetime convictions, exorcising all logical objections with minimal comprehension.

What hope for mankind? Far better to leave things to womankind, I thought.

CHAPTER 7

A FLEMING CLASH

I slipped back into The Citadel routine as if I had scarcely been away, which was, of course, true enough. Fleming seemed mildly relieved by my return, sound in mind and limb. The casualties to Woolforce had clearly shaken him. He needed news, and grilled me for an hour. As I was clearly going to be 'an occasional warrior', he said, I could meanwhile return to helping Margaret in The Citadel. The RN pay-bob was temporarily but inextricably involved with the aftermath of the Woolforce tragedy.

Within an hour of returning to The Citadel I realised how deeply the 30AU casualties had affected Fleming. He came down to the underground HQ to seek further info as if the unit would be sending follow-up signals by the hour. Quite clearly, he was holding himself ultimately responsible for the unit losses. Quite an unreasonable and unjustified reaction, but understandable. He was, after all, basically officer-in-charge of all elements in the unit although comfortably seated in Room 39.

The contrasts of my own life were emphatic. Within a week I had been translated from The Citadel to the battlefield and now back again to the admiralty. Within twenty-four hours, however, these disparities were shadowy memories. From my Fleet Street flat, I could be in The Citadel within ten minutes. So I settled once again into The Citadel routine with our Cambridge history don. She seemed to be coping extremely well, with occasional help from the lieutenant pay-bob, who was absent during most of the day. She had certainly shown how an accomplished academic could swiftly become a first-rate executive. This shy, sweet-natured scholar of serious mien was undoubtedly one of the more improbable and certainly one of the more successful appointments of the war. Quite coolly, she coped with all problems that came her way, including the comings and goings, adventures and misadventures of the piratical group to which she had been attached; pacifying irate senior officers; pleading with naval stores; filing; and forwarding and answering signals on the dot. And so on and on. She also kept track of private lives, answering anxious queries from wives, girlfriends and fond mamas.

Margaret soon had a few moments of unbearably rough introduction to the world to which she had been translated. The Cherbourg siege was proving the most exasperating of campaigns. An operation, expected to subdue the port within a week, was dragging on and on. And 30AU with it. The unit, having moved on from Sainte-Marie-du-Mont to Sainte-Mère-Église, might soon be moving on again.

Fleming was not only perturbed by the unit's losses but also by its thwarted movements. Two days after my return he came down to The Citadel very early, desperately wanting to know the whereabouts and movements of the unit.

Mapping the movements (if any) and the probable whereabouts of the separate elements of 30AU had now become, more or less inevitably, a major part of my day's work. From two messages from the unit's signals officer, received that morning, I had plotted the unit's likely whereabouts on the huge wall-map of northern France. Margaret and I had been staring at the map all morning as if it held all the meanings and answers we needed – if only someone had the key to a Cherbourg surrender. But not even Eisenhower had that. We were staring at stalemate rather than action. That the stalemate also had deep tensions for Fleming soon became only too obvious.

Inevitably, my plottings had been surmises rather than bull's eyes, but I had been used to those less-than-exact estimates of our oceanic whereabouts on Atlantic convoys, with dominant clouds and seas at mast-height, sextants useless and even dead reckoning a dead duck. Indeed, my commanding officer had once suggested that I was the mariner who had put the word 'dead' into dead reckoning. Nevertheless, in common with most navigating officers, amateur and professional alike, I rather fancied my talent for what I secretly termed 'intuitive calculation'. Most navigators will probably give a nod of shared agreement to this confession. Most shore-huggers will shake their heads. Had a bookie been nearby, I would have handsomely backed my guesstimate of the unit's whereabouts to within half a mile or even less. With upwards of a million men now landed on the coast of northern France, I was perhaps immoderately satisfied with this pinpointing. Within a couple of hours, my dead reckoning was to be confirmed as near-par.

But I was less knowledgeable at the time of Fleming's query. I took up a rule and pointed to my estimated spots in the Cherbourg peninsula and said: 'These seem to be their likely positions.'

That Fleming was undoubtedly under severe strain was soon evident. Now that stalemate threatened, with the further threat of oncoming German reinforcements from the east, and with his NID operational unit wholly committed, he clearly saw himself increasingly and even more responsibly involved as nominal head of the whole shooting match.

'"Seem" and "likely" are not words I'm prepared to accept,' he barked. 'Coming from a so-called topographical specialist and a recent observer of the battle, they are simply not good enough! Sheer guesswork, in fact.'

'Any pinpointing claiming to be more accurate would be just that,' I responded.

My response probably bordered on insolence to a superior officer, but these were taut times. I was prepared to stand my ground.

Fleming, however, was in no mood for a viewpoint based on luck or likelihood. He had what I can only describe as the most explosive brainstorm I have witnessed. His fearsome blasting of what he termed my incompetence verged on manic fury. Fortunately, the pay-bob was out of the office, but poor Margaret, as I could see from the corner of one eye, had lowered her head down on her desk as if determined to burrow her way through its stalwart timber.

Thankfully, Fleming then left, his shouting fury still echoing in the corridor.

Later that day, I decided that, historically, I had been accused and abused as few naval officers had been since Captain Bligh blew his now-historical top. The image of Fleming's face, distorted as if in apoplexy, inflamed as if doused in red pepper, eyes blazing with homicidal fury, has remained in my memory. At any moment, I had thought, a blood vessel would burst. What would poor Margaret do then? Or myself for that matter? My first aid know-how was negligible.

Had her head been bruised by her apparent determination to seek shelter in her desktop? She returned a wry wan smile, and said she was OK.

'I think we both need coffee.'

She seemed relieved beyond measure to return to the everyday world and to have so humdrum a task to aid her return, moving swiftly across to the coffee pot.

I see that I have written 'witnessed', and this still seems to me an accurate usage. At no point did I feel a victim of circumstance, unjustly involved in abusive, ill-founded accusation. I had become involved in a sombre wartime scene in which one man's emotions, normally tightly controlled, had suddenly snapped. In an odd way, I felt that he and not myself was the victim and accordingly felt sorry for him.

But not very. I judged that he might well have been sensing that the unit might soon lose far beyond its first twenty victims, the whole unit being wiped out within the next couple of days. His unit.

I wasn't unduly bothered to have been bawled out so fearsomely in the presence of poor Margaret. She, too, had clearly never seen so savage a display of rage, never heard so volcanic an explosion of sound and fury. And, hopefully, never would again.

Within a couple of hours, Fleming had learned that my pinpointing had been tolerably accurate. The following day he suggested lunch. We walked up Haymarket, talking over the news from Normandy with no mention then or later of his savage explosion. Indeed, I found some difficulty in relating this confident, self-possessed brass hat to the demented monster I had encountered the previous day. Years later, Ian's wife Ann mentioned that he had told her of his outburst. In turn, she told me, smiling her worldly smile, that she had suffered a few on her own account, but thought mine had probably been closer to an H-bomb than hers.

Over the meal, Fleming said that Curtis had, boringly but inevitably, requested my speedy return to the unit. 'Sooner or later, I suppose, I must seriously consider letting you go for the duration,' he groaned. 'The new pay-bob seems to have settled in and Margaret seems to be doing very well.'

'Very well, indeed,' I echoed.

'No need for over-emphasis. We'll see.'

As the attack on Cherbourg was falling far short of Montgomery's plans and assertions, 30AU's plans were changed. Although the unit was lightly armed, especially for possible action with forward enemy elements, the decision was taken to switch mobile and technically oriented force to three Crossbow sites, still being used for launching buzz-bombs on London. The Air Ministry urgently requested that, if possible, the unit should be made available to escort and protect RAF technical officers to these sites. The request was swiftly granted and the 30AU party in the British sector around Douvres was ordered down to the Cotentin Peninsular to take part in the imminent attacks. These were swiftly successful and much valuable technical data and equipment made available to RAF intelligence. This was 30AU's first success in the Overlord campaign and vastly improved spirits in Room 39, we learned, and certainly in the depths of The Citadel. But these additional operations were leaving the unit stretched well beyond the capability of their official resources. Fleming said he had had a further request from Curtis for my release. He certainly never gave up.

My few remaining days in The Citadel were doubtless usefully employed in dealing with the signalled results of the Crossbow assaults and forwarding details to those concerned and partly in aiding Margaret with the manifold signals that came her way. But usefulness was not enough. Active service had made these London days galling in the extreme, despite highly agreeable evening pleasures in the company of Silvertop during restricted hours away from the admiralty. I saw Fleming daily, seeking to conceal my continuing frustration and impatience. He doubtless saw through my affectation of dutiful composure, well aware of my thoughts elsewhere.

'If you had an ounce of true patriotism in you,' he said on one of his fleeting visits to The Citadel, 'you'd realise that you're doing a far more useful job for your country here than there. True or not true, Margaret?'

'Time will tell,' Margaret said, with her congenital gift for sempiternal wisdom.

Dunstan followed his request with a personal note to Fleming, saying that George McFee was so clearly in need of a reasonable time back home for recuperation and rehabilitation that his return to the UK was a must. Couldn't I be released once again?

To my surprise, Fleming agreed. 'If Curtis needs you again so soon, you'd better go,' he said resignedly. 'Margaret's worth her weight in solid platinum.'

'What about the pay-bob?' I queried.

Fleming's reply was so cool and so devastating I could see my future closing in. 'He's been seconded to more active service in the Far East.'

I wondered what surprise was about to be sprung. There had to be one – of substance. 'Fortunately, we've been offered what I had hoped to find in yourself: a naval officer with seagoing experience, a DSC who is wishful for an interesting shore job. He's also a married man and sensibly lacks this juvenile yearning to be swanning around the battlefields of history. You'd better take a couple of days' leave, see the transport people and rejoin the "cowboys and indians".'

'Why this continuing out-of-character preoccupation with the welfare of married officers under your command?'

'Who knows?' he said, grinning. 'Probably the innate kindness and consideration which you haven't yet recognised. Or acquired,' he added, for good measure.

'A shrink might have another explanation. Perhaps you don't want too many merry 30AU widows knocking at your post-war door.'

That, he thought, quite funny.

In this fairly casual manner, the unit was vastly strengthened by the addition of James Fawcett, an Oxford legal luminary who had also earned his DSC as a gunnery officer in the Mediterranean and who was to become a peacetime friend, a legal light and duly knighted for his post-war academic know-how.

Curtis was signalled that his request was granted and that I would rejoin the unit wherever stationed within the Cherbourg encirclement, and that McFee should be repatriated as soon as he had turned over his commitments to my care. I would now be regarded as a more-or-less permanent addition to the strength of 30AU.

I left on the following day, spared any spin-off from a sudden fearsome personal tragedy for Fleming. His long-time paramour, Muriel, the enchanting despatch-rider, to whom every naval officer in 30AU was devoted, had been killed that day in one of the final doodle-bug raids on London. Her mews house had been involved in a nearby hit and she had been killed instantly by flying shards of smashed masonry.

I learned of the tragedy from one of the RN officers in Room 39. Fleming had been utterly shattered, he said, and was unlikely to be back before I left, especially as he had been summoned to the poignant task of identifying Muriel. Her parents were fairly aged, apparently, living in Derbyshire and not up to the woeful task of travelling to London in the blitz and offering proof of identity of their darling daughter. Everyone in Room 39 was deeply depressed by Muriel's death. She had seemed so gentle and joyous a creature, all too rare in this world. Certainly all the officers in 30AU had, to some degree, regarded her as an enchanting and beloved mascot.

I took a taxi to Fleet Street, dashed into the flat, changed quickly into battledress and was away to Victoria station within minutes, cursing myself yet once again as a nit-wit to leave The Citadel for the cauldron.

Train to Portsmouth and motor-launch from Portsmouth took me to Arromanches in a blustery six-hour passage. The weather was grey and thoroughly depressing. My farewell telephone call to Silvertop from the flat had proved rather more moving than I had foreseen. Our friendship seemed to be shaping for a more lasting relationship than I had experienced so far. 'A man must be wary,' I told myself.

Inevitably, on such a day and such a journey, recollections of Muriel recurred. I had come to regard her as one of the few truly loveable creatures I had known: beautiful, sweet-natured, quick to laughter. Along with every officer in the unit, I had failed to understand why she had not become Mrs Fleming long since. After all, he had known her for a decade or more. She was clearly dotty about him. 'All that and lolly, too,' one of the Room 39 officers had said. 'He must have been off his rocker.'

'He's probably got another half-dozen like her in his locker,' another Room 39 resident had amended, to general agreement.

My own view, looking far, far back, is that she remained at the chilly heart of Fleming's affairs and affections through his twenties and early thirties. Continuing success with other ever-willing women, however, had persuaded him that Muriel would always be there: gentle, unquestioning, forgiving. He knew all that. Would he ever have married her post-war? I doubt that: slaves to romance rarely see their dreams come even half true.

Disembarking at Mulberry Harbour, I was directed to the junior officers' mess, where, to add to my gloom, I had a gruesomely inedible supper. Why, when naval cooks are able to produce reasonable fodder in small warships in mid-Atlantic on just such a day as this, were we presented with this hotchpotch of an alleged shepherd's pie? Even the 30AU cooks were better value. But I was in that kind of mood, intensified by billets in the attic of a shattered quayside house where my likely companions for the evening seemed as dreary as I was. Fortunately I found relief in my tolerably warm sleeping bag.

The following morning, Hudson was waiting with the Jeep, ready for the 60-odd-mile journey to the 30AU HQ at Carteret. We took our place in one of those endless streams of US martial traffic, which seemed to move at a steady 35mph without jams or tailbacks, despite the recent rain and gales which had turned the roads into quagmires, getting quaggier by the hour from the pounding of this heavy military traffic: lorries, trucks, scout cars, ducks and the rest. Dozens of the lorries carried their titular scrawls: *Wun Wabbit Wun*, *Voulez-Vouz Madame*, *Oklahoma Kid*, *Texas Boy*, *Naughty but Nice*, *Maizy Doats*, *Never Say No*, and, of course, *Try Me For Size*. Several written-off gliders of the US airborne forces littered the fields around Sainte-Mère-Église, further sharp reminders of the vast and casual throwaway costs of the machinery of modern war to add to the ever-increasing totals of dead and maimed.

The seaside mansion which had been commandeered at Carteret was quite commodious, but, at the time of our arrival, housed only a score of officers, marines and ratings. I doubted whether, after the fall of Cherbourg, even so large a building would be able to accommodate the full officer strength of the unit.

George McFee had nobly insisted that I share his attic. I dumped my gear there and sought to catch up on news. We had a good deal to talk about. A piece of inspired scrounging by Hudson had unearthed a fairly sturdy German camp bed in one of the outbuildings, unaccountably overlooked by his ever-foraging comrades.

I gathered that Dunstan, under Fleming's daily urging, still hoped the unit might play a useful part in the taking of Cherbourg. McFee spoke of continuing strained relations between the naval and marine wings in the unit and of Dunstan's fury and frustration with what he termed Fleming's 'ceaseless lunatic bureaucratic interference' and so on and on.

He touched briefly on his own health. He was clearly living on a dodgy daily menu of willpower and K-rations. Sitting on his trestle bed he looked woefully frail. He hoped I'd be able to stay on so that he could have a month or so away from it all. He would like a couple of weeks in Perth before returning to the unit or carrying on at the admiralty or, perhaps, even in Littlehampton, helping to train the replacements for losses already suffered. He must relax, I insisted, and take all the leave the quack might suggest. Out here I would do my best to act as his reasonable substitute.

Early the following morning, Hudson drove me down to Cherbourg. I met up with 30AU in the early afternoon, thanks to his topographical sixth sense. The noises of battle were about us. I found Dunstan standing by one of the scout cars, as if lost in reverie. A warm welcome was touched by warning: snipers had killed two marines that afternoon and wounded two others, and Colonel Woolley, CO of the marines, had proved to be the luckiest man in France, certainly in Octeville, Curtis added. Standing by a US tank destroyed by a direct hit, the colonel had been concussed and wounded. The incident had proved a sharp shake-up for everyone around.

Dusk encompassed us, its density doubled by dust clouds, caused mainly by US shells exploding against enemy bunkers. I was offered cramped space in a scout car. Hudson, now among his cronies, brought more K-rations and coffee. 'American!' he underlined for reassurance. I sat chatting with three or four naval and marine officers. Heavy gunfire, the occasional crack of rifle fire and spasmodic bursts of machine gun, plus the glow of tracers, enlivened the night.

Curtis came across and suggested we talk in his staff car, parked well behind the scout cars. Crossing to the car, I told him of Muriel's death. He was clearly shaken. After a long silence, he said, 'I know you thought she was one of the most delightful creatures ever. So did I. Why she ever fell for Fleming beats me. What about him?'

'Shattered – so I heard.'

'That's one of the many troubles with Fleming,' Curtis said reflectively. 'You have to get yourself killed before his emotions become unduly involved. To his vast surprise he then remembers that he quite liked you. Poor Muriel. How could anyone so sane and so beautiful fall for that boorish bully and be selected by fate for a death like this?'

I forbore to add my own belief that death had probably saved her from years of middle-aged agony. Curtis recalled recent meetings with her and was saddened afresh by his recollections.

Later, we moved on to matters more relevant to our own immediate lives, with Curtis admitting that he was vastly relieved by McFee's imminent deliverance from current chores, and also relieved on my behalf that I'd been able to escape what he termed 'the Fleming dungeon'. I sensed that he had much more on his mind and was keen to talk about the present situation of 30AU and himself, in which Fleming would certainly figure. My foresight proved well based.

Although the unit had kept a low profile in the Cherbourg operations, some US staff officers were beginning to show signs of resentment towards the presence of 30AU, seemingly waiting to follow US troops into the Villa Maurice and then into the Cherbourg U-boat pens. I could see the US viewpoint. Also Dunstan's. He had official backing and clear instructions concerning material and data wanted by the admiralty. Further material was also undoubtedly lodged at Coutances, Granville, Avranches, St Malo and Rennes. To get to those targets, we would need to be well up with the US forward troops after Cherbourg had fallen. But would the Yanks play ball?

Much of this US irritation undoubtedly derived from the tough time the Americans were having in their efforts to take Cherbourg. They had lost a gruesomely high total of men, including several experienced officers. To have a small unit of possibly marauding English sailors and marines getting as close as possible to their own forward troops was galling. To know that the limeys were after intelligence material for forwarding pronto to the British Admiralty could understandably upset any staff officer. Less so the officers in the field. They had been thoroughly briefed about the unit and knew something of the value of its work. They also worked on the general principle that any front-line fighting man is likely to be a comrade: the average staff officer otherwise.

An hour or so later I left Curtis in his staff car and wandered gingerly across the few yards to clamber down into a shallow trench onto some rubber sheeting Hudson had scrounged. Curiously, the trench was not as damp as I'd expected and I decided to use my sleeping bag as a blanket in case of a sudden notice to quit. The night was humid and fairly warm, so why not? At intervals the sniping continued, but I doubted whether even the most skilled of snipers could direct a looping shot into a dug-out at the limit of his weapon's range.

Curiously, I had no desire for sleep, even after so strenuous a day. Inevitably, I began to reflect, yet again, on the tragedy of the Muriel-Fleming relationship. She had clearly been utterly infatuated with him. He, in his own steely way, had been deeply attached to her, but nothing to match the depths of her emotions. I thought that Curtis had been pretty near truth in his wintry observations. Currently, no doubt, Fleming was, as his RN colleague in Room 39 had affirmed, 'utterly shattered', but Muriel had clearly been far too sweet-natured for someone as self-centred as Fleming. But could she have been otherwise? Not a chance. Was he drawn to a tougher breed of woman? Someone along the lines of his dominant, frosty mother? I thought that might be the strange truth. Like the rest of us, he was a man of manifold contradictions, but in his case there were some rather outsize variants: his envy of the Curtis gongs, yet his willingness to stay put in Room 39; his apparent self-control, yet the sudden snapping of that discipline which I had so recently witnessed; and above all, his apparently carefree nature, which, as I had already guessed, camouflaged ambition of a high and steely order, as well as his innate and seemingly unconquerable depression.

Finally, sleep took over. The following morning, coffee and some extremely hard biscuits came my way via Hudson. My sixth beard of the war was already well beyond the stubble stage. I sat back against the trench wall and started a letter to Silvertop, plus a stab at the fairly sketchy but comprehensive journal I kept at odd moments throughout the war. That morning I had little enough to record apart from a few final thoughts concerning Muriel against continuing noise and no action.

Action came later that day. Midway through the morning, Hudson came hurtling towards the trench, shouting: 'The Krauts've called it a day, sir! Turned it in! Come and see the buggers!'

I clambered up and moved towards the Villa Maurice at the double, pretty certain no snipers would be evident on this day of days. In a yard outside the entrance to the underground command post stood a crowd of bedraggled Germans. One of them held at arm's length what was undoubtedly one of the largest white flags seen in any war, although perhaps they came larger outside Stalingrad. The commander of the German forces in Cherbourg, Lieutenant-General Karl-Wilhelm von Schlieben, in field coat, Iron Cross at his neck, stood as if disdainful of both his enemies and his plight: a grey, hopeless, washed-out shadow of a beaten warrior. At his side was his naval commander, Rear Admiral Walter Hennecke, his uniform also embellished with the Iron Cross.

Fleming should have organised a lightning flight to Cherbourg, I thought, especially as rumours implied that a royal marine officer from 30AU had been the first to take the surrender, but the US forces were now in lively control. Word soon gloomily circulated that the general had only surrendered the Villa Maurice HQ with his under-ground staff. Other outposts, loyal to Hitler, would continue fighting until the last man. 'Schicklgruber's last stand!' as one of the marine officers opined, somewhat in advance of actuality.

The following day, after the hospital wards had been cleared of occupants, I stepped inside the villa – but not for long. The stench of humanity on its uppers was revolting, well summed up by one of the marines: 'Piss and pus, sick and shit! Take yer choice!'

Despite the vainglorious declaration of the admiral, the remaining German outposts in the port surrendered during the next few days. Specialist officers of 30AU were ready to move in under the protective care of the marines. The Americans, officers and men, seemed to have too much on their hands to make any attempt to halt these prospectors. In the final drive into the U-boat pens, Lieutenant Jack Lambie, a US naval liaison officer, recently appointed to 30AU, had been shot through the mouth by one of the do-or-die snipers still remaining in the catacombs. Fortunately, Lambie's mouth happened to be open at the time and the bullet made exit via his cheek. Curiously, within a couple of weeks only the faintest scar was evident, and even that soon vanished. Along with his Purple Heart he got a merciless ribbing from his British comrades on his return to the unit: 'I suppose keeping your mouth open's part of US battle instructions, Jack?' And so on.

I came to know Lambie well in later months and post-war. He had had an odd career. First schooling in UK at Rugby. Then on to Johns Hopkins University as a law student. Then back to UK for further legal study in the Middle Temple. Then back to the US to run, of all projects, a gigantical theme park somewhere in Ohio, which he'd left to join the US Army. Post-war, following these adventures in the picaresque, he moved to Florida to become one of the first patrons of the architect, Paul Rudolph, for a large, unusual and successful housing commune. We kept in touch until his death.

CHAPTER 8

A FIRST WHISPER OF BOND

After the fall of Cherbourg, 30AU was officially attached to the XV US Corps under General Patton, already flexing his martial muscles for a planned breakthrough towards the south-east, in furtherance of his determination to match his assertion that his would be the first Allied army into Paris.

The suspicion between US staff officials and 30AU which had surfaced before the final assault on Cherbourg increased rather than diminished after the battle. Reports concerning the growing dissension so alarmed the DNI, and, more especially Fleming – well aware that these niggling irritants could threaten future operations of the unit – that he arranged that the admiral, attended by himself, should fly out to meet Patton.

I surmised that Fleming had probably taken this decision well aware that Curtis was on a brief break in England seeking a solution to the problems of moving the vast quantities of captured material from France to the UK. Fleming doubtless had no wish to have the highly articulate Curtis present at so crucial a meeting with the US general.

Fleming had signalled the RM colonel to make all arrangements for a specified landing spot reasonably near the Patton HQ, and to keep me informed. A staff car would meet the DNI and Fleming. I took the Jeep with Hudson, delighted to have demi-semi-official authority for what promised to be a touchline view of the proceedings. I had heard and read so much about the legendary Patton and his imperious ways that I hoped he would be around, sufficiently close for innocent spectating. Fortunately, I was enabled to enjoy a sizeable slice of an exotic day.

Patton received his visitors with what I learned from one of his junior officers was yet another of his well-practised displays for such occasions. He undoubtedly had the physique and presence to carry off any scene he wished to dominate: Olivier playing Henry V came to mind. I was riveted as I saw the already legendary warrior stride out from his HQ to greet the admiral. His welcome was warm, even effusive. He could afford such a performance. He had all the aces in the pack.

With the admiral, Fleming, and attendant US officers, Patton made the way towards his tent, or rather marquee, dominating the HQ canvas complex. I hung around. An hour or so later, the party reappeared. Judging by the widespread, pervasive smiles, everything had seemingly gone well. Fleming certainly looked relieved. He had possibly known more about the background to the matters they had been discussing than anybody present. Above all, he knew something of the tangles in which the eager-beaver members of 30AU could enwrap themselves and others. No outfit could have hoped for a more persuasive and informal counsel. That I well knew.

Then followed an authentic Patton public performance. We stood as if in audience for an open-air Shakespearean play in Regent's or Central Park. The general undoubtedly delighted in such moments of grandeur, parochial or global. His legendary performance, of which this was certainly one, were rare gifts to the world's voyeurs, media men, cameramen, fellow officers, troops, the lot: a tall, impressive warrior, duly dressed for his heroic part in appropriate heroic garb, complete with those renowned mother-of-pearl-handled revolvers at his hips.

I was glad I had stood my ground. What I most admired was Patton's obvious enjoyment of his role. This was a truly natural, highly polished performance, every bit as hypnotic as Max Miller at the Holborn Empire or Gigli in the Albert Hall (both of whom I had witnessed hypnotising their patrons). Patton spoke to a couple of his junior officers, took the admiral by the arm and escorted him along the carefree rank of his senior officers. Bonhomie was certainly the keynote of the morning's consultations.

I could see that the admiral and Fleming were equally hooked, as were the young colonels and majors around their general, but I wondered how convincing the tall, diffident, stooping, schoolmasterly British admiral found the performance. He certainly seemed mildly mesmerised. Then the act was suddenly over. Curtains. The warrior was suddenly the diplomat. Would the admiral and his aide lunch with him?

Fleming opted out, claiming imperative naval problems to be settled. Within the marquee he would certainly have enjoyed first-class fodder and been able to contribute his unique knowledge of 30AU to help in any Rushbrooke versus Patton contest that might blow up. The admiral would need all the support he could get. But Fleming was wishful to escape the luncheon performance and crossed, to onlookers' corner, querying what chance of nosh and a wayside snack.

'All laid on,' I said, delighted by his determination to escape.

'Good. We've a few things to discuss.'

The day was perfect: sunny and cloudless after the recent rains. We crossed to the Jeep and the waiting Hudson, who, following my hopeful instructions, had scrounged a sufficiency of K-rations plus a bottle of Calvados in readiness for a likely call for provender, plus – for he was a young man of foresight – an expansive groundsheet.

I gave Hudson instructions after a few brief words with Fleming. 'Drive out for a mile or so. Dump us somewhere pleasant. Grab some fodder for yourself. Return to collect us in about an hour's time.' Hudson, clearly revelling in every minute of the music-hall performance in which he was so actively involved, saluted and went to get his Jeep.

We drove out for about a mile along the road and then branched off about 20 yards into a side lane, rising above the surrounding bucolic scene beyond: woodland on one side, wide fields on the other. A perfect spot for escapists. Hudson put down the ground sheet, the K-rations and the Calvados, saluted with marine precision and turned towards the Jeep.

'Back within the hour, sir!'

Fleming and I covered more subjects during the next hour than in any other meal of the war. The one subject left untouched was any reference to Muriel's death and/or its aftermath.

I asked how the morning's gabfest had gone. 'Patton was at the top of his legendary form,' Fleming recalled, near laughter. 'He said that one of the reasons he moved so fast in battle was that he left no time for politicians and bureaucrats and their pettifogging squabbles to catch up with him. As far as 30AU was concerned, he had only one decree: "If they're also fighting men they're welcome: if not, keep them out. My men are the fastest-moving action troops in the world and want no hold-ups."'

'A modest assertion,' Fleming said, grinning. 'Under the world's fastest-moving general was also clearly implied.'

'You enjoyed the bravado?'

'Absolutely. But what I really enjoyed was his unabashed pride in his men. That was something worth hearing. He's got his mealy mouthed critics and enemies, but I'd wager his troops are for him all the way.'

'Much the same view as Marlborough's: the faster you move, the fewer you lose.'

'You must elaborate these strategic theories in a martial monograph one day,' Fleming replied, sardonically. 'Do his men dote in similar fashion on Curtis?'

'Not noticeably. Certainly no doting. After all, he's not consistently with them, but the marines certainly cherish and cherished – oddly enough, I think that's the right word – a couple of their officers: Huntington-Whiteley, killed on D-Day and Geoffrey Pike, happily still around.'

'Back to Curtis. Is he a good leader?'

'He's courageous, conscientious, considerate. Aren't those the basic qualities for leadership?'

'You sound like a self-appointed defence counsel!'

'Versus Fleming-appointed prosecuting counsel would be more accurate, but why not? I like him and he's in a tough job.'

'So are we all. I sometimes think of him as a vain, romantic egotist. But let's leave him for the moment. How soon d'you want to come back to The Citadel?'

'Not at all. You've got Fawcett. You can't do better, as I'm sure you've discovered already.'

Fleming smiled. 'You're probably right. I've written you off, anyway. You seem to be a fixture here.'

Returning again to the subject of his *bête noire*, he said, 'Romantics have no place in modern war; and that's exactly what Curtis is. A thorough-going romantic, straight out of some farcical paperback.'

'Isn't Patton a major romantic?' I queried, and went on to say I clearly had a somewhat different view of so-called romantics. So had others. I rather agreed with a one-time girlfriend who said that, in her experience, alleged romantics were cold-blooded characters with a ready reckoner in one hand, a dance card in the other and a hard-on between the legs.

Secretly, I thought her description might be well suited to the frequently labelled 'romantic' squatting on the other side of the ground sheet.

Fleming laughed and said he rather agreed with my one-time girlfriend. He then returned to Curtis. What was my view of the Curtis career?

'He's got his beard and his gongs. He wants to finish the war with all-round approval for a first-rate performance that will guarantee him a successful post-war career with a sufficiency of lolly.'

'Maybe. But it's the current Curtis career I'm concerned with,' Fleming riposted. 'He's quite incapable of seeing himself as a cog in the naval wheel. He has to be the whole damn outfit. His sea-dog notions sometimes have me hopping mad.'

'That's very evident. He knows your views. He thinks of you as a higher civil servant with a brass hat and a reefer jacket.'

Fleming laughed. 'Grain of truth,' he admitted, but went on: 'Anyway, he seems to regard you as one of the few level-headed characters he's come across out here. God knows why, but I get a glimmer of what he means. Do try to make him realise that the admiralty knows best, starting with far more lines of communication than he'll ever have at his disposal.'

'For admiralty read Fleming,' I said. 'I'll do what I can, although I shall probably be seeing him less frequently.'

'That's probable. Curtis is also apt to upset Lewes with some of his notions,' Fleming added as a final touch.

'An easy enough task.'

Fleming smiled thinly: he knew my views on that fairly senior officer, now chief of staff (intelligence) with Allied naval commander, Expeditionary Force (ANCXF).

A divergent note here will suffice. Captain Lewes was an ex-submariner I had come to know fairly well during my short spell in the admiralty. He was known as 'Ginger' Lewes, a moniker of derivation doubtless from more hirsute days, for he was bereft of hair when I met him. He was then a lieutenant commander RN, passed over for promotion, probably due to the grounding of a submarine he had commanded pre-war. Due mainly to Fleming's manipulative skills he had been promoted first to commander, then to captain, a rank far above any D-Day expectations he might have entertained. In this rise and rise, however, he had changed from a genial and fairly relaxed character to an extremely touchy and frequently pompous official, suspicious of overmuch enterprise on the part of junior officers and rather over-aware of his new-found rank. He had also become a tetchy stickler for traditional naval discipline and dignity. Following one visit to the unit he had sent a top-secret memorandum to Curtis, which included the following comments:

> I was very surprised to see one officer going about duty in bush shirt and corduroy trousers. I consider this a bad example to the men. Fancy rigs are at all times to be deprecated and the practice of wearing them must cease. I notice that some of the men do not appear to address officers as 'sir' or to refer to them by their proper military titles. I consider that when on duty and in the mess this service custom and ordinary politeness should be enforced. And I wish this point to be brought to the notice of all officers.

I wondered how these starchy views, derived from an RN background, would have gone down with the Desert Rats. Such instructions certainly stood little chance of activation in 30AU's daily rounds.

Fleming suddenly switched as he so often did when quizzing: what was I proposing to do post-war?

'Probably what I was doing pre-war: designing books, magazines, advertisements and other printed ephemera. Probably start another typographical glossy along the lines of *Typography*.' He nodded as I went on: 'Anyway, hopefully I foresee an entertaining and agreeably profitable career. And you?'

'In due course, I am proposing to write the spy story to end all spy stories!' was his cool and immediate response. 'I've got the know-how, the background and, with a bit of luck, I may also find the time and, hopefully, the talent to tell a tale and a publisher to make it all public.'

This quietly expressed plan of ambitions seemed more like a programme of preposterous grandeur and ambition. I almost choked on my K-rations, but managed the solitary: 'Noted!' We went on with our gossip. His words have stayed lifelong in memory lane.

Inevitably, he returned to the subject of the unit. I was his sounding board, he said. Normally I was first cousin to a nautical clam, but prepared to comment when required. This seemed such an occasion and we talked about the unit, its members, objectives and likely future for a further quarter of an hour until Hudson arrived and parked nearby. We'd eaten and drunk well, thanks to his forethought, I said as we rejoined him. As usual he blushed like an usher at a local wedding when Fleming complimented him on his skills for coping successfully with the demands of the occasion.

Driving back, Fleming said: 'Frankly, I miss your presence if not influence in The Citadel. Fawcett is first-rate but somewhat withdrawn. Margaret looks after the need for efficiency, but we need a lighter touch around the place. Gravitas is a serious drawback in service life.'

'Service life is probably the trouble not its servitors. Aren't we all pacifists at heart? Isn't that the basic flaw? Do you really feel that uniforms, salutes, yes-sir, no-sir, have any sensible or even logical part to play in any so-called rational lifestyle?'

Fleming grinned. 'For some, that's the only conceivable way of life, but let's leave the philosophical, philological, sociological hairsplitting on which you thrive until that future lifestyle crops up. We're almost back with the American Attila.'

We had timed our arrival well. Within five minutes, Patton and Rushbrooke re-emerged from the marquee, apparently on quite convivial terms. Fleming joined them as if he had been present for the past hour. Patton escorted both to a large American staff car.

'You'd better hop in, too. Get your Jeep to follow,' Fleming said, after farewells had been completed and salutes exchanged.

Once in the car, the admiral closed the dividing glass screen between ourselves and the driver. 'Well, that seems to have proved quite a successful excursion,' he said, clearly exhilarated by his day. 'A very sound idea of yours, Ian. Our exchanges went extremely well.' In his thin-lipped, shy, mildly pedagogic manner he was also clearly well pleased with his own performance.

'What was the final fling in conclusion?' asked Fleming, ever the diplomat.

'Mainly that the unit will continue to keep close to American forces. That's the most efficient way they can escape the attentions of the hangers-on. All that's really needed is to make sure that we send a surfeit of top-secret signals to a surfeit of US staff officers concerning the surfeit of targets we have in our sights. And keep them in touch with all our findings when and if possible.'

'We do that already,' Fleming said.

'Recurring emphasis is always useful,' said the admiral. 'That should suffice. I don't know what you both thought, but I thought our host seemed unduly histrionic for a high-ranking general.'

'I daresay Alexander the Great made similar flourishes,' Fleming said. 'Pouring out that gourd of water in front of his sun-sodden army must have been a performance of similar scale. Guaranteed to impress the troops – don't you think, sir?'

'I think you may have a point,' the admiral agreed, chuckling.

He then began a series of queries, some of which, I thought, suggested that one or two points in his exchanges with Patton had found and left him in the dark. In the main, however, I thought he seemed quite well informed about 30AU for a fairly recent arrival with a good deal on his plate. This was mildly comforting. After all, this dry, diffident schoolmasterly brass hat – known to most of us as Rush Admiral Rearbrooke – was, short of the First Sea Lord, the authentic commanding officer of the unit: above Fleming, Lewes, Curtis, Commodore Tom Cobley and all. The realisation was apt to surprise: mainly, no doubt, due to the contrast between Rearbrooke and Godfrey, the probing, intellectual, intimidating, even occasionally ferocious predecessor.

Fleming's departure proved something of an anti-climax. I was beginning to find him one of the most agreeable companions among the few I had come across in recent years. He seemed prepared to discuss virtually any subject: martial or peaceful, factual or fanciful, without reservation. I also enjoyed the strong element of genial sparring throughout our exchanges. Above all, those explosive gusts of laughter.

Driving back, having seen their plane airborne, I reflected on Fleming's curious confession of his major post-war ambition. Certainly nobody had better credentials for such a test. Special correspondent in Russia for Reuters. War service under two directors of naval intelligence. Daily dealings with MI5 and MI6. Intimate knowledge of top-secret matters, from the interrogation of captured U-boat commanders to the scope of 'black radio' under Sefton Delmer. And so on and on. All this, plus the fact that the preparation of thousands of signals, memoranda and appreciations had taught him to write a spare and simple prose. Above all, he knew how fictionally preposterous are the true espionage stories. All in all, I thought he had a fair basis for a start on his post-war fantasy. But did he have the drive? Despite his apparent energy, Fleming admitted that, unless driven, as in wartime, he was inclined to be a somewhat idle fellow. And would his preoccupations with the ladies limit his time for fiction, or at least writing fiction?

As an alternative post-war career I thought he might prove a useful and welcome recruit to the Conservative Party. But that would mean that his obvious lack of interest in politics would somehow need to be quickened. Highly improbable. Yet, with his wartime background he could well be in the running to be Foreign Secretary some ten or twelve years hence. After all, few foreign ministers of the present century had had so useful and needful a training in political mechanics and mendacities as Fleming had experienced in Room 39. But most had been born with invincible political ambitions. Fleming's yearning was clearly for literary fame if overmuch desk work could be avoided.

I was becoming fanciful. Or was I?

I decided to wait and see, especially as I had no other alternative.

Far more important was that each time we met and discussed the world around us we both seemed to have enjoyed each other's views, however jaundiced.

CHAPTER 9

PROBES AND PROBLEMS

Although I was now apt to regard myself as a fully paid-up member of 30AU, Fleming made one final fling to seek to lure me back to The Citadel. In a 48-hour break during which I had delivered to the admiralty some allegedly especially valuable technical papers, we lunched – at Scott's, as usual. Halfway through the meal he asked what it was about 30AU that appealed to me as a way of wartime life.

'Novelty and carefreedom,' I said without overmuch reflection. That simple answer covered everything.

'No wish for promotion?'

'Not especially. I could have had that in India, thanks to General Lamplough. I was flattered, of course, but relieved that your signal got me back and into this somewhat unconventional naval finale.'

'Not the way it's turned out. I had you in mind as a right-hand man to overlook, on my behalf, the whole damned outfit – from The Citadel! Apart from the novelty-and-carefreedom line, does the unit offer any other appeal?'

'I led a fairly informal peacetime life. I think 30AU offers a comparable informality in war. I shall probably return to a post-war life similar to my pre-war existence. This has been an unexpected and quite lively interlude. Anyway, that's my belief and hope!'

'The words you use!' he scoffed. 'Comparable! Lively interlude!'

'I find the relationship between you and Curtis intriguing enough for any would-be novelist,' I said, grinning.

'So that's also what you have up your peacetime sleeve?'

'I doubt it. I suspect that typography and graphic design will remain my major interests. Each is something of a drug. Last time I met Shand – on my last leave – we discussed a post-war glossy to be entitled *Alphabet & Image*. But fiction has its own powerful pull, as you hope to discover or have probably discovered already.'

He shook his head. 'Thousands of other men now at war would give a lot to have something as sound and satisfying to look forward to as your alphabets and images, which I'm sure will duly surface in their own glossy formats.'

'Probably. But what about yourself? Apart from what you told me on Patton day?'

'I've told you of my hopes. I think my reality will be more akin to a bank manager's. But I've hopes of Kemsley extending a helping hand. Agreeable peace jobs are in his gift.'

'I'm sure they are, but isn't your wartime career going to help you in that spy-story future you've also got in mind?'

'If I have the energy,' he said laconically.

We moved onto other matters less concerned with the dodgy ways of war. He was clearly enjoying quite a social life in his evenings despite air raids, rationing and the rest. Happily, I had been able to spend my own brief break with the ever-obliging Silvertop.

My return to Carteret was enlivened by the arrival of Peter Scott, artist, ornithologist and now commander RNVR, and wartime friend of Dunstan's. They had both served in motor torpedo boats (MTBs) operating from south-coast bases in the early stages of the war, and had come to know each other well. Scott was still serving in these craft and in command of what appeared to be the several flotillas which had been deputed to operate off the French coast. I was doubtful whether any German craft of consequence would now be frequenting these waters. Nothing had been heard of E-boats since D-Day when, according to signals, one had been sunk by HMS *Warspite*. Scott, however, had his admiralty instructions which he was determined to follow in his best naval tradition. To that end he was wishful to find a base somewhere well down the French coast where he could berth his MTBs and prove to his superiors that he was operationally alert. I had been studying the local cartography and thought that Granville, due to fall within the next few days, might well provide a practical harbour for Scott's purpose. I was due to leave almost immediately with a marine detachment to link up with the US force about to attack the port. I assured Scott that I would report any parking possibilities.

I departed the following afternoon, the last day of July, with a small party of marines, three scout cars, a couple of Jeeps and a 15cwt lorry. My orders were to stay close to the advancing US military and report back anything of note. Otherwise I would be expected back well within a week. I foresaw a longer spell.

We made good progress, sleeping that night in a field a couple of miles or so outside Granville, rumoured to fall the following day. Despite the recent heavy rains which had held up the advance and dislocated Monty's plans for the great 'Cobra' breakthrough under General Bradley, the ground was surprisingly solid – far too hard for digging foxholes – yet so rutted that we decided we could bed down without overmuch fear of snipers, although several shots were heard throughout the night.

I see from a bedraggled notebook that has come gamely through the years that I wrote on 30 July: 'US have broken through. Probably in Granville tomorrow' – which they were and we were. The main American forces, however, swept through, leaving a ghostly port and no more than 100 or so scattered US infantrymen in and around the town. We drove down to the harbour. Outside a small, stone-built caisson, which I took to be an ammunition store, I noticed a bench covered by a dark tarpaulin sheet. Lifting the tarpaulin I stared into the white face of a German trooper, probably in his mid-twenties, still in uniform, seemingly about to wake from a forbidden forty winks on duty, yet clearly never to wake again.

Hudson, alongside, said: 'No blood around, sir. Not that old either. Wonder how he bought it.'

'Probably by being in the right place at the wrong time,' I said, replacing the tarpaulin for the medics. 'The usual wartime epitaph.'

Hudson mediated with that laconic fatalism-cum-optimism of English fighting men. 'Waiting for all of us, sir.'

'Not so lavish a use of "us",' I corrected.

He laughed. 'We're all in it, sir. It's the one equal chance in the whole business.'

Two RNVR specialist officers drove down to the jetty in the other Jeep. They waved and went into the harbour offices. I sat on a stone bench against the harbour walls and thought again of the young German along the harbour. In the four years of the war, I had half seen many men die, mostly leaping, in the blackest night, from torpedoed tankers, missing our warship deck far below, and swept away in the wildest seas. Yet somehow this young German prompted equally poignant thoughts.

Waiting for the two specialists to reappear, I wandered around the harbour, seeking to evaluate its worth as a base for Peter Scott's flotillas. The scene was strangely peaceful. A few local fishing craft were moored alongside the quays. The harbour seemed ready-made for the reception of a lively new fleet of MTBs. I signalled Dunstan to that effect. Whether Scott's craft ever did use Granville I never learned.

After Granville we were to proceed south to Rennes, thence to Vannes, making en route a diversion to St Malo if that *Kriegsmarine* stronghold had fallen.

St Malo hadn't. I reported our presence to an unusually youthful-looking US colonel lunching with a group of officers under a marquee while watching the effects of the shelling of the port by his gunners. He had the mildly detached air of a film director watching the making of a Hollywood western – even seated in the appropriate director's chair. The whole scene and scenario had a macabre quality. He gazed approvingly as shells hit the island, followed by bursts of smoke, then silence for a few seconds. Under field-glass scrutiny and direction he was clearly enjoying both meal and vista. He bade me welcome, invited me to join his table and eat what I wanted. As usual, these American officers were doing themselves and their fortunate visitors proud. If this army could prove how successfully an army could press forward on first-rate nosh, suitable for hungry stomachs, why couldn't other armies take the hint? I puzzled over the enigma. Not for the first time.

A US major, also at the table, said he thought I'd probably find Rennes and Vannes quite clear. I could press on. We found both towns in much the same state as the major had forecast, reported to the US HQ and were found billets in Rennes. As the scientists had targets foremost in mind, they sought and got clearance to explore and examine. Off they went, and I became a tourist for two or three hours. Then on to Vannes the following morning.

Our journey south was made memorable for me by passing through what I still believe to be one of the prettiest villages in France: Roche-fort-en-Terre. Revisiting the village in the post-war years those first impressions were confirmed: picturesque, stone-built cottages and houses with many of the qualities of a Cotswold village.

Three days were spent by the scientists in Vannes, one of the most historic and picturesque ports in France, with unspoiled domestic architecture set around a maritime square. The scientists yearned to explore the naval secrets of Lorient, but the U-boat base had not yet fallen. Meanwhile, I was fully prepared to spend my waiting days in this first town of consequence I had come across since D-Day. Above all, the port, oddly enough, seemed quite untouched by war.

But not all hours were for leisure. Auray, halfway house between Vannes and Lorient, was at the edge of a veritable no man's land. I drove out early the following morning with Hudson and two marines. Within the town, the tension of the French inhabitants was clearly apparent. Here, no welcoming Union Jacks or Stars & Stripes were fluttering. Townsfolk moved around in silence and obvious fear. Few among them made the V-sign and only children in quest of boiled sweets or chocolate moved among Allied troops with any confidence.

The tension throughout the town was strangely oppressive. Locals clearly thought that if the Germans broke out from Lorient and returned to find that US troops had been welcomed, German revenge would be merciless and swift. At the town's southern limit, US scouts covered the approaches. Dwellers in the side roads, returning from shopping in the town, moved hurriedly into their houses, clearly wishful to ignore American soldiery moving in the nearby orchards or seated on the turrets of their armoured cars beneath the apple trees, chewing gum or munching K-rations, gazing always along the long, straight road towards Lorient and Hennebont.

I decided to venture a mile or so beyond Auray, for we had been given a report of naval stores in the vicinity. I made our number with the two US outposts and proceeded, but the quiet, forsaken road somehow held an eerie sense of doom, despite the pleasing landscape. At least, it did for me. I had never thought of myself as possessing even a grain of psychic pretension, but I then decided that the stillness was acutely unpromising and ordered a turnabout, trusting that the marines shared my belief that I was demonstrating basic elements of martial discernment. During our return, I reflected on my decision. I was not disobeying orders. The excursion had been my own decision. I was not taking flight in the face of the enemy: I had none to face. I was displaying discretion, I decided, without overmuch conviction.

That afternoon three US naval officers, including a four-ring USN captain, pressed on in their Jeep along that same road and were shot to pieces. The Germans had a gun emplacement east of Hennebont.

Later, I learned from Hudson that after hearing of the American tragedy, his comrades had decided that I must have a hotline to the Holy Man and had proved – to them at least – that I was clearly an officer to string along with. Hudson, grinning the while, said he seconded this view. 'No need to hot up the Jeep for the quick getaways,' he had told his cronies – 'No. 1 was psychic.'

Would Fleming have decided that I was mildly psychic or preferred me to have pressed on into a self-made duty?

Twenty-four hours later, a signal ordered our return to Carteret. We were ready and prepared. The specialists were a happy pair, having collected and despatched what they regarded as important material from Rennes and Vannes. And now Lorient.

I got back to Carteret the following day. Curtis was in London. I was to await his return later that day. The following day I would be supervising the onward journey of further material from Lorient to London. Signals were despatched to the effect. I also received a signal: to report to Fleming the following day.

Aided by a conveniently timed Channel crossing, concluded by a swift run from Portsmouth, Hudson reached the admiralty with his usual efficiency and punctuality by late afternoon.

Most of the fairly weighty load of captured papers, plus many of the scientists' annotations to their finds, were already in England and doubtless in appropriate hands. I had addenda more directly addressed and in need of a modicum of professional help, fortunately forthcoming from the duty officer who took charge of everything, also pointing out a note resting on Fleming's desk.

My visits to the near legendary Room 39 had been few and far between. That afternoon the normally crowded and busy centre of worldwide naval intelligence was distinctly quieter. More akin, I thought, to a lull between editions than a wartime storm centre. The usual bustling splinter groups were now quiet, with only a murmuring half a dozen present. Beyond the windows the parade ground of the Horse Guards seemed as serene as any city churchyard.

The envelope from Fleming held no note, but a rough sketch map with brief instructions – 'Proceed here pronto' – with an arrow directed to the address of a cottage in the village of Buscot in Oxfordshire.

'When did he leave this oddment?'

'The usual Fleming efficiency would suggest that your missive is timed and dated,' quipped a nearby amused RN commander from an adjacent desk. 'He left midday yesterday, allegedly to Oxfordshire. Staff car.'

I was still mildly muzzy from recent travels and hoping for a lengthy siesta. My informant was correct. Necessary data was all there. I mentioned my hoped-for forty winks.

'What a hope with Fleming as majordomo!' said the commander. 'You should know by now he doesn't believe in such self-indulgence by others.'

'I'm not off on another secret Bletchley, I hope.'

'We had the impression he was off on a jaunt with another of his lady-loves. Just an impression, mark you.'

Laughter again. Room 39 in a moment of relaxation.

Hudson drove me to Fleet Street. I explained, somewhat vaguely, our new objective. He was unsurprised as usual and waited in Fetter Lane while I shaved off my beard, exchanged battledress for blues and rang Silvertop in the hope of arranging a meeting for the following evening, a hope happily agreed. Well armed with the produce of Brittany – three Camemberts, four bottles of Cognac and two of crème de menthe – we set off. Bed and board were doubtless assured, I hopefully told Hudson.

He'd be OK, he reassured me confidently.

CHAPTER 10

RAMBLE TO KELMSCOTT

Around 1900 hours on that blissful summer evening we reached our destination: a quiet, typical English village. I had had an enjoyable run from London through the seemingly peaceful countryside while listening to Hudson, who had proved an entertaining raconteur recalling recent events on the marine side of 30AU.

A minute of semi-final map-reading brought us to the village green; a further minute of local enquiry took us to the cottage listed in Fleming's note. A beaming elderly woman opened the door, and then a smiling, extremely handsome youngish woman followed her into the small hallway and took over. 'You must be Robert. Come in.'

In this manner I met Ann, then Lady O'Neill, yet to become Lady Rothermere, and, still later, to become Mrs Ian Fleming. Happily, to remain a friend until her death, still Mrs Fleming. That evening she was the lively, merry and welcoming woman I came to know so well post-war: slim, dark-haired, fine-featured, with a mildly imperious profile and presence. She was clearly a woman possessed of looks, vivacity, wit, vitality, charm – and brains. A woman well aware of these facts and factors. My guesstimate that she was in her earliest thirties later proved correct.

She showed me to a small bedroom on the upper floor. 'We're a bit crowded at the moment. I've rented this place for a couple of years. Marvellous for the young. I take it you've got your things with you. Gear, isn't that the word?'

'The exact word. In the Jeep. Now I know I have an overnight berth, I'll bring my gear up here. Will my driver be able to get a bed somewhere?'

'Ian's fixed him up at the local pub. All very cosy. Over on the corner of the green. He's expected to leave the Jeep here and make his own way over there. Meanwhile, get your gear and then come and have supper with us: that's me, the children and their tutor. After that, you're to drive us to our destination. I think I know the way, more or less.'

Hudson was highly appreciative of an arrangement whereby he got bed and board. He pulled out his knapsack and went, delighted with the unexpected novelty of his outing. I, for once, had the Jeep.

I had been wondering where Fleming might be. Returning to the small dining room, Ann half explained: 'Ian's up at one of the Buscot Park lodges, one of seven I'm told, sited at different points on the periphery. Isn't that the word? We're joining them later. Let's eat. You must be starving. Meet Fionn, Raymond and Roland, who has the toughest job in Britain: trying to instil basic academic know-how into their darling heads.'

Raymond was dark, self-possessed and around ten or eleven; Fionn was also dark, shy, pretty and watchful, a year or so younger. Their tutor was in his earliest twenties, doubtless an undergraduate awaiting call-up.

I produced my Camemberts, one of which was opened, tasted and deemed by the children to be quite awful, but welcomed as a rarity by my hostess and the tutor. Merriment governed the table as we ate our scrambled eggs, followed by apple tart.

At the meal's end, Ann stood up and declared: 'Let's go! Roland will hopefully get them up to bed in due course. Not later than ten, Roland, please, whatever hour you have in mind for yourself.'

Kisses and goodbyes.

'Ian seemed to assume we'd travel in your Jeep,' Ann said, wrapping a silk scarf around her head. 'Is that right? I've got a small car here but I'm all for saving petrol.'

'We'll keep to the Jeep. The Cognac is still aboard.'

'You'll be very popular.'

So, in the dusk, we drove off to the lodge, or rather one of the several lodges of Buscot Park.

'Has Ian put you in the picture?' Ann asked, as I swung the Jeep about.

'Not this particular picture.'

'He rarely does. He tells me you're one of the few people in the admiralty who talks his language, which usually means he expects you to be something of a thought-reader.'

'The language of carefreedom,' I said, recalling my recent usage.

'Possibly. He claims you're serious *au fond* and light-hearted all the rest.'

'One never knows oneself. I trust that the rest is around 98 per cent. One never knows.'

She laughed. 'I rather share your view, but I suspect Ian thinks he does know himself. Inside out.'

'He's certainly a more serious citizen than I shall ever be. He tells me that he sees himself as a melancholic Lowlander.'

'I think he does rather. Quite often I think he's dead right. And what are you?'

'A well-practised metropolitan escapist would probably be the verdict of a shrink, if I ever need to consult one.'

'What does escapism do for you?'

'Well, currently, enjoyment from this present moment to the next. Then on to an extended light-hearted journey, one hopes.'

Ann laughed. 'A practical, cosy philosophy. Ian thinks you're basically serious but possessed of more than a fair share of enjoying life as it unfolds.'

'As I said, one never knows oneself. One leaves that to neighbours and friends. And what about you?'

'I think I believe in something or other called destiny. Is that good enough?'

'Well, it covers most things in war and peace, life and presumably death. Meanwhile, tell me more about where we're going now and what we're likely to find there.'

'Well, it's one of the lodges that has been rented for the summer by Esmond Rothermere, newspaper tycoon, as you probably know: *Daily Mail* and all that.'

'The paper on which I started life as a trainee – and left, quite untrained, a year later.'

Ann laughed. 'But why?'

'I thought the alleged training was taking too long and the salary too meagre. I was in a hurry!'

'Well, Esmond is rather a friend of mine. Long-time. He'll be there. And a big cheese at the *Mail* called McWhirter. And Frank Pakenham.'

'I've met Pakenham.'

'Oh, when and where?'

'About five years ago he apparently came into some money from an aged aunt and was playing around with the notion of starting a left-wing monthly. Rather more to the left than the *New Statesman*, I gathered. He needed graphic guidance. I drove up to Oxford with a friend – the intended publisher-printer – to discuss the design of this projected publication, but soon realised that Pakenham's wife – Elizabeth, isn't it? – was far too realistic to let her husband's legacy and journalistic daydreams drift away into a guaranteed flop.'

'Sounds like the ever-practical Elizabeth. She's not here this evening, I gather. Mankind only at bridge.'

We reached the lodge to find a trio of cars parked in the forecourt.

I climbed out, shouldering the bottles I had brought from France. 'Do they deserve all this?' Ann queried, as a manservant opened the door and immediately offloaded my burden. I followed Ann dutifully towards a door within.

The quartet at the table rose as one. 'Hello! Hello!' greeted our entry. Ann completed introductions. Our host and his guests returned to their cards as Ann moved to a side table at the end and took out the bottles from my gift bag, now deposited in the room by the manservant.

Almost immediately the card game was resumed in silence.

'Robert brought some Cognac,' Ann announced, waving me to a large sofa set in a window bay. 'I'm assuming it's the right drink for the right moment.'

'More action, fewer words,' Fleming said over his cards.

Ann took glasses from a small sideboard, poured and dispensed. As she returned to the sofa, Fleming barked out, presumably to his partner: 'Oh, Frank, you're such an ass!'

To which outburst Pakenham meekly replied, 'I know, I know.'

'Let's get on with the game,' said Rothermere, clearly a man of peace and purpose.

As I knew and still know nothing of the game of bridge, I was surprised by this yobbish touch on Fleming's part, but play continued. From time to time the players sampled the Cognac, unanimously saluted as excellent. The game at table continued with no further outbursts.

Ann moved across to the sofa and we continued with our gossip, interrupted only by her attendance at the table to replenish glasses. At last the games were over.

Half an hour or so of general gossip followed the conclusion of the card game until Fleming announced that he had to be on his way early the following morning and needed to be seeking sleep. Pakenham added that he, too, needed to get back to Oxford. McWhirter was presumably staying. I was also hopeful of a fairly imminent bed. Happily, the party broke up within five minutes.

I had been impressed by Rothermere's persona. More akin to that of an academic than a press lord, I thought, listening to his pleasantly low-pitched voice offering unusually authoritative comment concerning the progress of the war. McWhirter contributed with an occasional Scottish-vowelled comment. Pakenham, as usual, was deceptively deferential in offering what I recall as tentative but quite reasonable views. Fleming, the man in the heart of the admiralty, let them talk without interruption. Ann had proved a dutifully attentive hostess.

Outside, Fleming commandeered the Jeep. Despite his abiding interest in cars, dating back to close association with Donald Healey and his pre-war racing ventures, his recent experience with the Jeep in our Oxford–Woking excursion had clearly made him an enthusiast for this novel runabout, an ideal transport for an outing on a summer night. He said he wished he could commandeer the vehicle for his visit to Oxford on the morrow. I let that semi-suggestion die on the midnight air.

Back in the village, Ann said goodnight, expressed her pleasure that we'd met and crossed to the cottage. Fleming parked the Jeep nearby and suggested a turn around the village green. He needed, as usual, to be brought up to date with the activities of the unit. After all, I'd come straight from the Carteret set-up.

I answered his queries with, I hoped, appropriate truth and brevity, for I was far more interested in being brought up to the minute with his own affairs, or perhaps more accurately, the particular affair that I judged I was seeing from the touchline. I had heard rumours that Ann O'Neill was Rothermere's mistress, yet here she was, sharing cottage and, no doubt, bed with Fleming. A brief survey of the first-floor accommodation had shown the improbability of overmuch space to spare for too many bachelors: the tutor, Fleming and now myself.

I began with a carefree suggestion that I was delighted by his invitation, but wasn't the cottage rather overloaded?

'Only a deaf mute could miss what you're implying,' Fleming replied.

'My implication's based on the simple belief that the cottage I'm to stay in isn't much larger than my simple cottage in Wales, and seems pretty tiny for at least seven or eight occupants.'

'Such a seemingly bizarre social situation is far beyond you: is that it?'

'Probably, but in my existence, seemingly bizarre set-ups usually have extremely simple explanations at journey's end.'

'You probably have a point,' he said, but laughed dismissively, adding: 'Only someone with the outlook of a tabloid columnist would advance those views.'

'So might an MP, a soldier, sailor, tax collector or even the local curate. An alleged intelligence officer should get there a trifle more speedily.' He chuckled as I went on: 'As the situation hasn't even a glimmer of innocence for me, what about the opinions of others?'

'They're probably not so warped in their thinking, or so convinced they're so worldly wise.'

'Always possible,' I agreed. 'But how do you counter unworthy or other worldly suspicions on the part of other enquiring acquaintances? I imagine one or two have surfaced.'

'I've always worked on the belief that if a friend bestows an unabashed kiss on either cheek when parting from an attractive woman outside a church or restaurant, any onlooker, including the husband, will think the whole show's above board. A touch of modest blatancy always helps.'

'I'm too old-fashioned. But aren't fond farewells far more agreeable indoors? Especially as most attractive women I've encountered seem to possess at least four kissable cheeks – each worth a far more beguiling kiss.'

He laughed. 'You're getting off the subject. Mature etiquette giving way to randy juvenile sidelines as usual in your arguments and/or reflections.'

'You should put aside that spy book you've got in mind and get started on a Boy Scout's guide to the quashing of all suspicions of fornication.'

'Enough of these cheap jibes,' he said, laughing loudly. 'Anyway, we both need a good night's sleep.'

'Too true!' I agreed. 'My own day started well over twenty hours ago.'

'I've got an admiralty car collecting me in the morning for Oxford, and propose to pop in to see Sam Bassett. Care to come along?'

'Not this time.'

We crossed to the cottage, parting on the narrow first-floor landing. Three bedrooms the limit, I decided. I hoped Fleming wasn't too tired, lucky fellow. And, where was the tutor bedding down?

After my own eventful day I needed no answers to my self-set social queries. I would probably be asleep in something under thirty seconds. I probably beat that.

I went down for breakfast with the family; Fleming had left, an hour earlier. Afterwards the children were to take a walk with their tutor. Then back to an essay based on the excursion.

'Why shouldn't we walk across the meadows to Kelmscott?' Ann suggested. 'Let's take a chance the house is open to respectable visitors. Your uniform should guarantee that. We could get back for a late lunch.'

I thought her own mildly imperious persona might prove far more successful than my uniform in gaining entry to any house of historical interest, especially if a susceptible curator were in residence. I walked across to the pub and found Hudson. With his usual demonstrative bonhomie, he was engaged in discussing the war with his host. We would be leaving between three and four o'clock that afternoon, I said. I needed to be in London by six or thereabouts. He was delighted with the prospect.

In much the same way that a chance partner in an aeroplane or railway carriage will indulge in confessions untold to long-time acquaintances in a drawing room, Ann opened out as we meandered across the meadows, talking as if she needed a sympathetic listener, not necessarily a close friend. She seemed to possess to the full the rare talent for transforming a listener into a confidant. Within minutes our chit-chat was as wide-ranging and somehow as intimate as if we had know each other for a dozen years and had previously exchanged many such confidences.

She confessed that she was inextricably involved with Rothermere, who, however, would not consider her seeking a divorce from O'Neill. But she was also deeply involved with Fleming. Indeed, she had been infatuated with him from the moment she had first seen him in a Swiss hotel almost twenty years before. The arrogant hero figure, entering the foyer, had totally ignored his teenage admirer. She more or less swooned, she said, but had also sworn, between her semi-swoons, that at some point in the not-too-distant future she must and would have him, and so on.

And now, ironically, she had them both, plus a husband. A trio on her own terms, more or less. 'But not quite,' she added. 'Esmond's fear of scandal is fully equalled by Ian's fear of marriage.'

'Fear?'

'Something along those lines. He can never make up his mind about this side of his life, and I'm not sure he'll ever get Muriel out of his memory. It may sound a trifle cynical, but I think he had more or less got her out of his mind while she was alive but cannot now she's dead. His sense of guilt is probably quite a help to him: now he's able to curse himself that he treated his dear Muriel so heartlessly. But that's not my problem.'

'What is?'

'The usual. I want the lot,' she replied coolly, smiling appreciatively at her self-knowledge.

'Usually impossible, but I imagine that most of your women friends would think that you've come quite close to having got the lot.'

She laughed as if in full agreement, but with personal reservations: 'I suppose you're right, but I think that the other party's earlier love or loves are always a bit of a preoccupation for oneself.'

'Happily, an emotional depth I haven't been called upon to experience so far,' I confessed.

She laughed. 'Well, you're lucky. I suspect Ian's earlier women always stay in the minds of his later women,' she said, mildly gloomily. 'Some of them will become old maids in the process. God knows what would have happened to his Mu if she'd gone on living. Everyone says she was a lost soul, thanks to Ian.'

'I'd go a long way towards agreeing with that view. Why do you all put up with so crippling an affection?'

'On first encounter I think Ian probably seems the man most women have been waiting for all their lives. And then they find there's nothing, or, at best, very little truly worth having. Yes, nothing is the word! What you get while you're with him is all you're ever going to get.'

I silently recalled the views of the guest Fleming had squired to the Gargoyle party. I laughed, querying: 'Nothing?'

'Absolutely nothing,' she repeated, and then to my astonishment, went on as if she were attempting to answer a query that clearly puzzled her. 'Esmond's a better lover: more considerate, more attentive, more unselfish. And a far nicer character all round. And he genuinely likes women. Ian doesn't really like them. That's his main trouble. He's too busy trying to live without them – like so many Brits. I think he even resents them because of his sexual dependence on them. He resents the way women complicate the rest of his life.'

'You're not suggesting Ian should become castrato and sing in the choir at St Georgio?'

Ann laughed. 'I don't see Ian in a surplice.' She paused and then said: 'He says you genuinely like women. About the only one of his friends who does. Yet none of these friends is queer. They just want women as sidelines.'

I agreed. 'I think that there's a lot in what you say about Brits and their women. For myself, they give me more pleasure than any other interest in life. I think Ian's well aware of my beliefs, but he'll never get anywhere near sharing them.'

'I think he believes such an admission shows signs of weakness.'

'I'm sure he does. We've discussed the subject from time to time.'

Ann nodded absently as we rambled on. Then she said, rather sadly, I thought: 'Ian really does believe in the battle of the sexes. I'm pretty certain of that.'

'He's not alone in that. It's the view of millions of supposedly worldly wise types. Women as well as men.'

'I think you're probably right,' Ann almost whispered. 'What a world!'

Kelmscott Manor was locked against all-comers, respectable or otherwise. We cased the joint, but all was bleak and blank. I think we were both unconcerned. Too interested in our discussion, we turned to wander back. Ann continued with her ruminations, wholly absorbed in the endless emotional maze and apparently delighting in a fully attentive audience. And, most flattering touch of all: never a single request for confidence concerning the confessions reposed with her listener. Or did she assume that such confessions and admissions were subject to further discussions elsewhere and with others? Everyday chit-chat. No more than that.

And so we returned to the cottage to lunch *en famille*, merrily, even vociferously. And then *au revoir*.

Hudson had had his ploughman's lunch at the pub and was ready to leave. He had enjoyed his excursion no end, he said. The pub was all a pub should be. He'd been treated like a hero and told his bill was settled. He felt a bit of a fraud, he confessed, but wholly unconcerned, as I told him, adding: 'You'll soon begin to think the hero part of these outings fits you like a glove.'

He laughed. 'Well, I didn't tell 'em how I got the squitters when the Kraut snipers were out and about round Cherbourg.'

'Most heroes feel that way at times, I'm told.'

'Worth knowing,' he said, nodding sagely. 'I'll remember that.'

We set out. Once again he seemed determined to demonstrate the road-holding qualities of the Jeep and was soon hitting 80mph. Upon reprimand, he dropped to 65. We got to London in what I suspected was a fairly record time.

I had quite a few items to record to bring my journal up-to-date before leaving Fleet Street for a highly agreeable supper at the Café Royal, delighting once again in the companionable and beguiling charms of Silvertop. I recalled Ann's personal complication volunteered so comprehensively earlier in the day, and hoped that my partner for the evening wasn't coping secretly with similar problems of the heart and head. Such possibilities were her own affair or affairs of course. Meanwhile, anyway, I didn't enquire. There were too many other more carefree aspects of our current lives that I hoped would be duly explored in the near — and possibly distant — future.

The following day, at ISTD, I set about dealing with demands Curtis had made for further 'user guides' — his own usage for the target guides he had initially decried. He now wanted guides for Marseilles and Toulon and, oddly enough, also for St Nazaire, a request doubtless touched by memory. So too, perhaps, was his request for a new large-scale plan of Granville, presumably for Peter Scott, although he admitted that he had had no further news of that possibility. I put the miscellany in hand at the press.

In the meantime, the battle had moved on. Paris was now so much the object of the exercise that Curtis had claimed, before I left, that a 'user guide' devoted to the Seine *Bateaux Mouches* might be both appropriate and timely.

With four days' leave granted, I decided to travel up to Beddgelert to view my cottage and to scramble among the less demanding Welsh hills, especially as Silvertop had received approval for a last-minute break from her Harley Street boss she served so devotedly. She was agreeably surprised by the cottage I had acquired and furnished so hastily. 'So cosy,' with not a single sign of dampness despite the close proximity of the river. Above all, the place was extremely well tended by the elderly neighbour living on the opposite side of the village street. I decided to keep the place for a while if I finished the war with most of my faculties still in working order.

Those four days wandering among the mountains followed by

evening meals and armchair sessions exchanging views of the world around us, followed by shared 'good nights', significantly lessened any desire for a return to 30AU. My partner also expressed no great wish to return to helping her boss repair the psychological upsets and short-comings of mankind and – increasingly, she affirmed – womankind.

Yet, dutifully, we returned on time, to our respective, hopefully temporary, careers.

CHAPTER II

BEGINNING OF THE END

I returned to Carteret. McFee was looking far too wan and worn for front-line tasks, yet, was nobly holding the fort, having offered to stay with the unit for a further week or so. Curtis had returned to the admiralty at the double; whether by his own decision or by Fleming's was anybody's guess McFee said, but thought the latter. All he knew was that an unholy admiralty signal had headed Dunstan's way. He outlined all he knew.

Despite the adequate time the German defenders in Cherbourg had for the destruction of virtually anything of value to the Allies, the specialist officers in 30AU continued to uncover material deemed useful to experts mainly concerned with radar equipment and weaponry of advanced or curious design. These finds were assembled for swift shipment to England. Captain Lewes and Fleming had taken over the arrangements for these cross-Channel shipments via local launches between Cherbourg and Portsmouth.

Who made the decision for one of these craft to make an overnight passage was something of a mystery. Needless to say, Curtis contended that Fleming had made or should have made all the arrangements, while Fleming contended that he had proof of Curtis's guilt at all points. Lewes merely fumed and spluttered.

'Altogether a typical cock-up by the Testy Trio,' McFee opined, smiling thinly yet definitively.

The episode had certainly sponsored both fiasco and fury. Nobody was prepared to supply background data concerning responsibility for the requisition of the craft or even authority for the rendezvous.

After hours of desultory searching, the master of the launch had returned to Portsmouth. Fleming had, apparently, gone berserk on receiving the news. Hence his recall of Curtis to London. The fulminations took both sides of an OHMS foolscap sheet, single-spaced, totalling well over a thousand bitter words. McFee had a copy. The merciless denunciation of Curtis and his ways of thought included the assertion that 'great trouble was taken to lay this craft on as you desired and it is indeed disappointing that the unit should have failed'.

Fleming then proceeded at length to outline the further shortcomings of the unit – primarily those of Curtis – in a lengthy critique, concluding with the crux of the continuing conflict between the two men:

> With the best will in the world I find it quite impossible to fathom your motives. I urge you not to continue questioning the decisions of the DNI and ANCXF, under whose orders you operate. The position in Brittany and also in regard to Paris is perfectly clear here and we are fully informed of the progress of the campaign. Why you should imagine that this is not so, which is the only possible excuse for your attitude, I cannot understand. The duties of the unit and its immediate role are also planned on the basis of more information than you can ever possess in the field. One thing is certain and that is that unless the unit obeys its orders without question during the future stages of the campaign, it will be quite impossible for me or Captain Lewes to prevent higher authority intervening drastically.

'Pompous nonsense!' had been the verdict of Curtis determined to defend his views in a sudden return to the admiralty. Meanwhile, the unit medico had declared McFee unfit for any activities in the field for at least six months. He was, apparently, still suffering from a recurrence of the malaria he had contracted at Salerno during the Italian campaign. He could carry out light duties in some undemanding naval outfit, if there were such an outfit, but active service was absolutely no go. Curtis had been informed and would doubtless have informed Fleming by now. Although vastly sympathetic towards McFee, I could sense that his return to the UK would probably sponsor my further service in France and beyond. But would this sensitive belief hold out against the gruesome expectations expressed in the Fleming missive?

The post mortem concerning the signal continued. The whole affair was, quite simply, a cock-up between Fleming and Lewes, Curtis contended on his return. Hence their venom towards him. Such mishaps were inevitable in wartime. Even in the Royal Navy, he added, with a typical sarcastic touch. As was the attempted offloading of responsibility.

Later that evening, having cooled down, Curtis said that in a brief and slightly more civilised moment he had been allowed by Fleming to outline the McFee situation and to advance a proposal, which he was now wishful to pass on to me. I waited, amused, doubtless half aware of what was to come. Briefly, Curtis had squared Fleming with the suggestion that I should take McFee's place – but, he added, he now had a semi-secret and sizeable request to make to me – already made to Fleming, he added apologetically. If I were agreeable and the details could be arranged – and he saw no problem – would I be willing to have McFee continue to be officially listed as the nominal No. 1 of the naval wing of 30AU and myself labelled as 'acting officer in the field', my links with ISTD duly underlined? Would I agree to this admittedly unusual arrangement?

'Why not "visiting cartographer"?' I asked, but this straight-faced suggestion was dismissed on the spot as cynical and typical word-banging on my part.

'That word "acting" was the important word for the characters upstairs,' Curtis said firmly. 'Let them mull over that.'

I always enjoyed watching Curtis's dexterity at work, first on himself and then on the beneficiary or victim of his proposal(s). Here was such a performance. I sought to hide my relish as his words proceeded to their conclusion. I then gave him my simple reaction: so long as I remained on somebody's payroll, he could make any pronouncement he wished. I wasn't in the navy for labels or glory, merely to pass the time until our unknown masters called it a day. The sooner the better.

Indeed, I would have agreed to this particular proposal even if I had been labelled 'supernumerary galley hand'. I had no naval ambitions other than to stay alive, preferably in sound physical shape, so that I could enjoy every scrap of interest and entertainment out of this appalling yet absorbing interruption to peace. Indeed, this imminent switch dispelled one or two desultory expectations I had occasionally considered, including being discovered long after the war's end as a uniformed skeleton deep down in The Citadel. Instead, I was to start, almost immediately, to explore a new twist to my naval experience. Curtis and McFee expressed themselves delighted with my speedy acquiescence.

Forty-eight hours later I was in London to further this new set-up. Fleming was diplomatically silent concerning the postscript to his Curtis letter. Indeed, he was clearly delighted with the new Citadel arrangements he had established. He now had a supremely efficient pair down there and suggested that McFee's convalescence would be more profitable to the unit if his time were to be spent in training new ratings for active service. Not exactly a conventional convalescence but welcomed by McFee, especially as strong whispers foretold that the unit might well be remodelled before the year's end.

I travelled down to Littlehampton to see McFee a week before taking over the foray that I was now to lead, and to take a glance at the mixed bag of trained and trainee marines he was preparing for my departure. Although showing welcome signs of improvement since my meeting with him at Carteret a week or so earlier, he still looked 'somewhat overdrawn'. 'Far better to be physically overdrawn than financially for any Scot,' he said, living up to the legend, as we strolled from his agreeable billet in one of the would-be Georgian houses on the promenade to the temporary HQ of the unit in a nearby Victorian mansion. With his dark, pointed beard, I suggested that he looked like a hollow-eyed hidalgo down on his physical – if not martial – luck.

'A downhearted Scotsman can be just as doleful as any Spanish hidalgo, but I'm on the mend.'

Why hadn't he taken sick leave and stayed home in Scotland for a couple of months?

'I'll probably push off there once I've seen you and your lot off,' he said, and merely smiled when I mentioned that masochism was a way of life for some Scots.

How soon would he like me to appear? Departure was booked for a week ahead in Dunstan's timetable.

'Why not come down the evening before. I think you'll find everything and everyone fairly ship-shape.'

Knowing my man, I agreed. Thankfully.

McFee's convalescence in Littlehampton rather than in London or Perth was to prove a major benefaction for the unit and above all for myself. His know-how concerning our needs, the replacement of vehicles and spare parts and, above all, the assembly of stores, was masterly. These convalescent chores were conducted as if he had been trained from his pram in the logistics of war. I asked whether his peacetime career as an accountant helped. He was dubious. 'Perhaps the Scottish aptitude for figures comes into things,' was his tentative suggestion.

Later in the week, I lunched with Fleming at the Etoile. I arrived to find him at a table set for three. Ann would probably be joining us for a few minutes en route to some fashion jamboree, he said, and then asked whether I had heard that her husband, Lord O'Neill, had been killed in the Italian campaign the previous week. I hadn't. But I immediately set to wondering what further upsets this tragedy might promote. I asked how Ann had taken the news. 'Brought pretty low, but recovering slowly,' he said gloomily.

I had no doubt that her sadness had probably been intensified, rather than lessened, by this reduction of her manageable threesome to a mere pair. A double life would undoubtedly prove more difficult to handle than the treble had been. But she was resilient and I was not surprised to note that despite the clearly evident sadness of her loss, she was *au fond* her usual self.

Her gift for prompting gaiety in others was unquenched. The effect upon Fleming, the self-confessed Lowland melancholic, was swiftly exorcised, even if temporarily. Indeed, he brightened even as she settled in her chair and opted firmly for: 'Salad. No more. I must be away in ten minutes!'

Half an hour later she left.

I watched her closely throughout that half-hour. I was surprised, puzzled and somewhat impressed by what I saw. Nobody, I thought, could have detected in her demeanour that she had been recently widowed. I could not help but begin speculation of what this loss would really mean to herself and her two admirers. Would Rothermere's wealth prove too enticing, or Fleming's more puzzling personality prove too tempting? I could certainly foresee no likely, clear-cut decision.

After Ann had left, Fleming inevitably turned to the subject of the unit, opining that its days as a basically British 'cowboys and indians' outfit were clearly numbered. The imminent exercise in which I was about to be involved could well prove the last of these useful admiralty-sponsored ventures.

He went on to confirm rumours which had recently been permeating 30AU. The unit, now so substantially enlarged, was already virtually under the complete direction of the intelligence wing of Supreme Headquarters Allied Expeditionary Force (SHAEF), which,

Fleming added, had expressed high opinions of the unit's achievements. Future forays would, however, be unlikely to involve more than a score or so of marines, each group hopefully protective of three or four scientists or specialists. United States intelligence needed to show its worth.

'How many marines are you taking on this venture? D'you know yet?'

'Just under 100, all in, I gather from McFee. More than enough, you think?'

'I imagine this is likely to be the last exercise of its kind. One of that size, anyway. You have a formidable list of objectives. I was shown the total yesterday. McFee seems pretty efficient in these matters. I wish you well, but I foresee an end to such exercises.'

'So our trip spells finito for 30AU?'

'More or less. Especially, as I said, for sorties of that size.'

'Yet McFee says we're not one whit over-manned, judging from the requests, orders and demands already received, and the number of alleged experts, scientists and boffins already promising to join us from time to time.'

'Best of luck!' Fleming said, grinning.

I then queried the likely place of Fleming himself in these imminent changes.

'I'll probably be retained on specific NID commitments – rather akin to the project I'm preparing for currently.'

'I won't enquire. What about Curtis?'

'He'll doubtless continue as nominal and operational head of the unit in the field. Who knows?'

'Splintered head of a splintered toy?'

'A cynic might put things that way. Just enjoy the last of your own "cowboys and indians" ventures. When d'you leave?'

'Friday.'

'How long d'you expect to be away?'

'A month, six weeks. Even somewhat longer, I'm told.'

'Have a good time. I'll probably be away myself most of the time.'

'Not with 30AU?'

'Far from it. I feel the need for a touch of sunlight.'

'Jamaican species?'

'Sadly, no. Briefly, I've been nominated by the DNI to make all necessary arrangements to visit our bases in the Far East. We've now had all British Pacific Fleet intelligence thrust upon NID. Frankly, there's damn little we know about the area as a battle sea. I'm being sent to see what's going on and what can be done – if anything.'

'When will you be going?'

'About the same time as your venture, I imagine, and I'll probably be away over a month, I guess. Somewhat less hazardous and basic as your own trip. Why not keep a log?'

'But won't this venture be more in line for you to keep a log?'

'That's always part of the exercise, but back to you.'

'Well, I do keep records en route: my own reactions to the places we get to and the characters – warriors and others we meet. Casual, personal, superficial.'

He laughed. 'So I guessed. Any chance of seeing a sample of your notes next month? I'll undoubtedly spare a few thoughts for the final days of 30AU while I'm sunbathing on some Ceylonese beauty or beach.'

'I'll see.'

He laughed. 'You can omit the reactions and dimensions of any adventuresses.'

'The only bits worth recording, but I'll see,' I said again, even more hazily.

Despite Fleming's seeming detachment, even nonchalance, in speaking of the probable changes in the destiny of 30AU, in the official recognition of the unit's worth and achievements, and his own forthcoming trip, I sensed that he was saddened by the oncoming break-up of the unit he had virtually created and fostered single-handed. His comments had certainly underlined the fact that US intelligence had recognised the value of this outfit and was taking it over, ready-made, for further and probably final forays.

I could sense his depression as the takeover neared, and was probably why he had set up what would be virtually a one-man, half-round-the-world trip, quite different from earlier ventures along with the then DNI. Nominally, as he had said, he was off to check the far-flung NID personnel and to estimate its capabilities for coping with intelligence demands likely to result from the setting-up of a British Pacific Fleet. He would certainly be seeing Admiral Godfrey and seeking his views on these prospects. Well, best of luck! He was putting Room 39 and 30AU well behind him as the war closed in.

Wandering back to the admiralty I was still preoccupied with our respective ventures and his departure from the unit, for that was clearly the prospect.

'General Lamplough wanted to keep me out there, so Godfrey will certainly seek to entice you.'

'Only if an entrancing Wren is part of the offer!'

In due course, Fleming did meet up with a witty, lively minded, easy-on-the-eye Wren officer, one Clare Blanchard, who was to become my highly accomplished post-war secretary, following Fleming's fulsome commendations.

My contact with the unit for our departure on that early December morning was so well timed that instead of an intending rendezvous with McFee for the previous evening, I arrived, with mutual telephonic agreement, an hour before the convoy was to move off.

'I hope she was worth it,' McFee, greeting my arrival. He didn't believe me when I said that a book, not a girl, had occupied me until the early hours. Before leaving, I'd been determined to finish a monograph I was writing on the wood engravings of Eric Ravilious, war artist and friend, who had died two years before in a plane lost off Iceland.

'Thanks again for your ready agreement with Dunstan's scheme, strictly on my behalf and for my benefit.'

'In return, thanks for what you've landed me in for here,' I said, surveying the quite impressive line of scout cars, Jeeps, signal wagon and the rest.

He handed me the loading and personnel forms. 'Wish you luck and all that, but I can't say I'm sorry not to be going this time.' He was looking appreciably fitter than a week previously, but still woefully thin.

I climbed into the scout car and the unit was on the move.

I consulted the personnel forms fleetingly. They included: a torpedo expert, attached full-time to the unit; two qualified diving officers from the Torpedo and Mines Division; a signals officer; and a US naval lieutenant liaison officer. This, happily, proved to be Lieutenant Lambie who had been wounded in so bizarre a manner in the German U-boat pens in Cherbourg. He was now fully recovered and, to the astonishment of all, carried no sign of the wound in his cheek.

The prospect ahead had its hazy outlines. A memo from Fleming to McFee, retained through the years, provides reason enough for my doubts concerning my qualifications for leading this field team of some sixteen vehicles, including four 3-tonne lorries; a pair of 15cwt wireless-telegraph signal vans, 'fitted with two crystal-controlled RN Type 65 jets, with power supplied by 12hp petrol driven generators, the frequencies to be 4150kcs with no alternative'. Our ciphers would be army two-way one-time pads with British No. 5 (SP 02105) as the basic book, which would not, as the basic book made clear, 'facilitate sending messages in cipher between two outstations: the control station of this net at sub-HQ would be open the full twenty-four hours'. Scarcely the set-up for an appointed leader so keen on small score-strong operational units.

Those notes meant little enough to me then, still less now. I include them for the possible amusement they might provide for a latter-day schoolboy who might happen upon this memoir. More for my own reassurance is a copy of a note of a succinct verdict by Curtis, penned a year later, with his succinct verdict on those 11/12hp generators. 'They are not only unreliable, they are also a menace.'

I would have preferred my departure to have been in Hudson's Jeep, but, needing some form of lookout post, I opted for the second scout car. We drove up through Sussex, over the Downs by way of Pulborough. Heavy rain had isolated small farms, but the countryside I had come to know so well in boyhood was as beautiful as ever. I had fresh views from the scout car, vastly different from those seen from a Jeep. Through Sussex and into Surrey, over London Bridge, through the East End.

The passing miscellany of green berets and sailors' caps brought forth waves from girls in the factories. 'You'd think we was Yanks or Poles,' said our driver caustically.

We offloaded ourselves in the parkland of an Elizabethan mansion down on its uppers and offers. This was to be our concentration area until the morrow's departure. We were fed, coldly and greasily, in one vast marquee, followed by sleep in bell tents rigged within another marquee. With a fearsome wind howling across the parkland, they were distinctly preferable to a berth in a scout car. We gratefully dossed down under the glare of the spluttering hurricane lamps.

In a dismal, chilly dawn we embarked on our specified TLC. Within minutes of clambering on board, I was presented with a clutch of 'regulations for troop embarkment'. I would be responsible, I learned, for providing duty parties for the ship: tank deck sentry party, galley party, fatigue party, store party. My task was to round up half-a-dozen men for each party from the three services represented on board, a problem soon settled by the time-honoured formula: 'You, you and you!'

I had the benefit of a cabin. Before falling into a doleful semi-wakefulness I made entries in the journal which had proved a mildly therapeutic escape on previous excursions. Needless to say, I was well aware that the top brass frowned on such secret confessionals, although I suspected that admirals, generals and air marshals would be shown post-war to have kept such journals throughout the war, even if only for the exclusive purpose of seeking to prove that they had been right in their views and actions and others dead wrong. Such suspicions proved well founded. Mine was for myself alone. Fleming might possibly get a glance.

CHAPTER 12

VARIANT JOURNEYS

The detailed official follow-up to the casual outline of my imminent foray, provided by Fleming, opened with what Curtis
termed 'a typical paragraph in the "lingo" of which Fleming
and Lewes were masters'. As follows: 'In pursuance of orders received
from ANCXF, you are to proceed by road to Tarbe and subsequently
to Bayonne for the purposes of carrying out certain investigations on
behalf of the Royal Navy, the French Navy and the US Navy.'

Then followed the names and rank of the half-dozen officers of the
three services who would accompany the unit and for whose well-
being I would, presumably, be responsible. Scientists and technologists
would join and depart from the unit as their chiefs requested – but,
in truth, decided.

Also listed was the route we must follow: Verdun to Marseilles,
thence to Bordeaux by way of Carcassonne, Toulouse, Toulon, Tarbe,
Pau, Bayonne, Brive. *You are not in any circumstances to deviate from
this given route* was the final injunction. Nevertheless, the instructions
seemed to promise a prospect of swathes of France I scarcely knew.

Yet, rereading the orders, seeking to memorise the details, I thought
– not for the first time – that too much official bumf was deemed
imperative in modern war. Did the demands of Hannibal, Napoleon,
Marlborough necessitate comparable accumulations? I regarded personal diaries, compiled by combatants so inclined, as of a completely
different order. Doubtless a touch of self-deception.

Although I was, nominally, to be in charge of this largest splinter
unit of 30AU, I saw a good deal of Curtis. He seemed to be spending
all his days and nights in his staff car, maintaining contact with the
other splinter units scattered throughout western Europe. Inevitably,
I came to know him better.

From an early entry in my diary, I am reminded of the piecemeal
nature of the exercise:

Besançon, 19 December 1944:

At the moment the only members of the unit here are Curtis; van
Cleef, signals officer; two French officers and myself. Lambie has
made what he terms important discoveries in the Metz area and
has gone to ANCXF in Paris; Hank, the other US naval officer, has
gone north to Luxembourg to dig about in the Siegfried Line in an
attempt to track down some reputed devilish devices there. Another
specialist has gone back to Epernay to meet an expert who has flown
out from England to inspect machinery of which we signalled a general
description; Besant has gone across to Nevers; Ronson and Pratchett
are still up in the factories around Metz seeking what are rumoured
to be new types of mines. Postlethwaite is still over at Strasbourg still
finding infernal German machines. And so on and on. At the day's
end, van Cleef pieces together the jigsaw of the whereabouts of our
scattered forces. News from the north continues gloomy with both
the Yanks and the Huns apparently hurling in fantastic amounts of
men and material. One of the scientists says roads packed with Patton's armour moving north at speed. Interesting to see what happens.

A few days later I see that I recorded another meeting with Curtis, typical of those vastly different events which helped to foster our friendship.

Barracks outside Dijon, 24 December 1944:

Into Dijon with Curtis to see a US colonel for various OKs. Saw the appropriate colonel. Our wishes granted *en bloc*. I always enjoy watching Curtis at work. Post-war, he should be made an ambassador. He is, without doubt, the most successful negotiator I have seen in action except vis à vis Fleming. We returned by way of Pontalier as Curtis wished to see the widow of a French officer attached to our SAS who had been killed in August. After the American breakthrough at Avranches, the Frenchman had taken a Jeep across country, through an area held by the Germans, to link up with the Maquis in his Burgundy homeland. Betrayed, ambushed and killed near his home, a small, pink-walled chateau in open country. Curtis wished to pay his respects. He has a rare concern in these matters. With his fluent French I thought he would be far better solo and I wandered off to sit on a low wall encompassing the stables. Our driver opted for a brief ramble. Two small boys approached, eyeing me suspiciously, doubtless wary. German paratroops have also been dropped on these parts, even recently. Battledress, paratrooper's jacket and black naval officer's cap was doubtless a strange uniform to find so far inland. They approached slowly and then scurried past the chateau towards the distant village.

The widow, handsome, slim, thirtyish, came out with her two small and pretty daughters – one five, other three – to say farewell. She was clearly moved by the visit. Against the distant hills and nearer vines, the chateau, with its pink walls, grey doors and window frames, and red-tiled roof, seemed a tranquil country home, not a house of infinite sadness and irreparable loss.

Scores of the entries in my journals covering the exercise recall the determined enquiries made by scientists and specialists, initial trips into the war zone for most of them. I am tempted to quote from these entries but most are concerned with personal experiences, responses and so forth, and have little enough to do with Fleming, far off on his own venture. Sideline visits to Carcassonne, journeys through the wondrous forests of Les Landes and so on are for one's reference in a couple of decades perhaps. I conclude with a final quotation from the journals:

Bordeaux, 25 January 1945:

A full section once again: scientists, specialist boffins, Uncle Tom Cobley and all. All seem delighted with the results of their quests. Most, however, are already back in UK with their findings. Reunited, we press on. My first destination will be the admiralty then my flat. Hudson claims he's prepared to break all continental speed limits to get to UK. We hope to be there within the next twenty-four hours.

We were. Happily, the results of the excursion were deemed highly successful, I learned from Curtis. Room 39 and the many scattered recipients of our frequent bundles – scientists, technical experts and their top-flight bosses – had fired in notes of approval.

Fleming had returned from his own Far East mission. I duly reported. He suggested we lunch at Scott's and spoke approvingly of the reports he had received concerning my own recent foray. Had his own trip been a success?

'DNI said it was a task that needed doing. Who was I to query his decision? Whether it or I was a success will be resolved within the next couple of months.'

'What was the particular problem he sent you out to solve? I forget.'

'Very funny. Prompted by his masters, the DNI was given the task of making closer contacts with our many representatives in the Pacific zone. With the American-Japanese conflict developing at such a rate, our own contacts were found to be somewhat threadbare. My job was to make sure in what respects our present arrangements need further zip. They did and do.'

'Did the job appeal to you?'

'From the moment the DNI mentioned the likelihood of such a trip.'

'He didn't propose to go with you?'

'I think he was tempted but he's too fond of his present job. Too many trips abroad and he might find himself back on the ocean.'

'Were you given the appropriate top-brass reception in his absence?'

'No criticisms there. Five star all the way: Colombo, Delhi, Perth, Melbourne, San Francisco.'

'Sounds omnipotent stuff.'

'On that level maybe, but I'm still involved in building up the intelligence side out there from here. The usual necessity for professional experts rather than so-called gifted amateurs. Anyway, the DNI and his masters upstairs seem to think we're on the right lines. Now, let's discuss our own respective life expectancies.'

'Starting with 30AU, no doubt. But I'm more vocal about returning to my erstwhile interests. Can't wait.'

'You'll have to wait. We'll keep to 30AU's future – if any.'

He began. Most of the remaining strength of 30AU was now concentrated in Paris. There was a good deal still to be accomplished. The scientists and others were awaiting their chance to be first into Kiel and Hamburg. The major factor, he added – somewhat gloomily, I thought – was that all that he had foretold was happening. The unit was now a subsidiary outfit wholly run by SHAEF. 'No doubt the change seems very logical to a group of staff officers sitting around a table in some remote HQ, but I doubt whether it will prove as mobile and resourceful as the 30AU we've known. Anyway, we're nearing the end of the whole dreary business. The best course is to take on whatever comes your way. I'm virtually out of the act and action. I'll be supervising one or two ops in the near future but that's about all. You'll probably be involved in one next week. I'll let you know.'

I thought I'd let details of my next foray surface in due course and remained unquestioning. Instead, I asked what he thought his own next move might be.

'I'm considering another off-the-map one-man mission. The DNI wants me to take another New York–Washington trip. Why not? I can add on a three-day Jamaican look-see. I'm increasingly interested in the notion of finding a worthwhile hideaway in those remote parts.'

This seemed a brand-new project. I was interested. Very.

'Have you contacts?' I asked.

'I can fix that. Ivar Bryce will be around. I've been sketching out the kind of cliff-edge hideout I want. Once again, I wish I had the graphic touch.'

'You could have it within a month if you set to. But why Jamaica?'

'Because it seems to have everything for someone hopeful of finding a place for the occasional self-indulgent break. Worth having at the war's end.'

'Is England going to be so doleful, then?'

'For five years, I reckon.'

'We've always been quite a resilient post-war race. I think we'll be on our feet within a couple of years – even if that.'

'We've had quite a bashing this time. We've taken most of the rap among the so-called victors. Winners always seem to be the losers in modern war. You watch Germany, Italy, Japan. They'll be our rich cousins well within five years.'

'Tell me more about the oceanic hideout you hope to find.'

He did for the next ten minutes. I then returned to immediacy. Had Curtis also learned the full extent of the changes to 30AU?

'He knew a week ago.'

'Disappointed?'

'Doesn't seem to mind one way or another. What you don't seem to realise is that inside the Captain Kettle exterior is a would-be high-flying bureaucrat, not one tiny scrap averse to finding an appropriate position in the open market – especially with his rank and wartime decorations. Mark my words, post-war Curtis will become an upstage civil servant. Probably a bigwig in a new-style League of Nations.'

I grinned. 'Curtis spoke of his post-war ambitions during one of our trips in France,' I recalled. 'Even hinted that he was seriously considering the possibility of opting for a post-war career in the navy.'

'He'd be stark raving mad,' Fleming said dismissively. 'The Royal Navy will be mightily relieved to be rid of every RNVR type in sight, especially anyone with a gong and high ambitions for advancement.'

'Rather what I implied. Not quite so ferociously, of course. I merely pointed out that his pre-war life had been part theatre, part law and wholly non-Dartmouth. Despite his gongs, he'd have quite a formidable quota of thumbs-down oddments stacked against him. He might even ask for a reference from you.'

Fleming grinned this time. 'Quite funny. 30AU has certainly proved an entertaining sideline to the horrors of the war. A set of memories to be treasured for old age.'

'Possibly. But won't you be busy with your spy stories long before old age sets in?'

'You never seem to forget the oddments others utter. You'd better wait and see.'

We switched back to 30AU, to what Fleming termed 'the terminal tail ends of the unit's wayward lifestyle'. He went on: 'I've had a request from MI5 for help in a task which might well interest you. A job suited to your well-tested talents. Details could be heading your way within hours of your arrival in Venlo. With Curtis somewhere between here and Hamburg, I think I can promise unusual interest. When are you due to leave?'

'Next week. Where's this Venlo? I keep hearing the word.'

'Not the kind of response I'd expect from 30AU's so-called topographical expert. Actually, it's an out-of-the-way hideout on the

Dutch–German border. You'll find the latest recruits to the enlarged unit there. Probably poised for the dreary clean-up tasks awaiting them. Anyway, you'll get instructions and plans for your next jaunt even before you've settled in there, probably the following day. I think you'll find the exercise unusual and interesting.'

'Any idea of what's entailed?'

'Rather along the lines of your recent outing but you'll probably be nearer the action, or what's left of it.'

'Do I set about making any arrangements?'

'Fawcett's already made them. Today's Friday. Venlo next Wednesday. OK?'

'Three more days of freedom. My eternal thanks.'

Fleming laughed. 'Keep your sarcasm for others. Happily, everybody else seems satisfied with his/her lot. Fawcett's agreeably married and sees his wife daily, I gather. Nobody knows your particular emotional or would-be pre- or post-marital set-up or set-ups.'

I remained silent. I had been speculating recently on that aspect of my life.

One of the letters awaiting my return from France had been a note from a one-time girlfriend. If my cottage in Snowdonia, she wrote, was proving somewhat distant, she had seen a cottage, known as the Mill House, in the Stour valley on the Suffolk–Essex border which was 'quite enchanting and just about an hour from Liverpool Street by train to Colchester. Just a dozen miles distant.' She had enclosed a snapshot of the cottage, owned by a lively middle-aged spinster proposing to move nearer London in the coming peace.

'Move quickly!' was the postscript from my enthusiastic informant. 'Too good to last unsold, and ideally suited for your oncoming middle years.'

This was scarcely the post-war background I had in mind, but my interest in domestic architecture was still active. Although Beddgelert's delightful cottage was in a beguiling setting, this new proposition seemed rather inviting and a more practical post-war proposition. Other considerations, far from architectural, were also beginning to prompt consideration.

As Silvertop had clearly enjoyed her visit to the cottage in Beddgelert, I thought that she should also visit this cottage so much nearer London. To simplify matters, I decided that Hudson and his Jeep, both now my responsibility for my imminent departure for Venlo, could step aside from naval forays for the even more imminent weekend. We would venture to the Suffolk borders with Silvertop given the rear seat and instructed to look as much like a Wren officer as possible.

We departed on the following morning, Saturday, and reached the cottage in little over an hour. We were entranced by everything about the place: the perfect weekend retreat and certainly a far more sensible setting in the East Anglian fields than the distant domain I had acquired in the Welsh mountains, beguiling as it was. The charming owner seemed quite keen that we should be the future owners of her cottage.

We drove back to London, discussing every aspect of the possible venture. Silvertop sought to remain a carefree yet serious friend with her comments and verdict. An ideal weekend place, she stated, especially for a busy man with an occasional companion. Hudson giggled. I grinned and nodded. Silvertop smiled. I seemed to be surrounded by enthusiastic supporters of this future bachelor life.

Hudson and the Jeep had no part in our Sabbath. Silvertop and I wandered around Covent Garden, lunched in a Leicester Square restaurant, with the cottage an entertaining conversational sideline during supper at the Café Royal.

Early the following morning, Silvertop was away to her medico. I spent a momentous solitary morning in the pleasant Fleet Street Kardomah tearooms. On an impulse, following my brooding, I took a taxi to the Moorgate Registry Office, introducing myself to the genial registrar, asking whether I could arrange to get married that afternoon. Rather a rush order, I admitted, but I was on call for a sudden dash abroad on the morrow.

He asked for details of my naval life, showing knowledgeable interest, and proved a rare and attentive listener. He then informed me that weddings, even those in register offices, must be preceded by banns, virtually a three-day pause before the ceremony.

'No good to me. I shall be gone tomorrow,' I declared, explaining my likely movements. He listened alertly and then said calmly: 'Your situation sounds a bit tricky but leave it to me. I think I could fix things. A bit of a squeeze, but the navy does a lot for the rest of us, so why not? See you both back here around two o'clock. OK?'

I thanked him fulsomely.

'Part of the job,' he said, grinning.

I took a taxi back to the Café Royal. En route the driver agreed to return to Moorgate. Silvertop was waiting in the entrance hall, smart as ever in a black spring dress.

'Not your garb of the weekend. D'you keep a wardrobe in Harley Street?'

'One or two essentials for special occasions. Lunch with you, for instance.'

'We're lunching elsewhere. The taxi's outside.'

'Not far out, I hope. I have to be back by three.'

'Possible, but doubtful,' I said, following her into the taxi.

'Where are we going? Do I know the place?'

'I doubt it. Actually, we're going to Moorgate. To my local branch of the registrar's office.'

'An odd place for lunch, surely,' said my guest, smiling as if this were a daily pleasantry on my part.

'I suspect that you're being deliberately ingenuous,' I said. 'We're meeting the registrar. I met him an hour or so ago. He was marvellous. We can be married within the next half-hour, if you're agreeable, that is.'

'I think it's a marvellous idea!'

'I thought it would suit us both.'

'The most sensible approach to the rest of our days,' she said, with ready-made confidence.

The taxi stopped. We were there. We were married by the registrar, who also provided two amiable cleaners as witnesses. He received our fees and gratitude with amused authority.

CHAPTER 13

TO THE ELBE

Our slumbers were terminated at six o'clock the following morning: Hudson telephoning to say that he was awaiting me in Fetter Lane.

I tottered into battledress, told Silvertop she could either establish her new status by staying in bed or be taken to Harley Street in the Jeep. She opted for a further hour's oblivion.

Our route was to Harwich, thence by sea to Ostend. Hudson had already sampled Venlo and was no advocate for what the place had to offer. He voiced his antipathies en route. 'A right real shambles, sir. Personnel officers who don't know their arse from their elbows, plus a right bunch of layabout trainees.'

Within half an hour of arrival in Venlo, I realised that this was an altogether different 30AU, changed beyond recognition. I knew none of the officers, naval or marine, all newcomers, most well into their thirties, presumably recruited under conscription. They were now parading as if they had, suddenly and, to their delighted surprise, been transformed into warriors in an assault unit unlikely to be assaulting anything or anyone in these last weeks of the war.

Fortunately, the data I had hoped for arrived the following morning: a telephone call from Fleming seemed to promise immediate escape from this curious encampment. I was to be responsible for escorting an army major and two specialist RNVR officers on a temporary assignment to a destination, which would be made known to me by a major who would introduce himself, probably that afternoon. I would have a Royal Marine lieutenant with me, two scientists, a lieutenant RNVR and about twenty marines and ratings; including two telegraph operators. Our vehicles would be two Jeeps, three scout cars, signal truck and 15cwt truck.

Later that afternoon an army major, just in from UK, sought me out: brisk, genial, straight-backed, strong-chinned, martial-looking, complete with military moustache; seemingly a no-nonsense regular in his mid-thirties. I sensed that he was MI5. He introduced the two Cambridge scientists now attired as RNVR lieutenants. 'I think you'll find them quite agreeable,' he said after the introductions. 'For them it's a real jolly. These academics quite enjoy seeing themselves in uniform, especially for an innocent outing such as this.'

I thought we'd get along well and went back to give my small detachment the once-over. They seemed typical of the stalwart, capable types I had come to know at Littlehampton. Indeed, two of them I recognised from visits to that genteel holiday spot. Hudson knew them and assured me that they were all good eggs. I took him at word. His comment that one was a first-rate mechanic was reassuring.

Later, in the mess, our two fellow travellers were clearly both determined to give passing imitations of long-service RNVR types: one a tall, fair, gangling, scholarly type, around thirty, too big for his uniform, the other shorter, darker, four or five years older, wary and given to frequent frowns.

After supper with the major I was further appreciative of his quiet authority and sense of humour, mildly sardonic. I asked our destination. He said casually that we were bound for somewhere near Magdeburg on the Elbe.

Rather a long way inland for a naval outfit, I commented. Had he any special route mapped out?

'No, it'll be a map-reading exercise. Generally speaking, our route is south-east. I've one or two enquiries to make en route. I propose to go by way of Hanover and Brunswick.'

'How far in all?'

'Something over 300 miles. Probably near 350.'

'And when d'you hope to arrive?'

'Friday.'

'Who or what are you after – if that's not a rude question?'

'I'm after a group of German scientists who were doing their stuff in the Ruhr. Now, we gather, they've skipped farther east to some outpost where they can continue, and presumably complete their endeavours. I suppose they hope to get everything ready to pop into some relevant archive for the next war or even destroy if their boss so decides. I'd like to be there before the Yanks or the Russians get in on the act. Both outfits are pretty nearby. It's all basically as simple as that. Our Cambridge friends over there are supposed to understand whatever we discover – if anything – and do some sorting out.'

'How d'you learn about the scientists?'

'Ready-made. Wished on me by NID by way of Fleming. I take it he's your boss?'

I nodded. 'Any possibility that these Ruhr characters may learn we're on the way and will be suitably prepared?'

'That's what we don't know. They may have the odd combatant unit guarding their well-being. After all, they're pretty valuable property. I take it your chaps are quite handy if that's the situation we find.'

'Presumably. I take them as they come.'

He laughed. 'You've been mixed up in this kind of endeavour since the beginning?'

'Not from the beginning. I was sea-bound. Then picked up by

Fleming. Hence what you term "this kind of endeavour". Turkey, Madrid, Stockholm. Usually in a blue suit. Nothing too obviously English. I rather prefer these excursions somewhat closer to the front.'

'The Elbe's now the current front line, but changing by the hour. That's why we need to be there on time.'

We spent half an hour or so chatting about the war so far. Then early goodnights. I set my alarm for 0530 and managed to write a couple of brief letters before turning in.

We did the journey well within the major's allotted two days. Although he seemed to know the exact route we should take, he needed a couple of halts at US command posts, to use their field telephones. I offered him the use of our fully fledged signals van but he preferred his own arrangements, presumably checking on his quarries and any potential changes in his programme. He returned from these trips looking fairly relieved, nodded and said we could press on, occasionally checking our distance from Magdeburg. Our overnight quarters were at a US command post.

Early in the afternoon of our second day, the major, now seated behind me in the Jeep, leaned forward and said: 'By my reckoning, I think our place is about a mile beyond the next village.'

Beyond that hamlet we came to a T-junction and stopped. Facing us, 50 yards away across a shrivelled, muddy moat, was a 20-foot high wall of dark stone, curving away on either side of a high solid door. Small deep embrasured windows, shuttered, were set into the thick walls. Even a drawbridge, now raised, had its part to play in this cinematic castellated setting.

'Well, we're here!' said the major. 'Will you see your marksmen cover the gates? Hopefully, I'm expecting a civil reception, but who knows?'

Each of the marines was at the ready. If the Krauts are hiding a few machine guns in there, we shan't be here much longer, I thought, despite the fact that the guns in the Stag car were of worthy calibre and the men certainly well trained.

The major clambered out of the Jeep and, covered by our small arms, crossed by a narrow footbridge, which presumably ran alongside the drawbridge if that were ever to be lowered again. I followed, keeping to the roadside. The major hammered on the great studded door with the butt of his revolver. A long pause and further blows on the door, and the small hatch in the door opened. The caretaker or whoever, doubtless viewing the armoured cars covering the great door, acceded to whatever order or request had been made by the major in his highly fluent, colloquial German. He returned to the Jeep by his narrow footbridge. 'Permission granted. Everyone inside!' he commanded. The drawbridge slowly descended with a clanking of ancient, blackened chains.

One of the scout cars covered the entrance. I crossed with the major. The rest followed. The drawbridge clanked slowly up again as we took over the castle grounds. The major beckoned his wingers, entered the building, and, within two minutes, reappeared. 'Left the boffins to an opening gambit. The Krauts are dead scared, as well as supremely surprised.'

'Not a suspicion you were on your way?'

'Apparently not. Let's look around and see what accommodation's available.'

The curved walls held several one-storey rooms with upper lofts. I chose one near the gate, which seemed fairly comfortable and already equipped with camp bed, table and a chair. The major chose another, nearer the Germans. 'Let's look in on the researchers,' he said, following our inspection.

We strolled along the gravelled path to a basic but efficient-looking office, complete with desks, filing cabinets, typewriters. The office overlooked the lawn and *schloss*. A group of two middle-aged and two younger Germans seemed to be sedulously occupied in demonstrating to their distinguished visitors the nature of their labours as if there were no war and this a rather uncivil incursion into their labours. The two Englishmen were looking into folders and studying papers, sitting opposite one another at a cleared desk.

The major now spoke to the German who had come forward as senior representative and spokesman for his colleagues. He was of middle height, grey-haired, grey-moustached and, I judged, in his mid-fifties. He introduced himself, preceded by the label 'professor'. He asked how we had discovered their whereabouts. The major's reply was one of the blandest throwaway lines of the war: 'A call from London saying you were here,' he said, genially, as if he had just been invited to drop in on a friend. The professor was clearly impressed.

I was equally impressed by the major's fluency in German, informing the professor that their work must cease forthwith; that they must make themselves available to answer any queries that might be addressed to them by the British scientists; that at other times they must adjourn to their respective sleeping quarters. They could continue with any food arrangements they had set up for themselves, presumably with their own service arrangements. Finally, they must consider themselves as prisoners of war and await further interrogation by American technical officers who would be arriving within a day or so. Following these doleful instructions, we went out and strolled along the path encompassing the lawn. 'These are the chaps, all right. All involved in lethal research projects in the industrial Ruhr and sent down here soon after D-Day. I can't understand why they've been left here. The panzers and the rest seem to have quitted in a rush.'

'The Russkies are just on the other side of the river,' I pointed out. 'No place for a panzer that's lost its way.'

He nodded as he opened a door into a small hall and more rooms. 'The three of us are on the other side of the Krauts,' he said. 'You're this side of 'em in the rooms you've chosen. That's some kind of protective sandwich. Plus your marines. Can you set up a round-the-clock lookout?' I agreed. He went on: 'Not that I think they'll try to escape. Where would they go? One prospect apt to scare any Jerry scientist is being grabbed by the Russkies.'

I returned to my room. Hudson brought in my gear from the Jeep. *En passant* he said that as one of the marines was quite a good cook, shouldn't they set about preparing an early evening meal? I agreed with enthusiasm. 'Lay a table for the major, the two scientists and myself in the room next to the office.' Hudson said he'd already made friends with a Belgian girl, erstwhile servant to the Germans. She would help in the cookhouse. I wondered how many cigarettes had already been traded for her favours.

Over supper, the major said we should reckon on remaining at least four days while his two advisors sifted through the archives.

Such was the first day in our anachronistic hideout. The Germans had been hiding from us: weren't we now more or less in hiding from the probing Yanks and Russkies?

'Not so much hiding,' amended the major. 'My preference is "evasive action". I think we've more or less avoided the Yanks. The Russkies are another matter altogether. Success in your exercise', he said, turning to the scientists, 'depends on speed, efficiency and general know-how.'

On that challenging note we adjourned for bed.

Halfway through the following morning, Hudson presented himself, came to attention, and asked whether he might make a personal request. The young Belgian girl, who had been virtually a prisoner of war within the castle, wished to help the marines with their meals. Did I have any objection? None at all, I said. She would hardly be a German spy.

Scarcely able to control his smirk, he asked whether I had any duties for her?

None, I said, he could go ahead, but, remember, willingly or not, she had doubtless been obliging the German garrison during her sojourn. He should consider that aspect of the matter. He grinned, saying that he was always careful.

Well within those first twenty-four hours, I had settled into my two-room apartment within the walls: small sitting room with smaller loft bedroom. I was at ease. Hudson, plainly delighted with his situation, said his Belgian popsy could easily help the cook to supply agreeable meals twice a day. He had already learned that the *schloss* had its own small, self-contained farm unit complete with resident cattle and chickens.

After breakfast – bacon and eggs, no less – I inspected my small, company of shockproof troops. The scout cars and Jeeps had never looked so spick – as if an inspection by at least a lieutenant-general RM were imminent.

That afternoon, I was presented with another irony of warfare. While sauntering out on the lawn, a tall, fair, handsome German – the quintessential Aryan, I thought – came from the house and called, 'Good afternoon.' He was dressed in grey flannels and a blue pullover and had a well-behaved Dalmatian nearby. We exchanged names and almost immediately slipped into what I could only regard as neigh-bourly exchanges. He explained that he normally worked in Berlin but was staying in the *schloss* until things quietened down. His Eng-lish was fluent and colloquial. He spoke as if he had decided to take time off in his country place after a fairly hectic week at the office.

As if following my thoughts, he explained that the house belonged to an aunt of his wife's. He asked where I lived in England and how long we thought we might be staying in the castle. I explained that I lived in Fleet Street – to his extreme surprise – adding that I had no idea how long we'd be staying.

'In view of all that's happening in Germany and around us, I'm rather relieved that we're living here at the moment,' he said. 'I gather we're in an American sector. I think that's vastly preferable to find-ing ourselves in a Russian sector. We hear terrible reports.'

As we've become accustomed to hearing terrible reports of the Germans, I thought.

Parting, he asked whether I would care to drop in for coffee after my evening meal and meet his wife, who knew England rather well. He assured me that the coffee would not be unduly ersatz. I said I'd be delighted.

'Around nine,' he said, calling 'Rex!' to the dog.

As the major and the two boffins seemed to have a good deal to talk about, I left them after the meal and called on the would-be friendly but still enemy Germans. A mildly eccentric form of wartime socialising, I thought. I was in for further surprises.

A middle-aged woman came to the door. My host came into the hall and welcomed me warmly, showing me into a pleasantly furnished drawing room, which could have been in Wiltshire or New Hampshire. His wife – a pretty, dark-haired young woman in a flowered summer dress – reclined in an armchair. I was ushered to another.

We began to chat as if we'd known each other for some time. First the marvellous weather, then London. Although Bavarian, my hostess, whose English was as fluent as her husband's, had been a pre-war student at St Martin's School of Art in Charing Cross Road. We compared notes: my own similar experiences at the Central School of Art and Design, and more recent experience tutoring young hopefuls in typographical design at the Reimann School, which had been transferred from Berlin to London after the rise of the Nazis.

Then on to the husband's career.

To my surprise he explained that he had been – and presumably still was – in Goebbels's press division, one of only two or three associates allowed to see the world's press, necessary for his job of making abstracts of international news for Goebbels and, presumably, Hitler. Further abstracts of news, more suitable for communication to the wider German public, were also daily duties. Inevitably, I sensed that he had been a Goebbels right-hand man. He said that Goebbels had been a demanding but fair taskmaster and had made no demands that top members of his staff should be or become Nazi Party members. I wondered how much he was playing down his career and job.

I certainly enjoyed my evening.

Over elevenses the following morning, I mentioned my meeting to the major, who had already made his own enquiries and had decided there was little enough that the sophisticated Germans in the *schloss* could tell him that MI5 didn't already know.

I visited the *schloss* for two further evenings. We scarcely stopped talking for a moment between nine and midnight. Scarcely a subject was left unprobed. What an experience Fleming was missing, I thought from time to time.

During the afternoon of the fourth day, the major joined me as I paced the lawn. He remarked that he thought the job was virtually completed: the Cambridge men had gained and assembled for their UK offices all that was available in the records and were ready to leave.

'And what will happen to the Germans? Do they stay here?' I asked.

He sidestepped my query. 'I've explained most of the background to the local Yanks,' he said. 'We're operating within their zone and I'm here thanks to their general benevolence, due mainly, I suspect, to the fact that not one of their own specialist intelligence officers is available. They'd like to see your Goebbels friend too, in due course. They think he sounds interesting. Thanks for keeping me in touch.'

I laughed. 'So when do we push off?'

'I was coming to that. D'you think we could leave tomorrow morning and make Venlo in a day?'

'As a couple of Jeeps or convoy?'

'Ideally the lot of us. We've got a lot of material I'd like to keep my eye on.'

'We probably could if you weren't so keen on your roundabout routes.'

He laughed. 'Not this time. I want to make the fastest dash possible. What d'you think?'

'If we left at six in the morning we could be there, with a bit of luck by, say, six in the evening. They're all first-rate drivers.'

'Good, that would be a great help. The Yanks are sending two or three chaps here to take over on a rota basis until the SHAEF types arrive. There's one other point…'

I waited. He seemed somewhat hesitant before saying, over-casually, 'I propose to take the senior chap back with me. The professor.'

'Where to?'

'UK.'

'Isn't there a hazy ordinance called the Hague Convention?'

'We need this chap back home. I've put it to him: would he rather be in the UK, the US or in Russia? He thinks he'd be far better off with us. He won't be away for ever. He can telephone his family from Venlo. And I've assured him he'll be able to call them from the UK.'

'Where do they live?'

'Somewhere near Frankfurt, I gather. Today's Wednesday. I'll have a flight to London laid on for Friday morning. OK?'

'OK.'

'There's one final point,' the major said, with unaccustomed hesitancy, as we continued on our perambulation. 'I may not be able to take our friend back. I've been in touch with your chief, Fleming, and if I can't – we've got a lot on currently – Fleming's not against your escorting the German. He'd like you back soon, anyway. Will you take it on?'

'If he says so.'

'Right. Six tomorrow morning. Sharp. When will your US successors arrive?'

'Two will be here this afternoon. Reliefs will be here around ten tomorrow morning. We'll be 100 miles on by then, won't we?'

'But of course!'

He grinned and nodded. We parted.

The convoy was ready to leave before 0600. I was passenger in the first Jeep, Hudson driving, the major a passenger in the second. The professor and one of the Cambridge types in one scout car; the other in the second car. The signal truck had driver and operator. The 15cwt truck was chockfull with documents, with the RM sergeant as guardian.

I had made my farewells to host and hostess the previous evening. We'd meet perhaps in London. A few locals watched impassively. The marines waved. We were off.

We arrived at Venlo at 1740, having stopped only once for K-rations outside Hanover. The 15cwt truck was put under immediate heavy RM guard.

'Not bad going,' said the major, climbing stiffly out of the Jeep. 'Thanks for everything. What shall we say about tomorrow?'

'There's little enough to keep me in Venlo.'

'You'll be met at Heston. Fleming says he'll have a Jeep waiting for you.'

'And the prof?'

'He'll be taken off your hands the moment you land.'

'You seem to have thought of everything.'

'We try. Meanwhile, many thanks. You've been uncommonly useful. I'm very grateful. I need to finish one or two jobs out here. I shall miss the protective care of your unit.'

'Glad to have been of help. Do I take the prof to the airport here?'

'No, I've already fixed that. I've borrowed a staff car. You'd better come, too. The plane'll be waiting.'

Next morning, I shared the staff car to the airfield. In the small military plane I sat with the professor. We talked intermittently. I thought, sadly enough, of his imminent venture into the strangest of worlds. Did he know any English scientists in his particular discipline? He said he knew one or two but had only the haziest idea how or where he might contact them. For a man into his fifties, possibly sixties, what lay ahead must have seemed a hazy prospect indeed.

At Heston we came off the plane and walked across the 100 yards or so towards the huts, and through what seemed to be recently erected barriers. As we moved towards a group of waiting officials, I noticed two men in dark suits, quite noticeable, in the surrounding world of khaki. The taller of the pair, hatless, blue-suited, stepped forward, crossed to myself and the professor, querying our names. The professor nodded. Blue Suit thanked me. They were gone.

I followed them out to the parking lot. A 30AU driver and Jeep were waiting. Just on noon.

CHAPTER 14

A QUERYING INTERLUDE

An hour or so later, I dumped my scanty luggage in The Citadel depths. James Fawcett and Margaret seemed almost submerged beneath the loads of bumf that was still arriving. The constant dumping and collection of papers and materials by the many scientists and others temporarily attached to the unit seemed to be growing daily.

Greetings were hearty and surprising. James Fawcett emerged from his collection of papers, signals and bumf to say heartily: 'Congratulations on your marriage, Robert!' His words were echoed by Margaret with the addendum: 'Why didn't you tell us it was to happen? We could have been at the registry. Even witnesses.'

'How d'you know about this happening?' I asked.

'In *The Times* last week.'

'Well, well,' was all I could say.

I took to the inner room and rang Silvertop. She was ecstatic. 'How wonderful to have you back. I'm afraid I did something you may have come across already.'

'I have.'

'Please forgive me, but I wanted to see a record of the biggest happening in my life in print. Am I forgiven?'

'Forgiveness doesn't even come into historical facts.'

She laughed. 'Gorgeous. When do we meet?'

'At the Café Royal. 6.30.'

'Perfect!'

I returned to Fawcett and Margaret.

Fleming entered. 'Hello! I heard you were around. All go well?'

'Very.'

'So I heard from my MI5 contact earlier this morning. Seemed delighted with the all-round results and grateful for your guarding the scientist you've brought back. I'm lunching. Any chance of seeing you at Boodles around five or so?'

I said I'd be there, leaving no later than six.

Once there and having settled into our armchairs with our drinks, he introduced the oddment I had expected.

'I saw to my vast surprise an announcement in *The Times* last week that you're now a married man. I was astonished. How come? Nothing as trad as an unplanned pregnancy, I trust.'

'All in due course. Preferably planned.'

'Why so sudden then?'

'Just seemed the right moment.'

'I like the name Phoebe, by the way. Quite a rare moniker these days, with all these Jennifers and Jills cluttering up the admiralty noticeboards. Will I meet her in due course?'

'You've met her already. At the Gargoyle romp.'

'I wondered whether that was the victim. The other of the two Silvertops. Anyone from 30AU at the ceremony?'

'No ceremony. No guests. An understanding registrar with a soft spot for active naval types. He was prepared to skip the three-day banns lark and found a couple of witnesses from his staff.'

'Good for him. But why so secret?'

'My view is that marriage is basically an affair between the couple concerned. If they want a crowd, let there be a crowd. But this was a fairly spontaneous decision and I had no wish or time for guests.'

'What about her parents and family? And your own?'

'She has only Mother, a brother overseas and a busy sister. I rang the mother who said she was delighted and if the marriage turned out to be a flop, Phoebe could always come home to her place in Sussex. I've nobody on my side.'

'A pretty rare set-up by any standards. Especially the mother's.'

'She's quite a rare type.'

'Does your Phoebe work? Another graphic designer?'

'Not a chance. She's PA to a shrink in Harley Street. Well known, I'm told. She wanted to be a quack, but, although she's by way of being quite a linguist with fluent French and German, fortunately her schoolgirl Latin let her down. Otherwise, we'd probably never have met.'

'What's the shrink's name?' he asked, rather casually, I thought.

'Strauss. Eric Strauss. Know him?'

'Heard of. I've always been interested in this psychiatric world. Even wrote a thesis on Jung when studying in Germany. Does she like the job?'

'Loves it. Likes anything concerned with medicos and their mumbo-jumbology. Runs in the family. Her brother's an army doctor now in the Middle East. I met him when I was in Beirut last year. Pleasant chap. Married to yet another medico, living in Hampstead. As does her sister.'

'Does your Phoebe want to stay in this engrossing career with its psychotic background? She seems rather keen.'

'Not a chance. She's looking forward to a shared life. She certainly seems to do everything for Strauss. Reception. Secretarial. Even assisting at a revolting kind of therapy called ECT, if you know what that is?' I queried, fairly certain he didn't.

'Electroconvulsive therapy I seem to recall,' he replied, quite pleased with himself. 'And she assists at these shock treatment sessions?'

'So I gather, but when medical mumbo-jumbology crops up I'm apt to switch subjects or leave the room.'

'Squeamish?'

'100 per cent. That's why I'm changing the subject now and why I think I've more or less persuaded her to quit her job. And she's paid a bare minimum.'

'And she's agreed?'

'She's given Strauss a month's notice. But enough of Strauss. How's your life among the ladies? How's Ann? And is that delightful Tiarks still around? What of them and others?'

'Both, and others, well and flourishing. But when do I meet this Phoebe again? I rather took to her, I recall.'

'Pretty soon, I hope.'

'You're evading. Proposing to keep her to yourself?'

'Not a chance. She's far more socially inclined than I'll ever be.'

'Was she provided with any forewarning of what was about to happen? That marriage was imminent?'

'Apparently not. I actually told her in a taxi on the way to the registrar's office in Moorgate. I'd met her at the Café Royal where she thought we were having a farewell lunch before I pushed off to Venlo.'

'Is it a marriage that'll last?'

'It's already lasted a couple of weeks. Admittedly, I've been abroad for most of the time.'

He grinned. 'Where are you proposing to live? Not in a Fleet Street hideout, I take it. I haven't been there but I gather it's a bachelor's one-room job.'

'Oddly enough, just before I went off on this Venlo lark, I saw and settled for a mill house – more a mill cottage – in Suffolk.'

'Why and where in Suffolk, for God's sake?'

'In the Constable country – near the River Stour.'

'Holy smoke, the things you do in secret! Marriage, house-buying, settling down in Suffolk … what next?'

'Probably those bambini you mentioned. Time moves on. I'm into my thirties and all that. This war's taken a six-year chunk out of our lives. Noticed?'

'Too true,' he groaned.

'And what about yourself? What about the spy story to end all spy stories?'

'You remember all your friends' failings. A truly civilised citizen would have forgotten such a slip of the tongue – at that Patton picnic, wasn't it?'

'You know damn well it was.'

He laughed.

'Well, I suppose it's still on. Hopefully. We'll see. Meanwhile, back to a subject you seem keen to dodge. What qualities did you look for in a prospective wife?'

'The qualities I'm still looking for.'

'Which are?'

'The persistent inquisitor, as ever. Did you pick up the technique in Russia?'

'Trying to get the truth out of a 30AU romantic is nearer the truth. Come on, more about those elusive feminine qualities.'

'Well, my main object was to avoid the three fancy qualities or gifts you once said you'd demand in a likely wife.'

'Tell me. I forget.'

'First, she had to be able to afford to buy her own clothes. No go for me – I've always been keen on buying the items I think would suit any current popsy. I shall doubtless continue on those lines with one popsy.'

'What a hope with a background of plunging necklines and open-gusset knickers, if any.'

'Why any at all?'

'Press on. What else was I demanding of a wife?'

'How to concoct a perfect Béarnaise sauce.'

He laughed. 'So I did. And the third if not the last?'

'That she should be double-jointed.'

He laughed even more heartily. 'A gift from the gods in any woman for any lover or husband with an authentic interest in sex.'

'Have you ever encountered this rare and fulsome attribute?'

'Once. Presumably that's why I include the memory in my trio. You're right about the rarity. A woman certainly has to be born that way. But let's cut the waffle. Let's deal with a few daily, real-life qualities and interests. What brought a self-sufficient, cold-blooded womaniser like you to marry this particular popsy, beguiling as she doubtless is? Not just because she's a bedtime speciality, otherwise she wouldn't be there. What else?'

'I thought she was unusually sweet-natured and easy on the eye. She contends that I'm the only authentic, well-balanced, cold-blooded, warm-hearted numero she's met so far.'

'I don't want your salient points. I want Phoebe's.'

'A sweet nature is the rarest of all feminine qualities. She has it in bulk.'

'Not the most lovey-dovey description, but that's the major feature in the kind of character you think you were looking for?'

'I think I rather agreed with a definition I heard from a naval type in Alexandria. He contended that most men – somewhere around 95 per cent – want Mrs Beeton downstairs and Eleanor Glyn upstairs.'

Fleming's burst of laughter was quite sharp for Boodles. 'A coinage worth remembering,' he said. 'With more than a touch of truth involved. I once met Eleanor Glyn, by the way. She had a cottage near Nettlebed.'

'Did she live up to her legend?'

'Come off it. She was hitting seventy when I met her. Anyway, back to basics. My belief is that bedroom know-how is inborn and rarely acquired. The zestful best are those born that way and stay that way, too.'

'Would your belief also include being, having been or likely to continue to be zestful with all men?'

'Probably. Who wants someone reserving herself for Mr Right? Who wants a virgin on a marriage night?'

'Most men, it seems. Preposterous, but there it is.'

He laughed. 'Jealousy, the dagger of love. We never know how basically possessive we are until the crisis crops up. Think you're free from it?'

'My simple and hopefully comprehensive view is that we can never own anyone on any terms. If that conviction's sincere, I think it subdues the possessive touch. Anyway, I contend jealousy derives from lack of confidence.'

'Probably – I'll talk it over with the next shrink I meet.' Fleming lifted his glass. 'Enough of speculation. My toast to your partner. The indomitable Silvertop. She must have a fair share of courage, taking you on. Best wishes to her.'

'What about the tasks facing the husband? Myself in this context.'

'I've long thought you've a rare talent for turning so-called daunting tasks into essays in entertainment. And as I regard marriage as a pretty daunting prospect for anyone – man, bird or beast – I think you probably stand a reasonable chance of success.'

'Well said. Why don't you set up as a post-war shrink?'

'Very funny. Anyway, I'll see if there's anything worth learning watching your double act over the next decade.'

'Forty-eight hours is enough, I always think. Time to go. I'm meeting the popsy in question at the Café Royal in ten minutes.'

We wandered out into St James's Street and up to Piccadilly. There we parted – he to his flat, myself towards Leicester Square.

CHAPTER 15

TRONDHEIM FINALE

Signals passing through The Citadel during the first days of May clearly indicated that the war was entering its final stages, but Fleming had what he termed 'a conclusive venture' to offer. Did I want it? 'You seem to have carried out the MI5 job pretty well, I gather,' he said across his Room 39 desk. 'That's the general verdict. I'm now proposing a final fling with a job in Norway. Seems well set up for you.'

I was interested. I had come to know the Oslo area quite well pre-war.

'You will need one partner in the venture. I hear of a 30AU newcomer. Veysey by name. He's been suggested.'

'I knew him in peacetime. An architect. I heard he was around.'

Fleming nodded. 'That's the chap. Highly recommended by MI5.'

He then outlined the content and intent of the bumf that he took from his crowded desk. Our job would be to report on U-boat and torpedo strength still existent in Norway and seek further data concerning German advances in the production of midget U-boats.

The venture would be under the command of Major-General Sir Robert Urquhart with the First Airborne Division, which was to drop in, so to speak, to free Norway from the still-occupying German forces.

The project had a mildly dicey side, as the German forces in Norway had apparently refused to accept the 'unconditional surrender' terms imposed on their countrymen in the final reckoning at Flensburg. Despite such obduracy, there was little doubt that Norway was regarded by the Allied top brass as something of a sideshow. The real battle had been won.

I knew Hugh Veysey fairly well. He was a Quaker, had volunteered as an ambulance driver for the Finns in their brief war with Russia and, after the Finnish defeat, had been expatriated via Stockholm and thence found his way into 30AU. Now, he was to be my helpmate in Norway.

Apparently, the North Sea had been so comprehensively mined by the Germans that a week or more would be needed for clearance before seaborne forces could safely approach any Norwegian port. Meanwhile, Fleming added, a grapevine report claimed that Churchill wanted UK forces in Norway pronto. Airborne forces were on standby. 'It'll probably be less of a jolly than the operations you're accustomed to, but who knows?'

'For me your projects seem to get cosier, anyway. The French foray needed over 100 officers and men for my guidance. The Elbe venture only needed fifteen or so. This one only needs two.'

Fleming laughed loudly. Other occupants of Room 39 looked up from their desks, smiled and returned to their studies, as if used to these merry outbursts.

'I see your point,' Fleming agreed. 'Probably the ventures now need sagacity rather than savagery. Brain rather than brawn. The old story in war.'

I grinned and took up the papers he proffered. 'See you soon, I trust,' I said in farewell.

'Hopefully. I've a venture on my own. More later.'

I departed.

Joining Operation Apostle proved another of those complex affairs seemingly inseparable from wartime projects. I contacted and met Veysey. We were instructed to proceed to an Essex airfield to receive directions for our embarkation with the airborne forces. At this stage we inclined to the belief that we would be towed in gliders and cast off over our destined Norwegian airfield. Hudson, now back from Venlo, drove Veysey and me to the airfield in what he now termed *his* Jeep.

Mid-morning, Veysey and I became involved, at the adjutant's behest, in an official and, apparently, unexpected lightning inspection by General Urquhart, who had suddenly descended on the encampment with scant warning. Despite our khaki battledress and peaked caps, Veysey and I undoubtedly gave the appearance of an improbable pair of interlopers in this impeccably martial parade. The general was an impressive character by any standards: tall, big, dark, with a heavy military moustache emphasising his strong features. As usual with high-ranking fighting officers at this stage of the war, his combat jacket was vivid with ribbons, native and foreign. He enquired of the adjutant the reasons for our improbable presence, took the adjutant's verification in his stride, nodded, hoped we'd be comfortable and passed on. Or rather out, for we were at the tail end of the parade.

Early the following morning we embarked on one of the several Dakotas on the misty airfield. Fractionally regretful, but vastly relieved, we realised that we were not to be cast off as we had apprehensively suspected, but would be flown in more conventionally. Three hours later, second-wave landing, we were over a port I recognised from the air as Stavanger, a town I knew well, for here I had frequently disembarked pre-war from SS *Jupiter* of the Olsen Line to rendezvous with a vivacious Norwegian blonde, then an occasional object of would-be romantic attentions if not intentions.

To our mild surprise and relief there was no evidence of any German opposition. We were driven to a quayside hotel, which, until a day or so before, had housed German officers. All were now prisoners, our guide told us with huge glee.

Early that afternoon, the brigadier called a conference with German naval representatives. As no senior naval officers were in Norway at the time, thanks to the North Sea minefields, I found myself in the curious position of being a lieutenant commander RNVR exclusively representing the Royal Navy in southern Norway with the authority to make any necessary maritime decisions.

The most significant instruction that I was delighted to pass on was that all ships' ammunition must be discharged on quaysides by six o'clock that evening. I retain a copy of a signal sent that day to Fleming after approval by the brigadier:

> From Harling, Stavanger, 10 May 1945, via army channels. No
> naval signal office or officers available. In absence of senior naval
> representation today ordered eight U-boats currently dispersed in
> Stavanger area to assemble Hillevag, south of Stavanger. Propose
> inspect tomorrow. Also ordered all trawlers and other craft to outer
> anchorages, leaving only minesweepers alongside main quays and
> at immediate notice. No damage to port installations. Naval sig-
> nal station intact. Propose leaving on Saturday for Christiansand,
> Arendal, Oslo. Zone commander urgently requests official naval
> representative be flown immediately Stavanger.

I pleasurably imagined Fleming's mild disbelief but genial acceptance of the contents of my signal.

No signal, however, could convey the eeriness of our visit. U-boats were moored in trots alongside the sheds. Torpedoes were stacked in steely array on giant racks. I recorded the types of boat, which, these many years later, mean nothing to me and no doubt little more to contemporary underwater specialists: five Type 23, two Type 1C and one Type 21. Of the sixty torpedoes, I noted that forty-five were suitable for firing from surface craft, plus fifteen Type 3 – what were these suitable for? – and, oddly enough, one British Mark VIII. Memories of early days of the war, when I had sought to help fish a fortunate few seamen from the Atlantic aboard our corvette after their merchantmen had been torpedoed, made this inspection further hideous proof of the idiocy of war as a means of settling any kind of problem.

Apart from our primary concern with U-boats and torpedoes, our sojourn in Norway was vastly enlivened by sideshows during this final break.

I had the adjutant's late-night request that I would seek to requisition a craft to collect and bring back into Stavanger a group of obstreperous German prisoners from one of the fjord's oiling stations.

I shared this bizarre midnight venture with Veysey, commandeering, complete with German crew, one of the R-boat minesweepers we had ordered to moor alongside the quays to be held at immediate notice. We proceeded along the Stavanger Fjord, myself in nominal command, cosily aware of a Norwegian pilot at my side and twenty stalwart British airborne troops, firearms at the ready, standing by the gunwales. We shared the bridge with a young German *Oberleutnant* keen to air his English, no doubt a practical investment for the future.

Alongside the oiling station we discovered that some fifty German sailors, apparently carried away by news of their senior officers' rejection of any suggestion of unconditional surrender, had been parading around the station, shouting abuse at the Norwegians, recently their slaves, threatening everyone in sight. As we came alongside the landing-stage, the shouting was heinous. Our searchlight was switched on and the Germans clearly saw the British troops. Their shouts subsided. I suggested to the *Oberleutnant* that he should go ashore and tell his countrymen that their day was done. They would be given five minutes to collect their gear. We would then be away. Any German left behind, or opting to stay behind, would do so at his own risk. Those preferring to come aboard would proceed in single file. Under the R-boat searchlight and the speculative gaze of our troops in their red berets the Germans skulked aboard, a well-fed lot, distinctly cowed but far from shattered. The R-boat was now a very crowded craft indeed, but curiously quiet. Neither prisoners nor captors were in talkative mood. The *Oberleutnant*, on the other hand, was determined to seize the final minutes of his unexpected English lesson. To my surprise, he wanted to learn all he could about London.

Returning to our billets in the quayside hotel, Veysey and I discussed the more bizarre aspects, which contributed to the dreadful fascination of war. We had both thoroughly enjoyed the midnight fjord excursion, our enjoyment ironically enhanced by our craft having been a German R-boat manned by a German crew.

Our next Fleming task was in Christiansand where we would examine U-boats and torpedoes at nearby sheds, recorded in my log as Maiken, Regellstelle and Slokai, although I can now find none of those placenames in the *Times* atlas. But what I do recall is our discovery of seventeen U-boats, one Type 21, five Type 7c and eleven Type 23, as my notes so incomprehensibly now remind me. In addition we noted over 100 torpedoes, including sixty Type T5, whatever that may now designate. Apart from those death-dealing items, there were over 800 mines. Signals were sent on to Stavanger. We then left for Arendal for what was virtually a repeat performance, mainly concerned with midget U-boats.

Then on to Oslo, which I had come to know well in pre-war visits. Veysey also knew the city quite well. We moored our craft in the Oslo Fjord, extremely close to the home of the Norwegian blonde I had pursued with such ardour during those pre-war years – but the grapevine which never fails, even in wartime, gave word that she had been too friendly with the Germans and was now socially ostracised and had been a victim of that abhorrent public procedure: shaving the heads of girls who had fraternised with the German forces. I had been sickened several times when passing through the market squares of France to see girls seated on high platforms surrounded by jeering men and women, faces distorted by venom and hatred as the baleful ritual went ahead.

The same thing would undoubtedly have happened in Britain, as barbaric as any other alleged civilised nation, had our land been occupied and then left.

All irregular operators have a sixth sense when officialdom is beginning to close in. We had completed most of the tasks we had been set. Only Trondheim remained. We knew that a flotilla of RN destroyers was likely to be in the northern port by now but doubted whether the examinations of enemy equipment, which we had been ordered to undertake, would have been carried out so soon. The prospect of a trip to Trondheim at this stage of the war was not only tempting, but one we could make with a conscience almost as clear as an archdeacon's diary. Early the next morning, Veysey said he would go ashore and seek out a car, so that on relinquishing our seagoing craft we could be on our way.

He returned after midday at the wheel of an open Steyr tourer. We collected our kitbags and, after hearty handshakes and waves all round, set off.

'I've got all the maps we need,' Veysey said. 'No need to break any speed records. I make it around 300 miles, give or take a furlong.'

'What about petrol?'

'That tonneau cover conceals Jerry cans galore. I now know the drill. What's your next contact with officialdom?'

'A signal to Fleming tomorrow should suffice.'

The Royal Navy was already evident in Trondheim. Ratings seemed to be on every street corner chatting up the natives. Parking our fairly ostentatious transport discreetly in a square well away from the quays, we reported our arrival and purpose to a lieutenant RN in the headquarters of OCNF, fired off an official signal to Fleming.

We were also presented to Captain D in command of the destroyer flotilla which we had already seen moored alongside the quays. The meeting was curt and formal. We had a distinct impression that as the war neared its end, RN regulars couldn't wait to get rid of those they hopefully regarded as amateurish would-be equivalents and seniors. Young Dartmouth entries in the first years of the war were now lieutenants RN. Many of them had seen active service and probably resented RNVR types of their own generation, who had probably seen far more active service and, in the process, had become thorough-going professionals of higher rank. Operational intelligence officers were certainly regarded with somewhat envious eyes by those trained in more strait-laced disciplines.

We were to see and experience more of the resentful aspects of this relationship within the next few days. Meanwhile, I said, we proposed to continue with our inspections of U-boat sheds and torpedo stores and trusted that launch and crew could be made available.

Agreement was inevitable. The lieutenant had Fleming's signals on his desk. He said: 'Ten o'clock here, then. Officers are being quartered at the Borg, by the way. You'll find a billeting office on your way out.'

'Must be hell, knowing that you must never, never put a foot wrong anywhere along the line if you want to grow up and be an admiral,' Veysey said, as we strolled back to the car.

'Nelson was quite good at putting a foot wrong from time to time,' I pointed out. 'Beatty, too. The trouble is that unconventional regulars need war. Nelson would probably have been court-martialled and dismissed from the service for some misdemeanour or other if he hadn't had Napoleon on his doorstep at the time.'

We were allotted a two-roomed, spaciously high-ceilinged suite at the Borg. We slept well in what Veysey termed our 'pine-panelled staterooms'. On some of our recent French jaunts such a room would have made a dormitory for thirty marines. We took these luxurious pleasures in our stride.

After supper we drove out to see something of the magnificent scenery within 10 miles of the city. We had a good deal to talk about and the continuing daylight was conducive to late nights, aided, of course, by our delight and surprise to discover the continuing exist-ence of those attractive little coffee bars, so congenial a feature of most Norwegian ports, with pretty girls sizing up the new arrivals. Arrangements to rendezvous the following day were easily made.

On the next morning we spent a good deal of time studying Hitler's yacht, the *Grille*, through field glasses; observing considerable activity as if officers and crew were keeping themselves in sound physical condition, despite the war's finale and their comparatively cramped quarters.

I wondered, with Veysey, whether all ciphers had been destroyed. The notion of making a first-hand inspection quickly became something of a challenge, especially as we completed our examinations of the U-boat sheds and torpedo stores within forty-eight hours and had sent the admiralty appropriate signals covering the lethal inventory. The war and our work were both nominally over, but we awaited a potential signal outlining any further enquiries to be made.

Inevitably, the *Grille* continued to exert an especial appeal.

We enquired of one of the RN officers in the office of the OCNF whether anyone had already been aboard the *Grille*. Apparently not. The matter was currently under discussion between Captain D and the German admiral, until recently chief of the German Navy in the Trondheim Zone. I mentioned our interest in the possibility of finding ciphers aboard. A lieutenant commander in the room said: 'Funny you should mention that. That's my interest, too, as senior signals officer for the flotilla. I'd certainly like the chance of getting aboard. But let's face it: everything worth our while will have been burned or be at the bottom of the fjord by now.'

We agreed that was doubtless the situation, but expressed the view that a boatload of resistant sailors concerned with their closest possessions might have overlooked a few papers.

I decided to contact Fleming. After all, he had sent us here and was our immediate superior, and the most conversant with the set-up.

I was tempted to take the signals officer into our confidence and seek his help in contacting the admiralty, but then requested the pretty desk girl at the hotel to get the British Admiralty. Fortunately, Fleming was on the blower within five minutes.

I put the modest problem to him. He dismissed any would-be

objection from anyone concerning the *Grille*. Such a visit was essentially a 30AU task, he claimed. 'Your documented signals concerning the U-boats were warmly welcomed,' he added. 'You probably wouldn't have heard up there, but over 200 U-boats have recently been scuttled in harbour and a score more did the job at sea. So any extant craft are in demand, as is any oddment concerning their HQ up there. Go to it. I'll sort out any problems – if any. We still need all the info we can get, and you're there to collect all you can and get back.'

'I'll get down to it straightaway.'

'Good. Mention the DNI if necessary. How are things? Not falling for any northern fleshpots up there, I trust.'

'Quite a few on ready offer. We leave such ventures to the ratings.'

'Ha! Ha! Well said, but nobody'll believe it. See you soon. Or perhaps not all that soon. I'm off tomorrow on my one and only personal venture on behalf of 30AU.'

'Where?'

'Info on your return. We'll be back around the same time. *Au revoir.*'

I returned to the signals officer and explained that I had received the OK from the DNI at the admiralty to go ahead.

He was now rather hesitant.

'Well, go ahead if you like, but it'll have to be rather off the record.'

'Not for long. No visit of this kind is going to be off the record for longer than ten minutes,' I said, adding reassuringly, I hoped: 'As part of our job is to get hold of enemy secret papers, ciphers and the rest, we're going. You supply the matelots and rowboats; Veysey and I will do the rest.'

I foresaw no great physical hazard in taking a boarding party out to the yacht. Her crew were in no position to repel inquisitive but official would-be boarders. Neither did I see any great difference between a boarding party such as this and scientists visiting suspect factories in France.

Two hours later, we were informed that scratch boarding parties and two naval launches had been organised and were ready. So were we. I took over one; Veysey the other. Within ten minutes we came alongside the *Grille* quite smartly. I called out for a rope-ladder. One came curling down. I went up, followed by Veysey and a dozen ratings.

Once boarded, we were faced by a dozen or so German naval officers grouped together, shoulder to shoulder: smart, watchful, mildly menacing. To my surprise all were wearing sidearms, presumably to demonstrate that they had had no part in the national surrender of their country and their fleet. I called for an English-speaking officer. One stepped forward, formally aloof, plainly groomed in advance for such duties should they arise. I gave him instructions that all sidearms and small arms were to be deposited on the quarter-deck forthwith and deputed a young petty officer from our boarding party to see that the order was carried out. I then went below, instructing the interpreter to follow. A rating conducted us along thickly carpeted corridors to a beautifully furnished cabin-cum-stateroom.

A sallow, heavy-featured man looking far more like a croupier than a naval officer, sat at a desk, bland and imperturbable. I introduced myself, explained the purpose of our visit and said that fellow officers were searching the bridge house, signals office and main operational areas of the ship. He nodded, shrugged his shoulders. I had the feeling that he regarded my visit as the most distasteful episode of the war so far, unforgivably arrogant on our part, even verging on the vulgar. Perhaps he'd been awaiting instructions to be ready to take Hitler to a favoured St Helena, and now, instead, he was under duress to deal with these vile Brits.

I asked to see his log signals. He pointed to a set of books neatly arranged on the table. Such a visit from somebody had been inevitable. I knew that I was being presented with material of no serious significance. I was certain that all ciphers and other records which might have been useful to us had been destroyed at least two weeks previously. I left.

Veysey and the signals officer had completed their searches and were already in the launches alongside. Perhaps I should have been

suspicious of the determined seriousness of our crew, each man looking innocently ahead or out to sea, ashore, anywhere but at a shipmate.
I gave the order: 'Back to base.' The launch swung round and, within
a few minutes, Veysey and I had been put ashore and the launches
were returning with prideful sweeps to their destroyers. The rating with the log and signals book had been instructed to hand them
over to the signals officer in the other launch with my compliments.
I would see him the next day.

Veysey and I sauntered back to the hotel, discussing the afternoon's
exercise. A shower and whatever substitute for tea was available seemed
indicated, and perhaps a stroll or drive before supper. This was to be
our last night in Trondheim. Or so we thought.

About seven o'clock, a serious-looking lieutenant RN found us in
a corner of the vast and virtually empty hotel bar, sipping rather than
drinking our innocent brews, hungrily awaiting the earliest possible
call to dine. He said: 'Captain D wishes to see you at base. Immediately. I have a car outside.'

We collected our caps in that species of silence preceding impend-
ing trouble, and went down the hotel steps to a staff Mercedes saloon,
complete with naval driver. The lieutenant got in beside him. At the
quayside HQ I was shown straight into Captain D's office; Veysey
was told to wait.

Captain D – whose name I propose to skip as he died some years ago,
and this memoir requires no imperative necessity for his identity – was
of middle height, black-bearded, red-faced, with dark intense eyes. He
clearly made a daily shot at looking like the sea dog he clearly hoped
he was. 'You took a party on board the *Grille* this afternoon?' he barked.

'Yes, sir.'

'A party of unmitigated looters, a disgrace to the service.'

'A party from your destroyer flotilla, sir.'

He paused fractionally. 'So I gather. Men follow officers' examples.
These men are scum, conscripts. One of the traditions of the Royal
Navy is no looting.'

'Not in my history books, sir.'

'Silence! I want none of your impertinent sallies.'

'I have the right to point out facts as I saw them. I saw no looting. The men seemed well behaved. Admittedly, I was below for a quarter of an hour. Some items may have been taken. One of the gruesome facts of war.'

'Nonsense! These are excuses made by an incompetent impostor of an officer.'

By then he was inflammable with fury, his eyes blazing, his face flaming, even more choleric in manner than anyone I have seen, even including Fleming. I could see that no words from myself stood a chance of being heard – and stayed silent. He went ranting on: 'You were in charge. I have had a report from the German admiral. I accept his word. I have called for a list of everything which was taken. This will be here tomorrow morning. Meanwhile, consider yourself under open arrest and prepare yourself for the inevitable court-martial. Now get out! Get out! Your companion, too. From tomorrow morning, you will report to my duty officer three times a day.'

We walked gloomily back to the Borg, wandered dolefully into the dining room, took our seats and ordered. 'We've got to try to eat something,' Veysey said. 'We've got a long night ahead. We shan't sleep, that's certain.'

Halfway through our silent and minimal meal, a tall, broad-shouldered, dark, straight-backed young lieutenant RNVR entered the room, escorted by the waitress who pointed towards our table. He crossed the room and introduced himself. 'I'm in one of the destroyers. I hear you're in trouble.'

'So it seems.'

'Through no fault of your own.'

'That's our belief.'

He smiled and took the offered chair. I invited him to join the meal. He said he'd had his supper, but wouldn't mind a drink. I ordered. After a pause, he said: 'Well, there was some looting. That's clear.

Irrefutable but understandable. Apparently the matelots saw Leicas by the score and whipped a few. I see their point. Wish I'd been there. But what I dropped by to say was this: before the show, I was at the Metropolitan Police College at Hendon. Reserved occupation and all that, but I thought I'd like a spot of sea service. I've enjoyed it. One of the things Hendon taught me was that there's little hope of any kind of prosecution if none of the suspect goods can be found. The buzz has gone round. Everyone's on your side but nobody will ever find a single bloody thing. I can promise that across my flinty heart. So stick to your story. You'll be all right,' he said, preparing to go.

I wasn't so sure, although duly grateful for his small mercies. We thanked him warmly, but I had a favour to ask: 'Have you a copy of *KR and AI* we could borrow?' I asked.

'Dead easy. I'll go and get it now and bring it round. Stay put.'

He was as good as his word, returning within twenty minutes with his ship's copy of *King's Rule and Admiralty Instructions*, the encyclopaedia of naval protocol. I did not ask how he had extracted the copy from his captain's cabin, but promised its return by the morrow's breakfast. I would leave the volume, well packed, in the hotel front office. 'I'll collect,' he said. 'You'll be busy.'

We went up to our rooms. Until three o'clock I conducted a one-man crash course in Royal Naval court-martial procedure that would have seen me successfully through any *Mastermind* quiz on the subject. Veysey lay on the bed in his room, mainly staring at the ceiling, dejected, becoming more dejected by the hour, he confessed. With the gradually comforting company of *KR and AI,* I began very slowly to be in mildly better shape. Some time after midnight Veysey dozed off. I had a further stint with my archive of naval lore and law.

Gradually, as a result of these hours of intensive devilling, I came to realise that Captain D had put himself into an extremely dodgy position, especially if, as I suspected, he was so vaingloriously ambitious. At its simplest, the admiralty holds that for an officer of superior rank to book a junior officer for court-martial, he needs to have one

Robert Harling (*left*) on the bridge of a corvette on North Atlantic convoy escort duty. During the early years of the Second World War, he served as navigator on several corvettes before joining the Inter-Services Topographical Division (ISTD).

'*Fierce opposition was still being encountered every yard of the way, enemy sniping still continuous and accurate.*' After D-Day, Normandy, 1944.

Robert Harling in 1945 with Lieutenant Holterdahl, en route from Stavanger to Oslo, on their quest to examine captured German 'midget U-boats'.

Post-D-Day 1944, Harling (*centre*) with Commander Dunstan Curtis RNVR (*left*), who 'was to become a close friend in war and peace'.

Robert Harling en route to Oslo, August 1945.

Robert Harling bought a cottage in Beddgelert, Snowdonia, and he would spend his wartime leave walking and climbing in the surrounding countryside.

© Rolf Richardson / Alamy

Joyce Grove, the rambling Jacobean-style country house in Nettlebed, Oxfordshire, built for Ian Fleming's grandfather Robert Fleming, founder of the eponymous merchant bank. Ian and his brothers spent much of their childhood on the 2,000-acre estate, which was completed in 1908.

'Fleming confessed that this was the most demeaning photographic session in which he had been involved.' Fleming leaving court with his mother, Evelyn St Croix Fleming, 11 November 1957.

'Fleming was certainly more at ease in Goldeneye than in any other setting in which I had seen him, with the possible exception of Boodles, where he invariably seemed wholly relaxed.' Ian Fleming in his study at Goldeneye in February 1964.

Violet, the 'cook-housekeeper' at Goldeneye, flanked by her two assistants. Robert Harling was not as receptive to the local cuisine as his host, a view shared by Noël Coward, who 'graced one meal with the opinion that the dish he had been offered and tasted had proved more akin to "armpits" than desirable food'.

'The duchess was tall, dark and extremely handsome, a sexy-seeming, effervescent woman of the world, clearly accustomed to getting her own way and ways.' Loelia, Duchess of Westminster.

Ian Fleming
in his study,
March 1958.

To Robert..
without whose constant
encouragement etc:
from
The Author.

CASINO
ROYALE

by
IAN FLEMING

JONATHAN CAPE
THIRTY BEDFORD SQUARE
LONDON

'*The spy novel to end all spy novels.*' A first edition of Ian Fleming's debut novel, *Casino Royale*, published in 1953. His inscription to Robert Harling reads: 'To Robert, Without whose constant encouragement etc. From The Author.'

Robert Harling's own 'Thunderbird', an Aston Martin DB2/4, which he owned from 1958 to 1974. It didn't have an ejector seat.

Robert Harling and his wife Phoebe, also known as 'Silvertop', painted by John Worsley in 1947.

'His portraits of the Flemings were first-rate character studies. Fleming was shown with his nose almost sniffing the weapon he held before him – a Ruger Blackhawk .44 Magnum, then and possibly still the most powerful handgun in the world. Ann was shown in an armchair, confirming the caption as "dark, handsome, highly strung", but here looking supremely relaxed and upper-crust.' Norman Parkinson's portraits, commissioned by Robert Harling to illustrate his profile of the Flemings in US *Vogue*, 1963.

Robert Harling
relaxing on the
Italian island of
Giglio, 1959.

overriding requirement on his side. Unless he has convincing proof that his accusations are well founded and will stick under the most intensive of cross-examinations, his future in the service will be smudged and jeopardised. The senior service seemed to me, after those hours and hours of homework, to be blessedly protective of its junior officers.

To add a touch of more positive, even forceful action, to my side of the story to clinch the data *KR and AI* had provided, I drafted a signal directed to Fleming requesting that Lieutenant Commander Karminski RNVR QC and Lieutenant Commander James Fawcett RNVR DSC should be flown out pronto to prepare my defence. Karminski, a peacetime acquaintance, had proved himself a highly capable pre-war counsel, and I had already gathered that Fawcett was on track for an impressive legal career in the post-war years. If I had to fire off the signal I would call Fleming and outline the situation.

After our somewhat fitful night, we descended to coffee and no food, left the copy of *KR and AI* in the hall and walked down to the quay to report to the first officer of the nearest destroyer alongside, a lieutenant commander RN, who was both Captain D's staff officer and also duty officer, too, we had learned. He was a tall, pale and some-what sacerdotal-looking. 'As you probably know, we have to report to you three times a day,' I said, introducing ourselves.

'I know! I know! It's all rather embarrassing,' he said. 'None of my wishes, y'know? Between ourselves, I think the old man's off his nut.'

'Nevertheless, these are his orders.'

'I know! I know! Look, I'll take your word as officers and gentle-men and so forth that you'll be around. What's your hotel? Good. Drop down here around 1800 hours and we'll have a drink. We'll take the rest as read, shall we? Same tomorrow if that suits you and this charade is still on.'

We crossed the quay to the naval HQ. I asked to see Captain D's chief of staff. I had met him fleetingly on my first visit to the HQ: a bluff, genial, round-faced, overweight commander RNVR, doubtless longing to return as soon as possible to the civilian life he had plainly opted for and preferred. I gave him a draft of the signal I wished to have sent to the admiralty. He shook his head after scanning my draft, plainly unwishful to be involved in this unwanted fracas.

'I can't send this!' he said, clearly bothered.

'With a threat of a court-martial hanging over my head, you certainly will. I need the best advice I can get. And don't forget the "QC" after Karminski and the "DSC" after Fawcett.'

'I don't like this. I'll have to consult Captain D.'

He left us.

'Captain D wants to see you,' he said, returning within a minute.

The captain stood up as I came into the room. 'I have the German admiral's list here!' he barked. 'Here it is. I want your answer to this within the hour. An answer to the slur you have brought on the navy and my command.'

I glanced at a very long list, mainly concerned with cameras, but with one surprising item: 40,000 cigarettes. I asked for a copy.

'That is your copy! You'll need it!' he barked.

By that time, I was well beyond any mood for overmuch service ritual and said: 'You can have my answer to this accusation now. No British rating in any British ship would dream of taking a single German fag. They regard them as horse manure or worse. Any member of your crews will confirm my words.'

That was the truth and the supremely assured logic of my words winded him. That was clear. German ersatz cigarettes were regarded by all the services in the terms I had used, albeit even more succinctly.

'That still leaves the cameras!'

'So your admiral claims.'

'Not MY admiral.'

'My apologies. The German admiral, of course.'

'Get out!' he shouted once again.

I stood my ground. 'I have just provided your chief of staff with the draft of a signal relevant to this affair.'

'I've seen the damn thing. A lot of good that'll do you. Now get out!'

I went out, knowing that I was leaving him in deep concern.

Veysey was waiting in the outer office. We walked back to the hotel. The *KR and AI* had been collected. We then drove out to the lakes again. At least there was visual pleasure there, although we doubt-less bored each other with our repetitious exchanges of views on our current burlesque.

I could see my gleam of hope beginning to glint and began to tot up the odds against Captain D. Ultimately, all members of the boarding party would be known to have come from the flotillas over which he had operational command. Could he allow that little item of news to come out? Then there was his chief of staff's refusal, so far as I knew, to send my signal requesting tip-top legal help. That wouldn't help his cause. There was also the telling factor that none of the items mentioned in the German admiral's loot list would be found. Their wholesale disappearance had been virtually guaranteed. Finally, what a day out for the popular press if English sailors were to be accused of looting from Hitler's very own yacht.

A note from the commander awaited us on our return to the hotel. I was to report to Captain D on the occasion of my afternoon report to the duty officer. I could scarcely tell Captain D or his chief of staff that I had been begged by that same duty officer not to make such a rendezvous, but I went. Captain D came to the point straightaway.

'I have had drafted an appropriate apology from yourself made out to the German admiral. Sign this and it will close the whole of this infernally irritating occurrence. I propose to drop my proposed court-martial proceedings.'

He handed me a note with the name of a German admiral written in block letters. I read his note.

'I wouldn't dream of agreeing to so preposterous a would-be con-fession,' I said, as quietly as I could manage.

Again his temper flared. Again he shouted: 'Get out!'

I got out. The only question was: when would he break?

A note was delivered to the hotel that evening ordering me to report to Captain D at 0830 the following morning. At 0700 I was up and ready for action.

Captain D made no accusations. No demands. Nothing. All he said was: 'I want you and Lieutenant Veysey out of this town before ten o'clock this morning.'

'We will do our best, sir,' I said, most dutifully, and left. On the way out I checked with his chief of staff that my legal plea had never been sent.

'As I suspected,' I said.

'Let bygones be bygones,' he said grinning, gripping my arm.

I walked slowly back to the hotel. Veysey was waiting in the reception hall. I told him we were on our way. We packed our bags quickly, signed chits for our accommodation and went out to the car. We drove out of Trondheim on a sunny day with a brilliant sky and scarcely a cloud.

Veysey was clearly thinking of other matters. After a long pause, he said: 'I'm not sure about the innocents abroad line: I have a rather embarrassing confession to make.'

'You looted a Leica?'

'Not exactly, but while you were seeing Captain D this morning, I had a visitor. A petty officer. Never seen him before. He put a sizeable parcel in my hand, said "Compliments of the season, sir," and vanished on the instant. When I got back to my room I found we'd been receivers of some fairly choice stolen goods: two Leicas, two viewfinders and a few other photographic items.'

I was silent, taking in our new career as fences.

'You're the *KR and AI* expert,' Veysey went on. 'What d'you suggest we do now, your honour? Turn around and go back to Captain D?'

'We drive straight on.'

'That's rather what I thought would be your decision. After all, if we hand 'em back we'd look like the actual looters. Even if our story is accepted, we'd land the ratings in trouble. Rather fascinating quandary, I thought.'

'A quandary suggests the possibility of choice of alternatives. I don't think we've got one. This was either an extremely altruistic move by that petty officer or an extremely devious one.'

'Wholly altruistic. I always like to think the best of people, especially petty officers, don't you?'

'You don't think the petty officer wanted to involve us, too, if the whole thing blew up?'

'Only a cynic would think so.'

'Perish the thought, then.'

We had a splendid trip back to Oslo, taking three days over the return excursion. The weather was perfect. The landscapes were fabulous. The natives friendly beyond belief. Why hurry with the war, or rather peace, providing us with this fabulous finale to our trip?

We flew back forty-eight hours later and, a couple of days after that, I met up with Fleming in Room 39. Lunch followed. He was keen to hear about the *Grille* episode in detail and highly amused by my troubles with Captain D, confessing relief that I had managed to settle the situation without recourse to himself. 'You certainly seemed to have ended your naval career with an unusually eventful couple of weeks.'

'Silvertop called it a service farce,' I said.

'She has her points,' Fleming conceded, smiling.

CHAPTER 16

FLEMING GOES SOLO

Two days after our return from Norway, Fleming returned from his own expedition into what he termed the Fenimore Cooper never-never land of Europe, traversed mainly, but occasionally, by the more imaginative members of 30AU. I learned the background to the story in due course.

Halfway through April, Lieutenant Glanville RNVR and his party had been investigating a school building in the small town of Naumburg in eastern Germany. The building had housed a branch of German naval intelligence but had recently been abandoned. One of Glanville's party had come across a charred piece of paper carrying an address: SKI/KA, Tambach. Nobody in the party had an inkling of the meaning of the initials, but the paper referred to the despatch of classified documents to that address. Glanville, a persistently probing officer, had decided that the information might prove of some significance and set out to see whether this seeming logogram could be defined. He thus became involved in one of those searches which more dedicated investigators of seeming mysteries so

thoroughly enjoy. Few men were better equipped by taste, temperament and training to take on the role of a wartime Sherlock Holmes
than this officer. The ensuing search took a week, but by late April
he had arrived at the Schloss Tambach.

News of what might prove to be historic material but scarcely current grade-one Second War material was signalled to the DNI. The
schloss might possess potentially valuable papers, especially as the outfit was under the care and protection of a retired admiral. With other
investigations on hand, Glanville needed to press on, having arranged
with 3rd Army HQ for a military guard to be laid on for the *schloss*
and to await the DNI's instructions.

Room 39 had heard vague reports of the collection: lorry-loads of
documents had been reported arriving at Tambach for several months.
The general assumption had been that these were records relating to
the current war and might be of considerable value. Other suggestions were that these were merely archival records. Fleming decided
that losing valuable archives of any war could prove a grievous loss
to future marine scholarship. Such a possible loss would prompt interest for any book collector of ambition and scope. On either score
– modern or antique archives – the *schloss* was certainly worth a visit.
Preliminary enquiries disclosed that Tambach-Dietharz or Tambach,
as the remote outpost was more generally known, was situated a few
miles south of Gotha on the E40 route, north of Thuringer Walk and
almost 150 miles south of Hannover.

In the course of our first lunch for a couple of weeks, Fleming readily admitted that his book collector's instincts had been aroused by the
thought of such a killing. He had arranged for himself to be directed
by the DNI to visit the *schloss*. For so chair-bound an officer, such an
excursion promised to be an unusual tail-end bonus to his personal
war. He had thereupon taken off with a bookish and scholarly RNVR
officer to view the hoped-for treasure trove.

'And was everything as valuable and interesting as a bibliophile or
intelligence officer would have hoped for?' I queried.

'Everything was worth having – as far as I could judge, that is. Let's leave it at that. One or two of the more fervently patriotic women working there had set about burning the records as they received them. Fortunately, Admiral Gladisch, head of the outfit, learned about this ongoing kamikaze fate for the valuable documents for which he was responsible and had it stopped, pronto. He had wanted everything shipshape and, hopefully, ready for approval on a promised visit by Admiral Dönitz at the war's end.'

'You inferred that most of the records concerned the First War?'

'A major part, but they continued into our own affair. If the worst happened, Dönitz would probably have wished to show the Allies how the *Kriegsmarine* always played by the rules.'

'This war or every war?'

'For Germans, life's one long, indivisible war. Dönitz is one of the few top-flight officers who quite respected Hitler and vice versa. I imagine he would have wished to show posterity a well-documented, clean bill of wartime behaviour by Germany's glorious navy.'

'And did he have a reasonable case buried in these archives?'

'God knows. I'll leave that for the naval historians. I left instructions that what we wanted were all the records, particularly any from the early and mid-'30s. I thought with those we might be able to see the way Hitler was viewing the outer maritime world. I left our dedicated, tame bibliographer behind to go through these treasures as best he could and organise the sizeable task of getting the stuff back to UK.'

'A job for Pickfords?'

'More or less. I'm told we'll need at least half-a-dozen 3-tonne lorries to bring it all back. We're expecting their arrival in a fortnight or so.'

'And who will be the archivist here?'

'Something will be arranged. Some willing German naval nutter, I gather. Along with an equivalent English nutter, of course.'

'A longish journey,' I said, recalling my own trip to the Elbe. 'What did you use? A Jeep?'

'What a hope! Staff car plus admiralty chauffeur. Plus two marines in a naval patrol car as bodyguards.'

'And what happened when you got there? Red-carpet treatment?'

'In a limited kind of way. The castle offered the usual visual pleasantries: mountain background, forest clearing, lake and so on. Rumour claimed the lake was in the process of being dried out for the intended blaze.'

'And you saved everything?'

'So it seems. If I were the donnish type I could probably claim preservation of all the German naval records for the past seventy or eighty years and settle down with a scholarly doctorate for my mature years.'

'Why not?'

'Any serious questions, by any chance?'

'Will these documents be much use for the next war, assuming this one is virtually over?'

'Such archives come under the heading of world history, of which you may have heard. For those of us interested in the past, this is one of the most significant and rewarding historical archive hauls of the war.'

'Noted.'

'The Russkies and the Yanks would certainly have welcomed such a haul. Think of all those sophomores at Paris, Harvard and Moscow, looking for subjects for degree dissertations fifty years from now.'

'I daren't think of it. Not one of my daydreams. Anyway, we've surely got our own share of sophomores. And what about the admiral?'

'The DNI has authorised that whoever comes here, someone more or less responsible for the archives, should be treated as an official guest of the admiralty.'

'I wish him well. What was the castle like – architecturally and so forth?'

'Cold. Dismal. Comfortless. Ghastly. Count Dracula stuff.'

'What was the old boy like?'

'Shattered when we arrived, but he soon became quite helpful. I had the feeling that the possibility of the destruction of those price-less naval records had been causing him quite a few sleepless nights.'

'He provided quite good practice for Fleming's German, no doubt?'

'More fluent by the hour.'

'All in all, you were obviously by way of being a white knight arriv-ing just in time to preserve these priceless records.'

'Something along those lines, despite your twisted view of the exercise.'

'Where will the German archivist be staying?'

'Probably in some naval quarters or London club. He'll be spend-ing most of his time with our own naval historians.'

'How long will he stay?'

'A month or so.'

'Did you enjoy *your* very own "cowboys and indians" interlude?'

'Up to a point. Finding old records doubtless lacks the lustre of finding new advances in German U-boat construction or plans for more destructive depth charges, but there it is: a modest contribu-tion to world history.'

'I hope the venture helped to persuade you to feel more compas-sionate towards the 30AU underlings you've been chiding for the past couple of years?'

'Not noticeably.'

Fleming had clearly opted to return after four days from a trip, which could easily and legitimately have sponsored at least a couple of weeks away from his desk. All that was now to become the respon-sibility of the scholarly RNVR type he'd left behind. Perhaps there was something in Ann's remark that Fleming could suffer anything but discomfort.

On hearing his tale, with its confirmation that he had so swiftly returned to Room 39 and the social life which, even in wartime, he had consistently enjoyed, I surmised that the somewhat basic and carefree life of 30AU in the field had been conclusively proven for him. Perhaps he had set out on the job thinking it might prove more exciting than it had. After all, even when presented with archives, which might become, in time, invaluable records for historians, he had cut the matter short. Certainly his experience, though interesting, bore little relation to the seemingly adventurous account which one of Fleming's biographers was to conjure up some twenty years later.

Somewhat later still, I got the full story from a helpful official in the Ministry of Defence. Contrary to that rather melodramatic biographical snippet, Admiral Gladisch remained in Germany and wasn't brought to England. Instead, a *Korvettenkapitän* had been deputed to assist in re-establishing the archives, and had returned to Germany a month or so later. The records then came under the care of a home-grown civilian archivist specialist in the German language and German naval history.

I hazarded a forecast: 'With a coup like that to your name and your brass hat and captain's rings, surely you'll be in the running for an OBE, at least?'

Fleming grimaced. 'My mother got one in the last war and Peter's got another in this show. If any oddments are on the tapis, I need something different.'

'Such as?'

'God knows. Whatever they dish out for wartime desk devotion.'

Which, alas, he never received.

'I hope you feel more akin to a fully paid-up member of 30AU after this somewhat piratical venture,' I suggested.

'I enjoyed the run. I'd never been to that part of Germany before. Apart from that, the trip confirmed my general view that you and your fellow activists probably enjoyed a far more light-hearted war than most characters operating in HM forces operating in any so-called martial theatre. Certainly far more light-hearted than mine turned out to be.'

'Plus occasionally harsher moments. Plus more than our fair share of casualties.'

'I agree that 30AU had its sharper moments and lost a dispropor-
tionate number of its men, but the rest of you got away with far more
than a fair share of unadulterated entertainment.'

With that statement I had to concur.

CHAPTER 17

RETURN TO FRESH STARTS

Peace, alas, seemed apt to sunder most friendships made in war. Divisive elements are limitless: differing social backgrounds; vast distances; marriages; lifestyles; jobs; joblessness; injury; death … and so on and on. I was fortunate in continuing friendships with Fleming and Curtis, those two polarities.

I left the navy late in the summer of 1945. I had lost contact with most members of 30 Assault Unit, due to my involvement in those late operations Fleming had foisted my way. The greatly enlarged unit, 'overloaded with land-based know-alls' as an old hand opined, had moved on to Kiel and Hamburg. Other specialist members were in Berlin. I had no wish to join them. I had enjoyed my far-apart excursions to Magdeburg and Trondheim, but had no wish for further forays.

Nearing the year's end, the unit was virtually no more. Members had moved back into their erstwhile civilian ways with, alas, no farewell party to match that pre-D-Day Gargoyle send-off. Hudson, I learned, was somewhere in Essex learning how to be a salesman. What of, I hoped to learn later.

Curtis remained in the navy for a few months longer and was then recruited by the Council of Europe, thus confirming the accuracy of Fleming's forecast that he would become a multilingual post-war bureaucrat. He set up home in Paris with his wife, Monica. We visited them the following year, and I also saw him from time to time on his visits to London.

Fleming's social life in peacetime London seemed little different from his wartime round: a workaday business life with an unusual concentration on evening commitments. He had retained his Athenaeum Court flat while he sought other, larger quarters.

He defined his working life as 'an old-age pensioner's version of Room 39'. This absence of novelty well suited him, he contended. He had been appointed to a top job – foreign news manager – in the Kemsley Group. I suspected that he had secretly hoped that he would also have been offered a directorship, but perhaps one step at a time was his plan or philosophy for peacetime.

At an early, post-war luncheon at the Etoile, which was rather superseding Scott's as our favoured rendezvous, he said he had insisted on his somewhat outlandish label on the Kemsley outfit as more befitting the job he intended for himself: directing the group's foreign correspondents around the globe from hot spots to hotter spots. He had declined the title of foreign editor – the original position he had been offered by Kemsley – convinced that he would be expected to pen a weekly think piece on the state of the world. Not his line, he said. He had neither the political conviction nor the pontifical prose suited to such a task. And neither dedication nor time such a task would have demanded, I thought.

He soon returned to his pre-war indolence, even persuading 'Gomer' – as Lord Kemsley was uniquely known to Fleming outside the family circle – to incorporate in his contract a clause whereby he would be able to take January and February as his annual paid-up holiday perk. He had decided that on these beneficent terms, the job would suit his peacetime needs: financial, social, and no doubt, sexual. He was determined not to repeat the gruelling demands of executive life he had experienced in Room 39. I wondered how he had persuaded Kemsley to agree to these self-indulgent requests.

He stood four-square by a personal belief that he was not the only one to find the top realms of newspaper life in Kemsley House fairly relaxing. He claimed that he had already 'counted fifty-seven varieties of executive doing fuck all', but was prepared to admit that he was only one of three or four 'doing minus fuck all'. This was doubtless by way of a carefree throwaway quip, for he was to continue in the job for well over a decade, to the apparent satisfaction of two successive owners and three successive editors. Years later, soon after he had sold out to Roy Thomson, I was invited by Kemsley to lunch at the Dorchester à deux. Probably, I decided, because I was one of the few outside retainers with whom he could discuss advertising and business aspects of a newspaper. I also thought that the invitation had arrived because he was just downright lonely, nostalgic and somewhat forlorn. He was, but cheered up after he began to talk of Fleming. I then realised, to my considerable surprise, that his lordship was deriving a curious latter-day pride from recalling the eccentric contract he had granted Fleming with those curious holiday arrangements. That those spells in Jamaica ultimately contributed substantially to the emergence of Bond was undoubtedly true. Kemsley clearly wished this seeming foresight on his generous part to be more widely acknowledged.

My own return to peacetime life was immediate and smooth. Weekdays I was busy in London; weekends agreeably relaxed in Suffolk. We were delighted by our mill house in Suffolk, and also retained the small Fleet Street flat which I had owned for five years and which was to prove a useful pied-à-terre for several years ahead. We delighted in our sabbatical explorations of the East Anglian countryside from Cambridge to Norwich, winter and summer. The house suited us supremely well until, eight years later on, a young and fast-growing trio necessitated a move to a more commodious homestead; a gothic rectory on the Surrey–Kent border.

I returned to my erstwhile career as a graphic and typographical designer and as 'consulting creative director' was vouchsafed a larger office in the large Adam Mayfair house occupied by the fast-expanding advertising agency I had joined pre-war. Thanks to Lord Kemsley's memory of the wartime dummy I had prepared for the *Daily Sketch*. I was also appointed design consultant to the *Sunday Times*. I was also invited by Lord Drogheda to advise on typographical matters concerning the *Financial Times*. Agreeably, I also became advisor to Stephenson, Blake, the international Sheffield type foundry, designing several types for that historic firm. Above all, I was keen to follow up the wartime publication of *Amateur Sailor* with a second book about the war at sea. I also had a modest ambition to start another typographical journal, especially as James Shand of the Shenval Press had retained his printing skills and maintained his enthusiasm for a return to such endeavours after wartime restrictions. In due course the first number of *Alphabet & Image* was published. My working life was as full and absorbing as I had hoped.

I also decided to establish a personal four-day working week in London to take care of this fairly comprehensive programme. Fleming was quick to point out that such a limited working week was rather more self-indulgent than the ten-month working year he had extracted from the Kemsley outfit. Speedy calculation proved that the two escapes were more or less in balance.

'What does the title "consulting creative director" denote?' asked Fleming, having heard of my appellation, and clearly still somewhat sensitive over that self-inflicted word 'manager' in his own early workaday title. 'That word "consulting", for instance. Who consults you? Or do you spend your days consulting others? Consulting about what, anyway? Slogans? Copy lines? Captions? Or what?'

'More likely about the exquisite legs of the latest recruit to the office staff?'

'More likely, no doubt. Furthermore, what about that word "creative". D'you merely have to say, "Let there be a layout," and, lo! There is a layout. Or what?'

'Something along those lines, but not quite so laboured. It's the language of advertising. Happily, our clients – the only people who really matter in advertising – seem to respond quite enthusiastically to our efforts.'

'The story of the ever-optimistic media world.'

He had more basic matters to discuss, however, and pressed on: where could he look for new living quarters? His current quarters in Piccadilly were too cramped for his civilian social life. He needed a more spacious domestic interior.

I made a few suggestions. Why not try for a flat in Albany? Couldn't he get help from J. B. Priestley, occasional contributor to the *Sunday Times* who was resident there? Fleming declined, dismissing the chambers as expensive quarters for occasional visits to London by pretentious millionaires.

Within a month or so he had left Athenaeum Court in Piccadilly, moving to what he declared to be a spacious, even resplendent west-facing first-floor bachelor pad in Montagu Place in Marylebone. I wasn't unduly surprised to learn that the Rothermeres were living nearby in Montagu Square while they awaited the completion of the refurbishing of their familial mansion: Warwick House, St James's, overlooking Green Park.

Commenting on the doubtless coincidental proximity of their current abodes, I was answered with a confirmatory but dismissive bark, and the assertion: 'Sheer coincidence. These things do happen.'

Apart from a further grin, I decided to wait until I learned the whereabouts of his next residential hideout after Warwick House had been made ready for reoccupation by the Rothermeres.

During those waiting weeks he drove down to our mill house. By that time we were more or less settled in. He and Silvertop became instant friends and remained so. She enjoyed his humour and apparent carefreedom. He relished her ready response and laughter to his quips and queries. She could not believe my view that he was one of the most inwardly despondent men she would ever meet, made for her ex-boss.

During his first visit to the Constable countryside, he asked whether we would venture to Jamaica during the coming year. Silvertop was keen to return to the island she had visited pre-war. I was more wishful to see more of Europe. We left the decision for further discussion.

Meanwhile, I visited his new home in Montagu Place, which proved a vast improvement on his encapsulated wartime life in Piccadilly. Space and luxury were now richly available.

Where had he acquired the handsome furniture? The splendid walnut bureau bookcase; the equally handsome mahogany dining table with appropriate chairs; plus a couple of ostentatiously comfortable armchairs?

'From my mother's overloaded house in Cheyne Walk,' he affirmed, sinking into one of the armchairs set by one of the large windows overlooking the square, waving towards its partner.

I congratulated him on the comfort and charm of his new home. Had he been responsible for this exercise in interior design and decoration?

'More or less.'

'You did most of the interiors?'

'Absolutely.'

'As in Jamaica?'

'Come and see for yourself?'

'Is that perfection, too? House? Climate? Situation? Islanders? Expats?'

'Every time I'm there I know in my ageing bones that I never want to come back to this metropolitan sink. And every time I'm there I realise I couldn't live there for longer than six weeks at a time or very little more.'

'Poor you! Such a problem!' And how was he spending his leisure time now that he was back in the city sink?

'The simple bachelor life,' he answered glibly. 'Kemsley House. Boodles. The Portland. Weekend golf at Huntercombe. Plus the occasional evening out and most evenings in.'

'Plus the occasional popsy also in, no doubt.'

He grinned, as usual dodging any direct answer with a querying aside: 'You've doubtless banished womanising and promiscuity from your own lifestyle.'

'I still have my Fleet Street flat and three nights on my own in London should my cast-iron resolution weaken.'

'And what are Silvertop's views on allowing her new husband, proven loner and womaniser, such latitude?'

'Ask her when next you meet. Basically, I think her views match my own. After all, she was the one to insist on my keeping Fleet Street. She scotched any inclination I might have had for daily commuting to and from Suffolk.'

'So you'd contend that you're both in full agreement on these normally highly controversial aspects of the conjugal life?'

I laughed at his persistence. 'You sound like some would-be worldly cleric dropping in for a counselling chat with a couple of local parishioners. We both had our several affairs and flutters in the near and distant past. Why not? Let's leave it that we both believe nobody owns anybody. Isn't that a primary requirement in all aspects of love and lust? Didn't I say that a month or so back?'

He laughed. Loudly. 'A rare and certainly an advanced domestic philosophy. Few wives and fewer husbands share such views, especially in the first year or so of fairly sudden matrimony. Which I still can't quite fathom. No pregnancy seems apparent.'

'None is. Currently. Ask again next year. Meanwhile, let's eat. Where's your local bistro or do we take a taxi down to the Etoile?'

We continued our exchanges over supper taken in a Baker Street restaurant he had sampled and approved. We were there until quite late. Curiously, for two would-be scribes, the written word was unmentioned during that evening and, indeed, rarely in future meetings. Instead, probably inevitably, the subject of women and their unpredictable ways were discussed, usually at some length. Certainly they were that evening.

I queried whether his proposed escorting of Ann Rothermere to

Jamaica the following month had prompted any direct and/or dodgy questions from his lordship, or, for that matter, from any of her several close friends.

He dismissed any need for such questions. She would be a visitor as would Loelia Westminster, who would accompany her.

'Ah. Your mutual chaperone.'

'Not at all. A visitor. As you will be next year, I hope.'

'Will Ann like Goldeneye? This is her first visit, isn't it?'

He nodded. 'She'll love Goldeneye, but probably find the place a bit Spartan for her tastes, rather more self-indulgent than my own.'

'Perhaps 55 per cent more indulgent. No more. And you still continue to see her in London. People talk. Doesn't that bother you at all?'

'We meet from time to time. I know you have your own odd views about the publicity side of our relationship, but she's one of London's busiest hostesses, plus family, plus hosts of friends and has more than a fair share of entertaining deriving from Northcliffe House. All utterly mad maybe, but she enjoys it. Obviously, such a round doesn't leave much spare time for gossip and anything else you may have in mind.'

'Enough spare time for Fleming is all I have in mind.'

'Not enough,' he confessed, and possibly thinking that my questions were beginning to probe too deeply, switched with a sudden question: 'Was your marriage deeply considered? I'm puzzled. It seems to be working out, but it still seems somewhat odd!'

'Most marriages have odd beginnings. Which one of the odd bits do you have in mind?'

'Well, the whole affair seems to have taken you less than a year – meeting, meandering, marrying, mating, moving. A trifle odd, wouldn't you agree?'

'Long enough to know each other's thoughts, desires, lusts, habits and so forth.'

'How long d'you think it took you to make up your mind?'

'The first twenty-four hours.'

'Including bed?'

'Forty-eight hours, then. No need for rushing things. Anyway, if that's no go, surely everything else is doomed, although some abnormal humans seem to get by without.'

He laughed. 'I think you're probably right. For 95 per cent of the globe, anyway. But why so sudden – all of it?'

'I think it may seem rather sudden to others, but not to ourselves. I soon realised that this was a one-off job and that I wouldn't easily – if ever – find another comparable.'

'Reasonable enough. How would you define the one-off touch?'

'One wants scores of women, but I think *wanted* and *needed* characteristics are imperative. I also think a wife should have shown herself possessed of qualities of friendship enabling her to remain a close friend, prepared to discuss any subject.'

'Go on. I'm genuinely intrigued. What were the qualities you thought you needed?'

'Patience. Understanding. Above all, a sweet nature. Gentleness and so on. Qualities I lack.'

'Just the qualities your selfish, ruthless, self-centred persona needs, you thought? And what did Silvertop want?'

'What most women want, above all, she says: a protective and generous partner. Both qualities usually go together, she says. Plus a man who moves her to laughter and orgasm.'

He guffawed. 'Not bad. Not bad at all!' he said. 'Presumably you provide all these benefactions?'

'Hopefully. Silvertop contends I do.'

'D'you think you'll stay married?'

'Who knows – but why not? We seem compatible, able to meet each other's needs and so forth. Is that an answer?'

'Of a kind, I suppose. So long as it covers everything in the relationship – from friends to fucking, for instance. You imply they do.'

'So far, so good.'

'You both seem to share all the same preferences and revulsions?'

I laughed. '*Most* rather than *all* probably. Makes life more interesting and durable.'

'You share the same interests in all carnal activities?'

I put his persistence down to the whisky taking him back to his wartime quiz tactics. 'As you seem to have switched from curate to quizmaster, the answer's a comprehensive yes. The same. Fucking. Fellatio. Cunnilingus. And any other spin-offs from simple old-fashioned demonstrations of sexual love and lust.'

'Quite a good title for a sex guide: *Marital Sexual Spin-offs*. You must write it one day. Plus a few chapters on sadism, bondage, flagellation, infantilism, sado-masochism and so forth. I suspect they're as widely practised today as they were in Sade's time, no doubt. And all still in use.'

'Happily of no interest for either of us and not much of a sexual recipe for long-haul marriages, I imagine. I'll leave those chapters to you. No appeal in Harlinghome. What about you, as we seem to be moving on? Will I be allowed to offer a similar set of probes in due course? After the Rothermere divorce, for instance?'

'We'll wait and see. I doubt there'll be a divorce.'

'So be it. In the meantime, what about listing your own sexual sidelines?'

'I just think I'm inclined to try out a few tendencies towards the more so-called sadistic sides of sex than you two seem prepared to practise.'

'*Chacun* and so forth. Beating about the bush or bum has never had any appeal for me – or us. Never seen or felt the need. I know kissing seems more zestful. I like women too much. I think one's born knowing these things. In any case, women are every bit as sexually experimental as men.'

'I'm not sure I like women in the close and confidential way you seem to anyway.'

'Most men interested in women and their bodies get odd propositions from time to time, I suspect. As I said, I believe women to be every whit as sexually susceptible and experimental as men. Rather more so, I sometimes think.'

'Agreed. But how experimental?'

I decided to opt for a personal recollection: 'Well, towards the end of our recent war I was invited to a party by a one-time girl-friend. She lives in a flat in Bloomsbury. On leaving, I shared the lift with a friend of hers, a pretty girl I'd seen there but hadn't spoken to. At the exit to the lift and then the building we faced the black-out. Could I help find her a taxi or share one? She laughed and said: "Didn't I overhear someone ask where you were staying while on leave and didn't I hear you say how you have a flat in Fleet Street? That sounded quite interesting. I'm in no hurry."'

Fleming took another swig at his drink. 'Not a bad start. Go on.'

'I was beginning to enjoy the oddity of the encounter. We found a taxi. En route I asked what we should do in Fleet Street. Casually, she said she didn't care what we did so long as I hurt her. That shook things up a bit, especially as she looked as demure and pretty as a choir girl. I shook my head and said no go, but we could sort things out when we got there.'

'Carry on,' Fleming said, well aware that I was well away.

'Well, we settled down in the two armchairs in the flat with our drinks and I opened with the observation that I'd gathered she was something of a masochist.

"Not something of," was her merry answer. "All of!"

I laughed but told her I had no interest in these extra-curricular entertainments. She then laughed and said: "Men soon learn." The first thing she did in the flat was to kiss me expertly and warmly, slip her hands inside my reefer and slide off my belt. "I love belts, especially leather belts," she said. "Especially across my arse. Any offers?" But it was no go. Not a chance, I said.

Did I have any shipmates also on leave? Couldn't I ring anyone? "As a girl with three ever-ready randy apertures, I like three men."

"No go," I said. Should I see her home? She said no, she wanted to stay the night so we settled for old-fashioned fucking. Later, she admitted that it had all been very agreeable, but there it was: well short of what she regarded as the real thing. Most of all, she liked bondage, being beaten black and blue, having those apertures filled. It was – and is – all beyond me.'

'Got her address?' Fleming queried, his grin followed by a thunderclap of laugh. He looked at his watch. 'Not all that late.'

My turn to laugh. Alas, I hadn't, I confessed. 'As I said, it was all beyond me. In the past couple of years I also met two other quite delightful women on much the same beat: one a good deal older than myself, and still very attractive; the other quite young and pretty. The older one – married to a colonel – even carried a folding telescopic whip in her handbag for what she called "occasions that just crop up". Again no go for me. The younger one also wanted a lashing. No go. Old-fashioned leisurely fucking – fore and aft if agreeable to both – still seems to me the most satisfying of all the pleasures nature's provided for our spare time. You don't agree?'

'As you said, *chacun…*' he said. 'Any other addresses would be gratefully, even joyfully, received.'

We settled our bill and wandered out to Baker Street to seek a cruising taxi. I was returning to Fetter Lane.

The taxi arrived. 'Pity you lost those addresses,' he said. 'If they turn up, let me know. I enjoyed this evening. I'd also enjoy the occasional evening out with either or both of the others you mentioned.'

'I'll bear the request in mind,' I said, getting into the taxi.

He waved and went his way.

Inevitably, we returned to these matters from time to time, but our inclinations had been decisively delineated in that evening's discussion. That was clear.

In the taxi, I speculated on the chance of the complex lives of Fleming and Ann remaining in their current separate but seemingly controllable entanglement for years ahead.

A few weeks later, Fleming took flight to enjoy the first of his annual two-monthly escapes from Kemsley House. He was duly followed, at what he thought a reasonable interval of a week, by Ann

Rothermere and Loelia Duchess of Westminster. In a letter, he said the holiday was going well. The chaperone/companion/carer set-up was 'perfection'.

Who could resist a grin when reading such word-banging?

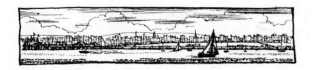

CHAPTER 18

EAST ANGLIAN REFLECTIONS

A week or so following his return from Jamaica, Fleming spent a weekend in East Anglia.

Once again he expressed astonishment at our remote rurality: 'A delightful house encompassed by fields to the far horizon.' His words not ours. The two-storied pink-brick mill house had been built in the early years of the nineteenth century, probably as separate staff quarters for a foreman at the grand weatherboarded mill, which, unseen by us, towered 300 yards down the lane above the River Stour. The mill, no longer in working order, was the home of an elderly widow and her son, a regular army major recently returned from war in the Middle East. They had already proved benign neighbours.

'Extraordinary move for a city slicker with a wife straight out of Harley Street,' Fleming observed as we wandered round the somewhat extensive garden for so modest a house.

'The Sussex Downs were part background to my boyhood,' I countered. 'And Silvertop's early days were spent at school in the Kentish countryside.'

He brushed aside so conventional a riposte. 'Little wonder you've wangled yourself a four-day week in London. What does Silvertop do during her days of freedom?'

'Gets to know the locals – she already has friends in Nayland, the local village – and she's also being spoiled by a temporary loan of her mother's housekeeper from Sussex.'

'All very cunningly fixed. I'm even prepared to admit it all seems to add up to agreeable days – and, hopefully, nights – in a happy-ever-after Mills & Boon mill house.'

'Let's hope your own domestic and literary endeavours will keep pace.'

'What a hope! Self-sufficiency is my simple motto for the years ahead.'

We gossiped on until Fleming's query: 'Doesn't Sefton Delmer live somewhere in these parts?'

'Nearer Sudbury, I gather. We could invite them over for supper in the near future if you can arrange to come down?'

Following our move to East Anglia I had been interested to learn that Delmer, remarried after a searing divorce – based on his wife's sexual misbehaviour with a colleague at Bletchley – had bought a secluded farmhouse a dozen miles or so distant from ourselves.

'Dead easy,' Fleming said heartily. 'I'd be delighted to see him again. Much to rehash.'

A month after that visit we set up another weekend visit when Fleming was free from golf or commitment to his paramour and keen to meet his erstwhile companion in Moscow and partner in 'black radio' projects in wartime Bletchley. Delmer was also delighted. They had quite a lot to mull over.

Delmer's wartime transmissions had acquired high renown among his contemporaries. These broadcasts, purporting to give lurid details concerning the scandalous private lives of the German political leaders and military legends had proved extremely successful, judging from reports by captured listeners.

I knew of Fleming's pre-war session in Moscow, covering the trial of British engineers, and of Delmer's gift for learning languages in double-quick time; a talent he had displayed on their Moscow trip. Fleming recalled how Delmer had met a Russian tart who specialised in indulging two stalwarts at the same time. Big-hearted Delmer queried whether Fleming was game to share her favours, proposing that they should toss a coin to decide which orifice the winner would prefer. He had also suggested that they should speak in French lest she happened to be a Soviet spy, deputed to befriend likely foreign spies. Fleming had declined, saying this wasn't his scene. His real reason, he told me, was that he couldn't guarantee an episode with Delmer's big, round, grinning moon face presiding over their charmer's neck and shoulders.

Delmer's success with his 'black radio' transmissions had so impressed all critics concerned with broadcasting to the enemy that Fleming had induced Admiral Godfrey to persuade Delmer to give instruction to two or three would-be naval broadcasters and/or scriptwriters to produce similar programmes to help undermine the morale of German mariners. Fleming nominated Donald McLachlan, pre-war journalist on *The Times*, then lieutenant commander RNVR, to head this unit. He also persuaded Colonel Bassett to sidetrack me for a few weeks from ISTD enquiries so that I could pen some of the earlier scripts to be broadcast in this naval venture. McLachlan and I were put under intense, even ruthless, instruction by Delmer in what appeared to be an empty and forgotten classroom but was indeed a one-time underground admiralty storeroom. Here at fourth-form type desks, the two pupils in their thirties sat before a mentor in his forties, learning the rudiments of 'black radio' scriptwriting.

Delmer, a larger-than-life character in every way – physically, intellectually, linguistically – had proved the toughest of taskmasters. Although he had been forewarned by Fleming that he had two experienced scribblers as pupils, he proved a quite different personality from the genial, world-travelled raconteur he was outside the school room. Within those cramped quarters he became a merciless critic. McLachlan termed him 'a man of the outside world who had become a master of the underworld'. I rather agreed. Yet, within a monstrous week we were virtually fully fledged scriptwriters prepared to do our best to undermine the will and warlike moods of the enemy.

That instructive week had certainly proved one of the most demanding spells of my wartime career. We had been put to work on half-a-dozen scripts dealing with the naval conflict. I recall that my major effort was an account of the sinking of the *Bismarck*, a story hopefully directed to undermining the will to win of any German naval types persuaded to switch on. This script was duly broadcast, and Fleming was duly impressed by the efforts of his two recommended Delmer pupils.

The secret admiralty broadcasting unit was based at Bletchley, one of the many Allied broadcasting units sited there. Here, McLachlan – later first editor of the post-war *Sunday Telegraph* – became a key figure in this extension to naval intelligence. Happily, the colonel sent word to Fleming after a couple of weeks that the Oxford topographical boffins had urgent need of my enquiring services in the Middle East for their own inquisitive reasons. Although I had enjoyed my tutelage under Delmer, I was relieved to return to my more *mouvementé* topographical enquiries.

Happily, these side ploys remain agreeable war memories.

The occasion proved a merry, loquaciously reminiscent evening. Delmer's new wife was a pretty and lively partner and the meeting of the two eminent wartime office practitioners was a hearty success, opening with Fleming's pertinent query: why did the Delmers live so sequestered an existence, even more remote than that of the Harlings?

Delmer was ready with his response: 'Basically because I've no wish for neighbours or intruders alike. Both groups sponsor strife.'

'How d'you know without meeting them?' Fleming asked.

'Instinct based on other people's experiences.'

We all laughed. I was quick to note that Delmer's comparatively new wife was clearly captivated by her husband's tale-telling talent. He clearly enjoyed keeping in top form.

'How d'you keep 'em away?'

'Our modest acreage is heavily fenced,' Delmer admitted. 'To the fencing, I've attached a couple of noticeboards bearing the legend "Valley Snake Farm", followed by injunctions and instructions: "Private property. No entrance. Beware snakes." Plus the addendum: "But if bitten…", then follow instructions on how to stagger across the fields to reach the local pharmacist in the nearest town, Sudbury, 3 miles off.'

'Even on Sundays?' Fleming queried, laughing heartily.

'Especially on Sundays. I've even invented a special sabbatical hospital number.'

'Any victims so far?' Fleming asked.

'We've never even had a week-day trespasser,' Delmer added, amid the general laughter.

He hugely enjoyed his tales. He was certainly well equipped to take centre stage, for he had both presence and voice for such extroversion. His voice was notably deep and possessed of dramatic touches when necessary. Clearly a born raconteur, accustomed to holding any audience enthralled.

'Upstage barnstorming,' was Fleming's later comment. He had a point.

They both had much to recall, especially their Bletchley memories. Delmer had been an important figure there, for he had early established himself as an imaginative and inventive 'black' propagandist and had been given virtually a free hand in his endeavours. Fleming, too, had been a keen if occasional visitor to Bletchley, even willingly broadcasting when needed in French and German, in which he was equally fluent. No one, however, was as fluent as Delmer, who could become a French aristocrat or German lorry driver on request. Fleming recounted how Delmer, arriving in Moscow with little Russian lingo, had been quite able to converse with the locals within a week.

Delmer put these skills down to the linguistic attainments of his father, a language teacher of rare versatility.

Round-the-world recollections by the pair held us at table well beyond the meal's end.

After their departure, Fleming had a good deal to recall concerning Delmer's marriages. I was surprised to hear him advance a belief that almost every man meets at least one angelic girl or woman in his life, usually in his early thirties. 'Forties are a bit on the late side for such juvenilia,' he added, before proceeding: 'He needs to make his decision fairly pronto: yea or nay. Normally, the girl doesn't contribute. Far too reticent. He begins to think she may be too gentle for the big decisions of life in this murky world: marriage, in-laws, tempestuous children, house-hunting, sexual and monetary differences, divorce and so on and so on.'

'What about his two wives?'

'I think he's better off with this wife than the former, who was a No. 1 heartbreaker if ever there was one.'

I agreed. Delmer's first wife had been, I recalled, quite legendary. Fleming claimed the breakdown of the marriage had left Delmer broken for months. His performance at our reunion supper seemed to suggest that he had fully recovered.

'Why does any couple ever marry?' Silvertop queried, clearly ready for some oddly held views.

'Because nobody ever learns a damn thing about love and lust,' Fleming opined. 'Three in every 10,000 are the annual exceptions.'

'A somewhat sweeping decision, surely,' Silvertop suggested, smiling, rising and quitting the room. 'Do reflect while I get our nightcaps.'

I grinned at query and response, and decided to fly a further kite for Fleming and said: 'I've found that gentler types of women are frequently the more strong-minded and supportive characters, frequently better able to cope with the manifold problems you've mentioned than flamboyant heartbreakers. Let's hope that's what Delmer has now acquired and welcomed.'

Fleming was inclined to agree, but, as usual, suggested my farcical views might well prove to be worth a monograph. What about it?

'I'll put it down on my list of never-never titles,' I said as our hostess returned with appropriate nightcaps, clearly ready to rejoin the exchanges.

Fleming, with one of his typical lead-ins, said: 'I was just about to congratulate your husband on a rare touch of sanity in his marriage. I'd got the impression he collected women, and then, after inflammatory attentions – to use his own phrase – disappeared into safer territory.'

Silvertop laughed merrily, adding serenely: 'But Ian, I've gathered from gossip and legend that such behaviour was/is also your speciality. My husband's the lifelong-friend type. He still contrives to take old flames out to lunch or supper in London. They call on him for advice on almost any problem. I'm all for these post-passion diversions.'

Fleming laughed. 'Don't forget the axiom: "Old embers can soon be poked into new fires"!'

Silvertop laughed. 'Like myself, Robert enjoys old embers as well as fresh twigs! Perhaps the logical course is to try to stay a tolerably fresh twig for as long as possible, especially at home, and then try to become a non-boring ember all round.'

Fleming laughed, nodded and then switched: 'A thoroughly sound philosophy. How did he meet you?'

She laughed. 'Old fashioned pick-up. He'd seen me three months earlier, a claim I was able to prove correct – strolling up Regent Street after I'd been to the cinema with a one-time school friend. He lost me that evening as he ran into an old flame near Oxford Circus. Five months later, just after he'd returned from India, he saw me once again, this time awaiting a friend and scanning a book. He thought I was probably waiting for some heart-throb, but decided to wait. Then up came my girlfriend. We were just going to see a film in Leicester Square. This time he decided to make no mistake and accosted me. I think that's the correct word, isn't it?'

'Certainly the correct word for the story so far. Carry on. Please.'

'Anyway, the accoster made due apologies to my friend, begged her to move on a yard or so and then said he'd like to take me out to dinner.'

'And you didn't slap his face?'

'Would any girl slap the face of a smiling naval officer in uniform making such an invitation? I just said he could see I couldn't dine that evening but I could one evening during the following week. Tuesday would suit me if he was still in London. I still remember my choice of day.'

'A pretty cool response.'

'It may have sounded cool, but it certainly wasn't. Why send this dishy naval numero out of my life with a flea in his ear? Anyway, I thought he was probably winning a wager with one or two naval cronies watching from round the corner. To my delight, he agreed. My gamble paid off.'

'Obviously you turned up on the Tuesday.'

She laughed. 'Here I am! Then I was at the Café Royal, eight o'clock sharp. I'd decided to give him ten minutes and then push off if he didn't show up. But he was there. We dined and talked and talked and talked. Afterwards he took me back to his flat in Fleet Street and we talked and talked still more.'

'And how long before he got you into bed?'

'I've been awaiting that enquiry. Well, I've never believed in rushing promising occasions. They're too rare. He was clearly setting out to charm rather than grab. Anyway, I think one-night stands are strictly for obvious one-night occasions. Generally, the signals are quite clear.'

'I think you've got a point there,' Fleming agreed.

'Hopefully, I thought this would prove a repeat job. We'd had a marvellous evening. Around midnight he took me all the way to Hampstead by taxi, kissed me farewell and said he'd like to fix another date. I had to wait a frightening week for that date, but, by then I think we were both yearning to discover what bed could offer. Does that answer your question?'

Fleming roared with laughter. 'Absolutely. To the dot. And things continued, just like that, from then on?'

'Why not?'

'All my best wishes,' Fleming said.

His listeners smiled.

We began to talk of other things, partly of his own complex life, but although he always sought to get the truth out of others, his own confessions were apt to prove somewhat evasive.

'You're a far better interrogator than interrogatee,' his hostess commented, smiling. 'Your answers verge on the threadbare as far as relevant facts are concerned.'

Smiling, Fleming agreed that this might well be the truth. Then, as was so often the case in similar query-and-answer circumstances, he switched.

'When are you both coming to Goldeneye?' He fired the question at his hostess, clearly bypassing myself. 'You were in Jamaica before the war. So you know the island. Why not come again?'

'I'd love to, I still recall what an enjoyable time I had there pre-war. Do you know the da Costas?'

'I've met them once or twice. Were they your hosts?'

'Just for a couple of days. Frankly, I'd love to come. I imagine we will, too. The da Costas were very kind to me and I'd love to see them again.'

'Good! Then it's settled!' he declared.

I had my protectress. She smiled and said gently: 'As you know, Ian, my husband did so much globetrotting in the war, he's probably a bit jaundiced about foreign travel in peacetime. We'll see. I hope we'll be there.'

'Think about it. Both of you. And now it's bedtime for me. I've had a gorgeous day – and evening.'

What fun he was, yet how sad he sometimes looked, said his

hostess as she returned indoors from our farewells the following morning.

'The Lowland melancholic!'

I decided once again that Muriel had indeed been the tragedy of his life. Like so many other lovers in this sad world he had only recognised the rare qualities of his beloved too late – after her death. He was now in a situation, which might, he hoped, lead to another partner comparable with Muriel, but I doubted whether that could ever be. Indeed, I also doubted whether he would ever be able to acknowledge that he truly needed any woman on any 24-hour basis. I judged his need to be either too basic or too complex for the mortals of this world; even if one of those rare angelic creatures, who might appreciate and even understand his persona, entered his life.

My speculations had their flaws.

CHAPTER 19

DOUBLE LIVES

A lthough the somewhat grandiose flat in Montagu Place provided an agreeably spacious home and background for Fleming's private and social lives, he soon began to find the place rather too expensive.

He was thus relieved and delighted when his mother offered him release on rare terms, even by maternal standards. He could have a three-bedroom one-time coach house in Hay's Mews, Mayfair, to the rear of the rather grand house Mrs Fleming had recently acquired in Charles Street. As this retreat was offered rent-free, the deed was swiftly completed, and the lease of Montagu Place sold at a miniscule profit.

My observations that the mews was nearer St James's and War-wick House, Ann's new home, and offered advantages of privacy and proximity were dismissed as 'poppycock on an Ethel M. Dell level'.

I accepted this rejection of my theorising and congratulated him on his bargain. With this he agreed. The cobbled mews offered the privacy which his lifestyle necessitated, plus the adequate parking space needed for his latest Thunderbird. That the rooms were noticeably smaller was a matter of modest concern against a rent-free future.

The interiors of the house were furnished with smaller pieces, presumably also from his mother's resources, the grander pieces having been returned to Charles Street. Within a month, Fleming showed his casual talent for making living quarters comfortable and colourful, agreeable to host and guest.

The oddest touch in this fresh chapter in domesticity, however, was that Fleming had mysteriously, and seemingly effortlessly, recruited a charming Czech girl, Sandra, as cook-housekeeper. On my occasional visits I speculated on how many activities that word 'housekeeper' might encompass. Or should the word be 'house-kept'? Had she, for instance, been vetted by Ann? Fleming dismissed all such surmises, leaving me with the thought that Ann may well have aided the recruitment, deciding that one disposable certainty was better than several might-be residents, semi-residents, and/or hangers-on.

Sandra was above middle height, slim and extremely pretty. She also seemed quite at ease with the British language as well as with her employer. And with her mini-apron over a far-from-lengthy black dress, I thought she could get any job she applied for, especially one with a fresh title such as 'stripper-secretary'. Fleming affected not to be sharing and acting upon these evident facts and practical possibilities. Sandra was certainly such a highly desirable element among the amenities of the coach house that, knowing her master, I could see no logical alternative to my belief.

Ann's own social life was undoubtedly severely demanding, especially her ambition – now in full spate – to be one of the leading and certainly the most publicised of London's upper-crust hostesses, as well as a queen-bee sponsor of the leading London fashion shows.

I was invited to a couple of her luncheons at Warwick House, each with well over thirty guests at half-a-dozen tables. Here I met up again with Frank Owen, former editor of the *Evening Standard* and now editor of the *Daily Mail* – a recent move, due, mainly, rumour claimed, to the machinations of Ann, a view hotly disputed by herself. Nevertheless, she was prepared to contend that a cabal at Northcliffe House was determinedly minimising her attempts to influence Rothermere and his newspaper empire. My view was that no cabal in history could get up early enough to carry out such a plan against so ambitious and determined a predator, operator, benefactor or whatever.

I had met Owen in wartime India where we had become casual acquaintances. He was then press officer to the Mountbatten SEAC HQ and editor of the SEAC forces newspaper, ranking as a colonel for the job. On our first meeting he told me that earlier in the day he had been vetting hundreds of official photographs. The 'kamerattzi', as he termed them, were always out in force whenever Mountbatten made a public appearance. Well over 95 per cent of all negatives were invariably destroyed, Mountbatten decreeing that they were not doing photogenic justice to any leader. 'Or his profile,' Owen added, proceeding to recall an incident from a Delhi evening two nights previously. Mountbatten had left a gathering around ten o'clock, apologising, saying that he had been too late to bed the previous night, studying field reports. 'Around two o'clock,' he had added for full effect. 'I know,' Edwina had put in. 'I saw your light go out, and wished you sweet dreams. I still had another hour's paperwork in hands.'

'God save me from a ceaselessly competitive marriage,' Owen had commented.

Whether the Almighty obliged I never learned.

On my first of these press luncheons, I was at the table hosted by Ann. A collective strike was in progress at the *Daily Mail*, *Evening News* and other Rothermere papers. Owen, as a pre-war politician – he had been a Liberal and the youngest MP in the House – was doing his best to settle the clash and, indeed, had been discussing possible settlement terms that morning. He was gloomy. He thought that the compositors and the machine-minders had the upper-hand in the negotiations and that the whole performance was moving steadily towards an unpredictably vicious finale. But, as a determined optimist, he had hopes that a settlement might be imminent. Within the next forty-eight hours, he hoped.

Ann scoffed at the whole democratic process. 'Words! Words! Words!' she scoffed. 'One settlement always followed by another settlement!' She was undoubtedly voicing the frightening truth. Well into her stride, she went on: 'I know what my settlement would be: machine guns.'

'Now, now!' Owen said, pacifically. 'You don't mean that and therefore shouldn't say it.'

'Why not? And I do mean it,' Ann insisted. 'I shall never be famous – that's for certain – so I might as well be infamous. And I certainly mean what I've said!'

Loud laughter around the table. All were relieved to note that guests at adjacent tables had apparently ignored or not overheard her ladyship. Most importantly, neither had guests at Rothermere's table at the far end of the room. The meal continued. Ann, clearly impressed by Owen's whispered 'Shush!' made no further inflammatory calls for strike-settling. None at the luncheon table, anyway.

Her remark had held more than a hint of her true character. She undoubtedly enjoyed the splendour of her life in and around Warwick House and enjoyed showing off its spacious interiors. Wandering around the mansion, under her guidance, I had been impressed by the size and contents of her dressing room. I had never thought of her as a leading figure in the world of fashion, although she seemed to enjoy invitations to head various publicity shows for London fashion houses. She dressed neatly and pleasingly to any appreciative eye, but not as a woman determined to rank high in the world of the major international couturiers. Yet here was a veritable treasure trove of fashion: rack after rack. She quashed my surprise, saying that she had to appear as the chairman's wife at a 101 openings, luncheons, dinners and the rest and therefore needed at least 202 complete rigs in her wardrobe.

I liked Ann and always enjoyed our meetings. Her abounding vitality and gaiety were irresistible and I thoroughly enjoyed her carefree non-stop chit-chat concerning her acquaintances in the *Vogue/Harper's/Tatler* worlds. She talked freely of her continuing intimacy with Ian and seemed somehow reconciled to the fact that the relationship could one day, not all that remote, blow up and end in a headline divorce. She faced up to this doleful yet fatalistic prospect despite the fact that she admired and respected her husband and needed the shekels provided by his millions. Why then, hadn't she married Ian when she had had the chance? Those millions, was undoubtedly the answer?

'I suppose because I wanted to be Lady Rothermere,' was the simple but undoubtedly authentic answer, despite the throwaway intonation following the frank query I once presented to her when we were alone. 'I think most women would have made the same decision. After all, Esmond is very undemanding, and has an agreeable temper. He also seems to like having me around.'

'And who would get your vote as the more agreeable and protective husband?'

'Esmond, of course!' she had declared decisively. 'Ian undoubtedly spells excitement, danger and the unexpected, even though his health isn't all it should be. All those headaches. Basically, I sometimes think, a juvenile infatuation never fully evaporates. I fell for him at seventeen.'

'Juvenile madness,' was my own view.

She laughed, admitting that there was possibly a grain of truth in my simple assertion. But little more than a grain, she insisted. I had my own doubts concerning the true weight involved.

Thus, once again, we moved into what was virtually a repeat performance of our casual ramble across the fields to Kelmscott. I mentioned my memories of that occasion. She agreed the situation hadn't changed. She had merely changed her husband. I wondered how many women in London at that moment would have agreed that the intervening death of one husband, marriage to another, and complications with a third possibility, posed no great problem.

'There's no changing the set-up,' Ann said as if mindreading. 'In a curious kind of way I think that the arrangement we've worked out suits Ian and me. I also think Esmond only sees what he wishes or decides to see.'

'The classic set-up, you think, for a non-explosive trio?'

'I'd like to think it is and will continue to be, but sometimes Ian snaps. Then I, too, snap and decide we've got to make a break for freedom. Then we decide otherwise. But if freedom's the word. I suppose something along those lines may happen one of these days.'

I had a passing thought that if that were to happen, Ann would be fully equal to take in her stride whatever chaotic circumstances might arise – apart, perhaps from the absence of those millions. Fleming would doubtless remain his melancholic self. But would her life prove as peaceful as it seemed currently? Fundamentally bogus as it might be.

Meanwhile, Fleming was seemingly reconciled to his sideline life, even if his Sandra had her part to play. But apparent pleasantry was not helped in any degree by his work. I occasionally thought that Kemsley House was one of the last workaday settings in London to which a Scots melancholic should be confined. The only redeeming element was that his break-outs, especially his luncheons, offered some scope for a modicum of self-expression.

A typical example surfaced later in the month after my Etoile rendezvous with Ann. I had just come from the nursing home in Welbeck Street where our firstborn, Nicholas, had been born the previous day. Fleming had already sent a duly ribald congratulatory postcard to the nursing home with best wishes for mother and son.

Within the next half-hour, he asked where we would propose to send our son to school.

I said this seemed a fairly precipitate approach to any boy's education – or a girl's, for that matter. Shouldn't parents wait awhile to attempt an estimate on what kind of character was emerging in an infant, what future interest the child might be seeking to discover in the world, what subjects he or she might wish to study? And so on and on.

My views weren't practical enough for Fleming who contended that such an outlook was verging on too casual an approach to parenthood and a son's future.

Would he have been so concerned had I been reporting the arrival of a daughter?

He grinned and agreed that his interests would probably have been mildly lukewarm. Meanwhile, this set-up was far more urgent. What was I proposing to do? Shouldn't I make sure of the boy's education by putting his name down for Eton straightaway? The pressures were considerable, he affirmed. Waiting lists were impressively lengthy. Timing was everything. He knew two housemasters and would willingly send an introductory note, which would, in due course, virtually guarantee relevant interviews.

He was surprised to hear our shared parental viewpoint: that we had no interest in Eton, or any other boarding school. The system was not for us. Silvertop had far preferred life, studies and freedom in her earlier Hampstead day school to later boarding experience at Benenden, and I had certainly enjoyed day-schooling at Brighton and in London, with no yearning to board.

'What will you do then?' he asked, as seriously as if we were now faced with the probability of a scholastic disaster.

'Nicholas and any future brothers or sisters will be pupils at the best day schools we can find. We'll probably be nearer London by then, anyway. I also seem to recall that you weren't all that dotty about your own boarding experiences at Eton, outside games. So why so keen now?'

'I was desperately unhappy,' he readily admitted. 'As you say, away from the hours I spent on the playing fields, I hated the place. Yet if I ever have a son, his name will go down on the Eton waiting lists within three days of his birth. It just shows what a conventional so-and-so I am at heart.' He grinned, adding: 'We're clearly worlds apart on this subject, too. As well as on aspects of sexual sadism, the place of women in daily life, Kemsley House and so forth.'

'So it seems. Anyway, we've decided we'd like to watch our son, and any future bambini we may beget, growing up. We'd want to hear their views on this and that across the supper table. We hope to welcome and enjoy any weekend spare time they felt they can devote to us. We look forward to their friendships. And so on.'

'Quite decisive views, it seems.'

'More or less. Even more important: unanimous.'

'I daresay there's something in what you say,' he reflected, smiling. 'Amaryllis contended the other day that Eton mainly sponsors stockbrokers and politicians and asked what men of the arts had Eton produced? I said Shelley and then, after a long and shameful pause, added Cyril Connolly. She guffawed.'

'You could have added Robert Bridges.'

'Didn't even cross my mind. In any case, such a questionnaire's scarcely likely to crop up again.'

'I suspect that Amaryllis could have other equally searching and revealing questions relating to most aspects of your life.'

He grinned. 'Probably. She's quite inquisitive and very incisive. Anyway, let's change the subject. Now you've got your first-born, you can come to Jamaica and start the second in that other Eden.'

I said we'd think about it.

'Too much thinking kills off action,' he opined. 'This time, make a big effort. I'm sure you'd enjoy Goldeneye and I'd be delighted to have you there. And, quite frankly, I'm certain Silvertop would like to see her Caribbean friends again and enjoy a dip in the adjacent ocean.'

'Venice is that much nearer and seems to have a good deal to please the eyeballs apart from a quite satisfactory beach across the lagoon.'

'On a miserable European scale under a doleful European apology for sunshine.'

'If we come, promise to show us the Kingston Venice.'

He laughed. 'That would be a bit tricky, but Goldeneye has its own private beach and, as Silvertop will tell you, Jamaica has some spectacular spots on offer. Anyway, think about it. If not this year, next year or when you're less smitten by worn-out corners of old Europe.'

'We're hoping to visit Venice again next month,' I said.

The news came as no surprise, he said, even if somewhat depressing to his own plans and hopes for us.

Yet we did get to Jamaica and Goldeneye in the early weeks of the following year.

CHAPTER 20

GOLDENEYE GAMBOL

The *Concise Oxford English Dictionary* defines 'gambol' as 'a light-hearted frolic', as apt a definition of our break in Jamaica as any non-Oxonian lexicographer could coin.

Despite our keen wish to see Goldeneye, we had certainly been somewhat tardy in arriving, following Fleming's first invitation, which came with a copy of the 1947 Christmas number of *Horizon*, to which he had contributed a feature on Jamaica in the series: 'Where shall John go?' The text was boldly confessional:

> I spent four days in Jamaica in 1943 … I went back in 1946, chose a site, designed a house, chased an agent and an architect and by last December all was finished. This year I had five weeks' holiday in the new house and wished it could have been six months.

In practice, he confessed that his time span preference had a two-month limit.

We had been enjoying post-war excursions somewhat nearer to

our Suffolk home: Oxford, Cambridge, the East Anglian coastline, Aldburgh and its manifold attractions, even way south to Chichester and Brighton. Plus, of course, those thrice-yearly four-day excursions to Venice, occasionally adding a week in Ischia, our favourite island in the Med.

There were also manifold inducements to keep breaks brief. We were enjoying parenthood and were also keen to increase our family, having left these considerations as well as our original encounter rather later than most couples. And, if successful, we would need a larger house. That was certain. Occasionally, I thought that Fleming had a point in deciding that I had stored up such a surfeit of wartime travels that I occasionally showed signs of wishing to become a home-based squatter. My defensive references to Venice were dismissed as 'architectural window-shopping expeditions to a cultural suburbia'.

Nevertheless, we had both remained keen on a future visit to Goldeneye, a project now made easier by the recent recruitment of Kitty, a reliable, trained, live-in nanny in her thirties, well educated, relaxed and clearly fond of children.

Thus, a year or so after Fleming's original invitation we prepared to visit his island paradise. We would be the only guests, apart from Ann, who had agreed to make the trip. Thus the Rothermere–Fleming tangle continued into still further entanglement and puzzlement.

Would we be acting as alibi or phoney chaperon and chaperone?

'You're too suspicious. I thought Silvertop would like to see Jamaica and the da Costas again, and skip Venice for a year.'

'My interest in Venice will be lifelong. We'll be back there in the autumn.'

'Try being unselfish for once. You'll both enjoy it. Don't let memories of your globetrotting war get in the way. You're becoming a fully fledged Suffolk stay-at-home.'

'Not while Venice is open to other Europeans.'

The real problem was that I was thoroughly enjoying my unfolding post-war home life. I liked our mill house and the Constable landscapes and I was enjoying my four-day working week and our various weekend excursions. In any case, another oncoming event seemed likely to jeopardise the trip: we were expecting another birth. Reassured, however, by the genial yet authoritative gynaecologist that the mother-to-be could fly the Atlantic at this early stage, we arranged to fly with Ann and Fleming to New York, where both parties would stay for a few days. We yearned to explore, once again, the city we had found so exciting and alluring at every level on previous visits.

We flew BOAC in the New Year and en route met up with Hugh Fraser, then husband to Antonia. I had come to know her quite well, for she had proved a talented forager for unusual prints needed for illustrating features published in *History Today*, the magazine Brendan Bracken had founded to add a touch of academic authority to his *Financial Times* set-up. I had been invited to join the venture as design consultant, working closely and agreeably alongside the dual editorship of Peter Quennell and Alan Hodge. Hugh Fraser proved to be a lively companion, an amusing and assured raconteur. Indeed, the flight seemed shorter than any previous transatlantic trip I could recall.

We decided to take separate taxis from the airport, as our New York destinations were well apart. Fleming and Ann already seemed to be moving somewhat surreptitiously, as if suspecting they were being tailed. We had arranged to stay at the Barbizon-Plaza Hotel, that well-loved wartime refuge for RN personnel which persisted for several post-war years as *the* hotel for one-time UK naval types.

Meanwhile, delight and excitement dominated our visit. A decade earlier, Silvertop had lived in the city for almost a year, had taken to the US way of life and had come perilously close to seeking US citizenship. She still had relatives in the city. These we visited and twice I met up with Fleming in the *Sunday Times* New York office. His trips to Jamaica were a convenient way of keeping in touch with his US 'stringers' and other correspondents. We spent four crowded days exploring the city; our evenings passed in seeking restaurants we recalled.

Then followed our airport rendezvous with Fleming and Ann for the flight to Jamaica. From Kingston airport, we shared a cross-country taxi to the north of the island, thoroughly enjoying the trip through the overpoweringly timbered and lush dark green interior, emerging onto the fabulous shoreline.

Goldeneye was much as I had expected in design and structure: 'mainly a sizeable living room with basic bedrooms tacked on', as I wrote to a friend, but its setting, poised high above a small private bay, was far more picturesque and appealing than I had imagined. I decided that it would be difficult to find any refuge from the bustling urban twentieth century to equal Goldeneye. Whether that is still the situation, I do not know, but doubt the possibility as I gather other buildings have been added to the scene by a later proprietor.

Apart from the *Horizon* feature, I was already aware of the background to Fleming's determination to get his house. Ivar Bryce, his closest friend from Eton, had married and settled in Jamaica, thus providing himself with an authentic springboard to a wartime career representing NID in the Caribbean, a position manoeuvred and supported by Fleming and Room 39. Bryce had thus spent his war on intelligence duties in the Caribbean Zone plus liaison work between the RN and the USN. Fleming later masterminded a trip for his chief, the DNI, Rear Admiral Godfrey to Washington which had concluded with a personal solo breakaway to see Bryce in Jamaica to discuss his secret dream for an island pied-à-terre.

During that explanatory wartime jaunt, Fleming had requested Bryce to find a plot above the ocean on which he could build his dream house. This project Bryce had successfully accomplished after much arduous questing. He had also found a builder prepared to erect the house for £2,000.

A local architect had certainly been involved in the design and building of Goldeneye, although Fleming maintained that, despite having been denied any graphic skills at birth, he had, towards the war's end, designed 'every square inch of the house' during boring lulls in Room 39. By this, I suspect that he had sent Bryce the roughest of rough scribbles with notes concerning the sizes of the living room and bedrooms he would need and that these notes had proved a basic guide for the builder to hazard a quotation. Fleming certainly had a friend in Bryce, who became virtually resident overseer on the job.

The privacy of the Goldeneye beach later prompted unexpected arrivals by occasional London friends. Fleming would put on a poor imitation of a willing and delighted host for visitors who had been too casually invited in London to drop by to view his private bay in remote Jamaica should they ever head that way. Ann never seemed averse to these invasions. Invariably congenial and welcoming, she was a delight to watch as hostess. Our host, however, was more likely to grit his teeth, grab his flippers and disappear down to the beach and the deep.

'How deep?' I once queried in frivolous mood. 'What's it really like when you get down really deep, say 6 or even 7ft or so? What depth do the local sharks prefer? How deep will an aqua-lung take you?'

'Very funny,' he had grunted. I had trodden on fairly sacred ground. Ann, however, thought the quip quite funny. She shared my own irreverent views about the scuba world.

Silvertop was quick to join in these sportive ventures, even in her *enceinte* condition, choosing early hours for privacy in her first dip of the day. Her husband was not. Although much of my boyhood leisure had been spent swimming round Brighton's West Pier even on wintry days, I had long outlived such oceanic appeals. Even with the water at 70F, I preferred a good book or gossiping with Ann.

Occasionally, Fleming would cross to the extensive seat outside the house, facing the sea far below, which I had virtually commandeered for reading or sketching. Although he had had the house for so short a time, the garden was already richly endowed, for which benefaction he took no credit. 'The great thing about making a garden here is to remember that everything grows at a quite astonishing rate. When I return each year I invariably find that actuality has far outstripped imagination. If a royal palm is left somewhat bereft but basically intact by the hurricanes, it'll grow again while you're looking. I'm only in my third year here, but the growth has been fantastic. On returning, I can never believe my eyes. With nature's largesse on this scale, anyone can be his own Capability Brown. I've just become a planner with nature as my right-hand man.'

'Then why live elsewhere?'

'The major drawback to *living* here is that the white society of the island is so thoroughly suburban: Purley or Golders Green. Anyone who comes here with notions of becoming a latter-day Gauguin with ample and responsive sex waiting just outside the front door and all cherished Christian taboos swept away will quickly find himself – and his mistress, if he brought one with him – left more or less lonesome.'

'I've usually found women more resilient and adventurous than men when faced with novel social situations: what about them?'

'No go. Not here, anyway,' he said, quite adamant in his summing-up of the Jamaican social scene, omitting reference to any home-based complications.

Goldeneye thus remained his annual two-month holiday retreat wholly lacking any prospect or appeal for even a modest permanency. 'I can't believe any white can become a tropical pagan merely by coming here,' he affirmed. 'The price would be too high. Growing up here probably makes a difference, of course – as the da Costas would probably claim. An adventurous dame would find Kingston a fairly tough and dangerous city. Far better if she finds a sugar daddy in the UK and brings him here for the odd month or so and then back to Kensington.'

These were obviously clear-cut convictions, repeated at odd times. I knew, however, that he started with grave disadvantages in any dreams of a Gauguinesque lifestyle. He was among the last of men to defy or opt out of home-grown conventions. Despite his pretence of upending normalcy, he lived well within its confines.

I asked about Ivar Bryce, most welcome of all visitors to Goldeneye. Wasn't he a fully fledged settler?

'What a hope! Ivar's the prize international playboy of our time. He's worked it all out to a nicety. His home's here – or more accurately, his wife's. Jamaica's OK for a relaxed escape from the European winter but as the European sun begins to perk up over the Côte d'Azur, or some other cosy European spot noted for its easy women, he's off. Above all, he leaves his wife here.'

'Doesn't handsome always do as handsome wants?' commented Silvertop.

'Probably one of the many reasons Ann's no great fan of Ivar's,' concluded Fleming.

On his next visit, a day or so later, Bryce said Fleming had told him that I was keenly interested in international domestic architecture and would I care to visit one or two of the local plantation houses? I could start with a visit to Bellevue, his own residence. I was delighted by the invitation, having heard something of the house.

We vastly enjoyed the visit the following afternoon. Bryce was always fun to have around: tall, dark, handsome, amusing, thoughtful, quick to laughter and to encourage laughter in others. My appreciative wife contended that he should have been forcibly deported to Hollywood and that there he would have been snapped up pronto as rival to Gregory Peck or Gary Cooper.

Ivar's wife, Sheila, was handsome, even beautiful, but, quite clearly, rather frail. We had learned from Fleming that she had been given a medical diktat to avoid both strong drink and the deceitful night air of the island. After showing us over the house, Bryce, to our vast surprise, had had strong drinks brought out into the garden where we sat. We stayed out there until well after dusk. We left in time for supper at Goldeneye. Needless to say, Ivar drove us back. He was also a guest for supper at Goldeneye. Poor Sheila.

As I had expected, Bellevue was an intriguing contrast to Goldeneye and, to my eyes, a far more attractive house for annual visits or year-round living. Indeed, I far preferred this enchanting eighteenth-century plantation house with its serene classical façade to any latter-day charms of Goldeneye. Bellevue's spacious central hall, the heart of the house, was an unexpectedly handsome introduction for any visitor to the house.

Bellevue was undoubtedly the most interesting building we saw in Jamaica, although we visited half-a-dozen other houses owned by expats. We then joined Ann and Fleming on a two-day jaunt to Negril at the far eastern end of the island. Negril is nowadays a tourists' wonderland, I learn, but then an off-the-map outpost for one of the largest of the island's banana growers and exporters. For our excursion Fleming had been loaned a house on the shore owned by one of the local tycoons.

While the others were swimming late on the first afternoon, I helped Ann with the modest chores involved in preparations for our evening meal. As we set the knives and forks, she asked whether we wanted another son or a daughter.

I said we had no fixed yearnings, apart from hoping for a healthy child or children, with the requisite number of fingers and toes.

She laughed and went on: 'What do you want your Nicholas to be?'

'No fixed ideas,' I said. These were early days. All I could hope for was that he'd have as entertaining and interesting a life as I'd enjoyed so far: a life providing adequate pleasure and profit.

To this carefree note, Ann made what seemed to me an extraordinary, yet clearly seriously intended rejoinder: 'I don't think it's worth having a son unless one directs him towards becoming Prime Minister.'

'You can't be serious. What about Raymond?'

She said she was dead serious. Her son, Raymond, was now at Eton, but this was her fondest hope and firm belief for his future. I carried on with my table chores, giving passing sympathetic thought to Raymond and Fionn, both of whom I had met on my trip to Buscot.

Secretly, I doubted whether her son would be amenable to his mother's ambitions. He had seemed far too independent a boy for such a cast-iron directive. And I doubted whether the young Fionn would ever wish to become one of the early women MPs, still less Britain's first woman PM. Anyway, the future would doubtless show interesting divergences from maternal ambitions-by-proxy. Of that I was certain. (I have, I gather, been proven a fairly competent crystal-gazer, at least as far as the futures of those two then-young O'Neills were concerned.)

Not all Ann's contributions to discussions were as single-minded or as serious as her thoughts concerning sons, but she had a rare talent for taking over any general discussion and infusing the chit-chat with her own highly charged, even explosive re-directions.

She was at her liveliest after supper, usually fairly late as Fleming and/or Silvertop wished to enjoy a final dip under the last rays of the setting sun or a final half-hour in the garden. Ann allowed no soporific leanings after supper. Pencil-and-paper games were the order of the evening, whatever the inclinations of the owner or his guests. Yet the games were apt to be concluded at a moment's notice if she suddenly found herself stymied by flower names beginning with Z or the title of Tolstoy's first novel. She would switch ruthlessly to another track.

One evening, when Ed Stanley, Lord of Alderley, ex-RNVR and a still-active womaniser, was a fleeting guest, Ann suddenly said she was tired of these pencil-and-paper games and thereupon decreed that Fleming, Stanley and I were to tell Silvertop and herself at what age and in what circumstances each of us had had his first women.

We duly made our respective contributions to this record of adventure and misadventure.

Fleming, in a break from Eton, had picked up an enthusiastic amateur in Slough. Taking her to a local cinema he had been caught by the manager *in flagrante delecto* and subjected to a torch-lit blasting and a swift rearrangement of clothing while en route in banishment from the premises. Fortunately, Fleming added, not before his, if not her virginity, had gone for keeps. (Fleming used this schoolboy fling in a later Bond book: *The Spy Who Loved Me*. He has his hero sexually involved with a young woman on the floor of a small, old-fashioned cinema. 'One of the few instances in all Bondery,' he confessed, 'of fiction copying fact.')

Stanley's contribution looked back to a fairly giddy life begun in some out-of-the-way southern corner of Australia, where his father had been governor-general. Travelling in the outback in an old banger he had sought sustenance and rest at a farmhouse and fixed terms for the night with the 'oncoming' (his word) wife of the absentee husband obligingly distant for at least three days *and* nights masterminding their far-flung acreage. Stanley got far more for his coinage than he had reckoned. 'Absolutely first-rate bed plus better than first-rate bawd,' he recalled and spelled.

My own contribution concerned my long-ago music teacher: a sad, attractive spinster in her forties. When I mentioned to her that as I would soon be eighteen and was proposing to devote more time to specialised typographical studies than pianoforte, she became tearful, took me across to a large sofa, then into her arms, then into her bedroom, then into herself. All with rare and irresistible aplomb after she had dried those early, easy tears. I need hardly add that I continued with my musical studies for at least a further six or seven months. What she taught me during that time proved invaluable experience for ensuing decades, well beyond any charms extended by Chopin or Rachmaninov.

On the conclusion of the last of this trio of recollections, Ann said, coolly settling back in her chair: 'Very, very interesting, don't you agree, Phoebe? Now I'll tell you all how I had *my* first woman.'

Although she had this desire to shock, she was effectively shockable in her own right. Prior to supper two evenings later she mentioned that she had heard giggling from our room during siesta time earlier that afternoon. What rich joke had prompted the laughter?

'Just the normal pleasures of any siesta hour,' I replied. 'A tropical version of *cinq à sept*, no doubt.'

'Oh, not that!' cried Ann. 'Not that! I've spent too many boring afternoons having said OK to a *trois à quatre* at lunch.'

'Happily, other women seem to enjoy siesta pastimes,' I suggested. Ann smiled faintly, clearly unconvinced.

I was surprised, for Ann had some reputation as a woman of the world, sex and all, yet I always had the impression that, for her, sex was an occasional social offering or expected indulgence rather than a physical or emotional 'must'. In view of Fleming's occasional remarks on the subject from time to time, I had begun to assume that he had his own special sexual entertainments, possibly mildly masochistic and/or sadistic, lacking in appeal to most of the rest of us. I hoped they appealed to both.

Earlier in the year, during a meal at the Etoile, speaking of his brother Peter, renowned traveller and author, married to the actress Celia Johnston, Fleming had advanced a belief that couples who live in the country are apt to have simpler sex lives than those who live in cities. 'They're also much more secretive about the whole subject,' he added. 'That's indicative, too. Don't ask me why I think this: I just do. Despite having all those afternoons free I think they prefer working in the garden, thus getting tired earlier than city folk, and so to bed that much earlier – to sleep.'

'Most Brits are extremely secretive about their sex lives,' I pointed out. 'Not just country dwellers. City slickers too. You are and so, probably, are most Greeks and Swedes. Even Froggies and Eyeties. No matter whether its sodomy, bondage, beating or the missionary-position four times a day, they're apt to stay quiet about these matters as far as personal confessions go. You've never expounded any of your own possible indulgences or departures from conventional sexual attitudes and practices. Never.'

'Perhaps I have the belief that such confessions are apt to drift into old-fashioned boasting.'

'Maybe. Or could it be that the indulgences rather demand basic secrecy?'

He pressed on, skipping my implications. 'Unlike you, I'm more inclined to the belief that women react more favourably to master-ful types of mankind, whether in the living room or the bedroom.'

'And masterful types prefer secrecy?'

'Until he has one drink too many.'

We would doubtless return to the subject later, I thought. (As we did, of course.) In common with any born quizmaster Fleming was as highly inquisitive concerning others' lives as he sought to be secretive concerning his own.

Only one aspect of Goldeneye marred the visit for me. Fleming had asserted in his *Horizon* piece that Jamaican food was 'delicious and limitless', but the cooking uninspired and 'English' unless you fight against it. That proved impossible. My somewhat squeamish attitude to Goldeneye foods was ruthlessly matched by several dishes clearly among Fleming's favourites, doubtless derived from his determined patronage of local provender. Hence first samplings of salt fish and ackee and calah soup were disasters for me. Far more adventurous in these culinary matters than most of her acquaintances, and certainly myself, my more experimental partner appreciatively sampled everything on offer. As an unenthusiastic sampler of Jamaica's indigenous dishes, I discovered that I was on par with one of Goldeneye's earlier visitors. Noël Coward had graced one meal with the opinion that the dish he had been offered and tasted had proved more akin to 'armpits' than desirable food. I rather agreed, although I too, had certainly never tasted his well-chosen comparison. Unreservedly. I occasionally thought I was subsisting almost exclusively on bananas and coffee.

These culinary experiences caused me to point out to our host that, apart from the local food which he seemed genuinely to enjoy, he never gave the same acclaim to local drinks. I never saw him drink any Jamaican concoction, whether coconut juice or even rum punch. He far preferred imported whisky, gin, vodka, martini. Plus, of course, a dash of soda water, also imported.

Fleming was certainly more at ease in Goldeneye than in any other setting in which I had seen him, with the possible exception of Boodles, where he invariably seemed wholly relaxed. I occasionally wondered whether this was due to a background which encouraged him to forget – temporarily, at least – newspaper offices; women, their ways and wiles; and to put aside his money worries which, at that time, were never far distant. He may have enjoyed a similar sense of relief on the golf courses he favoured, but as I did not play the game and never saw him thus engaged or in any clubhouse, I could not judge. Others have claimed that he was. Certainly, we sensed this rare sense of relaxation at Goldeneye. At that stage the house had no Visitor's Book. Had such a volume existed, I suspect that many disparate views would have enlivened the pages.

Patrick Leigh Fermor, in his book *The Traveller's Tree*, claims Goldeneye to have been the most practical house for a tropical lifestyle in which he had stayed on his extensive travels. Rare praise indeed, highly appreciated by Fleming. Noël Coward's view of the house was vastly different. He had rented the house at £50 a week after *Tonight at Eight-Thirty* had folded in New York. He needed a retreat to finish his autobiography and decided that Goldeneye might fit the bill, despite what he considered its comfortless interiors and the high rent Fleming extorted. Coward's memory of his brief sojourn sponsored a genial venom which never lessened during his lifetime, although his deep affection for the owner of Goldeneye never wavered.

With Fleming, I visited the playwright's own house, Blue Harbour, built virtually on the beach at Port Maria, and passed an amused hour with the master after Fleming had opted for a swim. Fleming's departure was saluted by Coward's wave from the balcony and the comment: 'Off goes our dear friend! Three cheers for the man who, against all the odds, still remains the barracuda's faithful friend!'

As we settled back in our deckchairs on the balcony, Coward asked what I thought of Goldeneye. We were enjoying ourselves immensely, I assured him.

'But what about the house itself?' he persisted. 'I'm told you write about houses and modern design for the *Sunday Times*.'

I'd already coined my own label: I thought of Goldeneye as something akin to a Caribbean Bauhaus.

Coward chuckled appreciatively. 'Far too flattering,' he said. 'Not a single touch of sound design in the place. I prefer "Caribbean Cowhouse"!'

I laughed, of course, but thought he was being rather over-critical. I was prepared to claim a few agreeable touches for any fortunate visitor, but before I had attempted to offer my defensive views, Coward was well away with his own splendidly disparaging discourse on the house. He had, in myself, what Fleming contended Coward most enjoyed: a quiescent and attentive audience. He was certainly fluent that afternoon. Ian and his architect – no name mentioned – had made serious basic errors, Coward asserted. Mainly in the sitting room. 'Merely consider those window sills,' he said, with a querulous chuckle. 'So high. Up to one's eyebrows. Guaranteed to do two things at once: give one a crick in the neck and deny free and fabulous views of the Caribbean. I think that takes genius of a highly individual order. I'm told Ian loves to see the sun rise, but he clearly hates sunsets. That must be the reason. Then again, Goldeneye's so badly angled, one can scarcely ever see a sunset from anywhere in the place. Perhaps we should enquire into the reason for this distaste. Perhaps Ian's mother never came to say goodnight and he spent hours awaiting her. What a hope! Have you met the old duck? Waiting for her goodnight kiss would be like waiting for dreams to come true or, possibly, awaiting the hangman's approach. Certainly she was the very last thing I'd have wanted, as a boy, to turn up in my bedroom for a goodnight peck. No indeed. Mrs Valentine was definitely not made for such gestures of goodwill. Perhaps I should appoint myself honorary shrink to the Flemings. They all need one, starting with Peter, exploring any old desert that comes to hand with some young Swiss miss.'

And so on and on… My afternoon host was clearly wishful to go on for ever and his listener certainly hoped that the egomaniacal raconteur might do just that.

Little wonder, in view of his dyspeptic views of the house, that Coward had coined his now well-known renaming of 'Goldeneye' to 'Goldeneye, Nose and Throat', adding that he always directed visitors to 'the first cottage hospital on the left after leaving the well-known banana port of Oracabessa.' In similar vein, he had written to Ann to say that Ivor Novello, another recent newcomer to the island, had, 'with rare Welsh cunning, built himself the only house on the island from which one cannot see the sea'.

Every moment of these continuous quips and observations sparked entertainment of a rare order. Certainly, that afternoon, as I sat there enthralled: 'a rare and highly responsive audience', as our host affirmed to Fleming on his return from the deep. Over tea and/or cocktails, Coward's chosen theme was Jamaica and its British settlers – headed by Fleming – and visitors. The following day, no doubt, the horror of the New York theatrical critics, a tribe he clearly loathed, might be his subject. As a word-spinner, he had everything: novelty, voice, gestures, fluency. Why should anyone seek to stop him? I certainly admit to chuckling appreciation of this ever-continuing performance by the master of the querulous. My only regret that afternoon was that Silvertop was visiting acquaintances elsewhere on the island.

The rest of our Goldeneye gambol was a day-after-day enjoyment of sun, sea and sand, enjoyed in our respective ways. I swam almost every day but came no nearer to the slightest appreciation of the scuba world.

The only shadow on this trip – and that minimal – was that I saw no sign of Fleming at a typewriter at work on that promised thriller, which increasingly seemed to be a goner.

I occasionally regretted not returning to Goldeneye, despite further invitations. The best news we had during those following years were postcards and letters from Fleming, and rumours of his novel. He seemed to have settled on a sound basis for sustained work on his typewriter, working intensively at the Bond books, frequently confessing that they bored him, but prepared to spend most of his leisure back in London in furthering the ever-growing legend.

But that was all much later.

CHAPTER 21

FLEMING AS PUBLISHER

During the early '50s, Fleming was still pondering – and post-poning – the future of his projected thrillers. Too many side diversions delayed starting 'the spy story to end all spy stories', which, almost a decade earlier, he had claimed as his major post-war objective.

We occasionally discussed – not at any great length – our respective scribblings. He was agreeably complimentary concerning the two books I had written about the war. Their success had prompted me to tackle a novel with a newspaper background; *The Paper Palace* was the prelude to others. Fleming's literary career, however, seemed to have been the piece he wrote about Jamaica for *Horizon* and odd anonymous paragraphs for the 'Atticus' feature in the *Sunday Times*.

I was puzzled by this literary forbearance, for I knew he yearned for fame and cash. His brother Peter was still writing and publishing occasional volumes and acquiring further renown for his percipient leaders in *The Times*. Above all, the dominant Mrs Valentine Fleming was still around, and still only too keen to emphasise the disparities in achievement of her two elder sons.

Our lunchtime chit-chat occasionally concerned Kemsley House, the bleak block in the Gray's Inn Road full of highly ambitious journalistic thrusters, commercial and literary. The leader of this pack was undoubtedly William (later Lord) Mabane, whose unashamed ambitions prompted Fleming to observe that big business only needed one such central character for those less-ambitious to be left in peace.

He clearly needed such peace for he confessed that he had the gist of a plot and hero for a novel and proposed to tackle the actual writing immediately, having noted what he termed my own 'excessively easy path to literary acceptance. I would then see, recognise and acclaim the economy of wordage needed for authentic suspense.' I grinned, nodded and awaited proof of this declaration.

I recall that on the same occasion, I happened to mention the words of Dashiel Hammet, that most successful of thriller writers: 'When action begins, suspense ends.' Fleming was silent while absorbing this injunction. He then said, with rare seriousness, that he thought the comment one of the most authentic advisory admonitions vouchsafed to literary would-bes, and went on to say: 'With two months on my hands I ought to be able to set about it. Each time I get out there – and I've had half-a-dozen trips already – I tell myself I'm going to start the damn thing straightaway. I've got the table and typewriter. I've even got the glimmer of a plot. All I need is a starter. Instead, I push off up to Bellevue or Ivar comes down to Goldeneye and the day's a goner. This year will be different, Annie notwithstanding. Mark my words.'

'But what about the island's other beguilements?' I queried.

'I propose to lock myself up, instruct the housekeeper to keep all visitors out and tell Ann to get lost or find a few new friends.'

'And you've got your plot lined up?'

'More or less.'

'Based on what, whom, when and whereabouts?'

'All will be made clear in due course.'

Although he was clearly hopeful to find the urge and energy to get down to this promised thriller as soon as he stepped inside Golden-eye, he had other delaying publishing ventures heading his way on his homeland plot.

In 1945, Lord Kemsley had bought the machinery, types and equip-ment left by Lord Carlow, diplomat and founder of the Corvinus Press in the mid-'30s, as a hobby. Carlow had been killed in an air crash the previous year. The Corvinus equipment had been removed to a small Georgian house in Bloomsbury, conveniently close to Kemsley House and owned by Kemsley Newspapers. Although his lordship never visited his private press, the outfit was inevitably renamed the Dropmore Press after the Kemsley domain in Buckinghamshire.

A smooth and persuasive Kemsley executive, Clarence Winches-ter, was appointed to oversee the business and the technical side of the press, and a respected and genially cynical journalist and poet, Edward Shanks, first winner of the Hawthornden Prize, was deputed to run the literary side. Their early productions were portentously innocuous: De Qunicey's *Revolt of the Tartars*; the funeral ovation of Pericles; a book of essays by Shanks; and, topping all else, a pro-jected unwieldly 12-pounder, *The Royal Philatelic Collection*, doubtless intended to underline Kemsley's devotion to the Crown, echoed by Winchester, also possessed of a deferential respect for royals.

The production of this book was proving costly and drawn-out. Kemsley's reaction to the situation was the logical response of any newspaper owner accustomed to dealing in thousands, even millions, whether readers or sterling. Instead of keeping to a limited edition of 100 copies of so rare a publication, he decided to increase the edi-tion to close on a 1,000. Almost immediately, the book was ousted from the catalogues of booksellers specialising in rare books. Disaster was certain. Several hundreds of this vastly expensive, red leather-bound publication were likely to moulder for years in the cellar of the Bloomsbury house. In many ways this was a bibliographical tragedy, for the sovereign's rare and regal stamps had been superbly reproduced in authentically impeccable colour by the printers, Cowells of Ipswich, and sumptuously bound.

Kemsley had learned his lesson. Another grandiose volume, tentatively entitled *The Holkham Bible Picture Book* was already under discussion between the British Museum, Lord Leicester and the Dropmore Press. This volume was certain to be limited to 100 copies. At this stage, Lord Kemsley turned for help to Fleming, hopeful that his foreign manager's contacts, worldliness and experience would help nearer home.

Although flattered by Kemsley's invitation, Fleming foresaw huge and niggling problems which could threaten his job, his lifestyle, his lethargy, his two-month annual break, and, above all, his recently revived literary ambitions. Inevitably, as typographical consultant, Fleming roped me into this sideshow.

Onerous death duties had caused the third Earl of Leicester to cede this valuable volume to the British Museum. Dr William Hassall of the Bodleian Library, also consultant Holkham librarian, had pulled strings and arranged for the original manuscript to be at Holkham for inspection. The proposed Dropmore version would be printed at the Oxford University Press.

Fleming was far from keen on this new task. Success might sponsor Kemsley's appreciation of his talents, but the hazards ahead were many and gruesomely remote from his own skills.

For starters, he suggested that we should drive up to Norfolk in his latest Thunderbird to meet Lord Leicester and his librarian. I had seen the house once and welcomed the proposal of a further visit. The chance to visit the library added further allure to the venture.

All went well in the wondrous William Kent library, although his lordship visibly paled when Hassall, enthusing over the unique pages open before us, seemed fairly carefree with his cigarette ash. I thought this showed the unbridgeable gap between one for whom a fabled picturebook represented a vivid contribution to the pleasures of daily life and another to whom it represented something around £100,000 in lieu of death duties. (Value now, probably nearer half a million.)

An hour or so into the discussion, Hassall informed us that he had to get back to Oxford. Fleming and I had been invited to lunch with the family: the earl, the countess and their two attractive daughters. Well before the meal's end, the Leicester family had left the table at the double, for Holkham was open to the public that very day. The earl needed to oversee arrangements; the countess needed to organise guides; Anne, the elder daughter, needed to assemble pots from her own Holkham kiln for sale to the visiting public; Carey, the younger daughter, would be needed on duty at the desk for souvenirs.

I was left with Fleming and the rice pudding, which would guarantee, I assured him, an agreeable finale to the meal. He, no sweet tooth and less appreciative than myself of the boisterous departure of the family to their battle posts, reached, of course, for his cigarette case. Our farewells to the Leicesters in the bustling entrance hall some fifteen minutes later were fairly scamped.

Our return journey to London was enlivened by a retrospective review of the day. Fleming opened the review by contending that, unlike any other supposedly dedicated book designer and typographer, I had been far more intrigued by the stately home with its rare architecture and bubbly siblings than the projected promised publication. I was inclined to agree. Handsome buildings and feminine good looks had far more to offer than antique lettering.

'You found the Leicester girls easy on your scanning eyeballs?' he announced, as if opening the case for the prosecution.

'Very!' I said. I had found them both extremely attractive: easy on the eye and clearly enjoying their open-day chores. A further bonus was that they had seemed relaxed and on unusually good terms with their parents.

'And what of the parents?'

'His lordship seemed somewhat out of his depth with the *Bible Picture Book*, I thought. I found her rather attractive.'

'I noticed those appreciative glances. And you've come away with her gift, a history of Holkham, I noticed. And what of Hassall?'

'I thoroughly enjoy watching these Oxbridge dons and profs struggling to enjoy or seeming to enjoy a day away from their bookish retreats, yet longing to get back as soon as possible.'

Fleming rather agreed. 'You were clearly keen on the house.'

'Splendido! But sheer hell to own. Would you take it on?'

'Probably – with the Leicester lolly.'

'Is any distant Fleming domain of comparable consequence?'

'Nothing of that order. Some modestly extensive oddments, but they're all in Peter's possession. An old-fashioned touch of primogeniture, heartily approved of by my mother, especially as she's not the financial genius she thinks she is. Peter got all the spare cash from my father's will. Hence the house he was able to build at Nettlebed. Not beautiful, I admit, but adequate for his needs. I prefer my mews… Or rather, my mother's mews,' he corrected, somewhat tardily.

I grinned. 'Our cul-de-sac retreats seem to offer adequate scope for our metropolitan needs?'

'Yours is a three-night refuge, single or double. Mine's a round-the-clock base. Maybe a house is waiting round the corner.'

He returned to the subject of the Holkham girls. 'D'you think girls like that can make worthwhile wives?'

'Why not? For men in their own circles, of course. Or shall I ring 'em up, claiming readers in the *Sunday Times* want to know whether they can cook, sew and screw to match the highest professional standards of the foreign manager?'

He laughed. 'Well, it would make quite a feature. I think the *Sunday Times* might pay quite handsomely for such a piece, although Ernestine might take a jaundiced view.'

Ernestine, wife of the bibliographer John Carter, who had originally introduced Fleming and I, was the fashion editor of the *Sunday Times*. She was also a well-known, well-practised American autocrat. I regularly – and enjoyably – designed her pages.

And so the exchanges continued.

A couple of days later, reporting on his post-Holkham discussions with Kemsley, Fleming said his lordship had been readily persuaded that the ecclesiastical picture book should be published. I had little enough to do with the production of the book apart from what might be termed the window-dressing: designs for the binding, title-page, prelims and text pages devoted to Dr Hassall's learned disquisition. Plus the money-no-object red leather binding. The printing by the Oxford University Press was impeccable on every count.

To keep the modest printing equipment of the Kemsley-Bloomsbury terrace house in some kind of action, Fleming then decided upon a series of reprints of sporting books which had entertained him at one time or another. He chose two small nineteenth-century manuals, which enabled him to commission brief essays from two mature journalists whose writings he admired: Neville Cardus contributed a preface to *The Young Cricketer's Tutor* of 1833; Bernard Darwin a similar piece to *The Golfer's Manual* of 1857. Both were small and interesting books, enlivened by appropriate wood engravings by John O'Connor. I enjoyed designing the formats for both *Tutor* and *Manual*.

Fleming's next move was to persuade a few of his literary acquaintances into providing essays or poems lying neglected in their desks and which they might care to see in print. He cast around. Sir Osbert Sitwell, his first target, had recently won the *Sunday Times* literary prize for the first two volumes of his seemingly endless autobiography: *Left Hand, Right Hand* and *The Scarlet Tree*. There was, however, a snag. Although Fleming had played a significantly persuasive part in the appointment of Osbert's brother, Sacheverell, to take over the 'Atticus' gossip column in the *Sunday Times* – and equally significant part in Sacheverell's later departure from the job – he was emphatically *persona non grata* with their sister, Dame Edith. She had expressed sharp distaste for what she deemed Fleming's facetious chit-chat at a luncheon presentation of the *Sunday Times* award to Osbert. Fleming had thereupon been well and truly banished to the Sitwellian doghouse – at least as far as the dame was concerned.

This upset was left to be smoothed out by the poet, William Plomer, close friend of both, and one of the most gifted social smoothers of his time. With his usual diplomatic skills, he sponsored a rapprochement between dame and foreign manager verging on the obsequious, Fleming confessed. Within a month, of course, he was one of the dame's most favoured gallants with invitations galore heading his way from then on.

After a strategically timed interval, Sir Osbert was tackled about the chances of the Dropmore Press publishing any forgotten literary gem from his personal records. Fleming struck lucky. The Dropmore Press would be allowed to reprint an essay by the legendary peppery Sitwell *père*: 'On the Making of Gardens', originally published in 1909. Fleming was no gardener outside his self-fructifying Jamaican plot, but he was hard-up for a text and this resurrected oddment by Sir George Sitwell provided an opportune latter-day memorial. Sir Osbert was keen to have his father's book reissued in a limited edition. I later learned that the original book had been a notable flop.

I was one of Fleming's two guests at a decisive luncheon at Boodles. With his jowly face, half-closed eyes and shaky but watchful mien, I thought Sir Osbert looked more like a cross between an occidental bookmaker and an oriental mandarin than the poet, essayist and battler against the philistines *Who's Who* declared him to be. Happily, he was also sonorously supportive to my tentative suggestion that John Piper should be asked to contribute drawings to the text. I had long admired Piper's work, especially his superbly evocative drawings of Renishaw, Sir Osbert's home in Derbyshire, and his lithographs of Brighton – so evocative of my own boyhood. Fleming said later that the Piper suggestion had proved exactly the touch to clinch the deal. He was duly grateful, as was Piper when the commission came his way.

Fleming then decided that as Sir Duff Cooper (later Lord Norwich) was known to scholars as an able commentator on, and practitioner in, the rare craft of translating classic poetry, he would move in on him, especially as their ladyships, Rothermere and Cooper, were close friends. No arm-twisting of any kind was needed. Nobody had been known to resist a reasonable or even unreasonable request from either siren. Then, too, no writer of prose who has dabbled in verse can resist the opportunity of being seen as a master of both skills.

A typical instance of Duff Cooper's underrated literary insight was a comment in the introduction to his ensuing book: *Translations and Verses*. 'A critic might seek', he suggested, 'to offer reasons for considering such a simple line as "I am dying, Egypt, dying" to be great poetry. But they are unlikely to prove to be the right reasons. The truthful answer to the question *why is it so good?* is that nobody knows why: just that it is. If it had run "O Cleopatra, I am near my end", the information conveyed would have been the same, the metre more regular, and the English equally good, if not better, for a pleonastic repetition would have been avoided. But the poetry would have disappeared.'

Literary criticism is rarely so magisterial or convincing.

Sir Duff was delighted to have a dozen copies of the books as gifts for friends. This plenitude of free copies, plus half-a-dozen volumes selected from the crowded shelves of Heywood Hill, the Curzon Street bookshop, was Fleming's usual pay-off to his authors. Never the coin of the realm. Thus Ellic Howe, whose book on *The London Bookbinders 1780–1806* was published later by the press, chose second-hand sets of the *Dictionary of National Biography* (twenty-two volumes) and the *Oxford English Dictionary* – 'a mere dozen', as he pointed out in a later edition of his book published by the Merrion Press.

Having completed these early and comparatively straight-ahead negotiations with Sitwell and Cooper, Fleming decided to turn his persuasive talents to a far more newsworthy literator. Evelyn Waugh was a close and devoted admirer of their mutual friend, Ann Rothermere. To his surprise, Fleming found Waugh genially inclined towards the mooted co-operation – on condition that the book would not upset his publishers, Chapman & Hall.

Hitherto, Fleming had had a high regard for Waugh's prose but a far dimmer view of his persona, dismissing him as a snob, bully and social pretender. 'The only way to deal with Waugh is to sock him first – as with all bullies,' he had opined. 'After that he'll be more or less bearable.'

This somewhat aggressive view possibly derived from Waugh's unabashed devotion to Ann and his regular attendance as a guest at her dinner parties. These were festivities which Fleming never attended, far preferring his bridge-table encounters at the Portland. On her side, Ann took unabashed delight in Waugh's undoubted devotion to herself and his dyspeptically caustic views of the world and its denizens.

Waugh suggested for publication a collection of sermons by his Catholic mentor, Father Ronald Knox. Fleming was delighted. As Waugh expressed the wish to discuss the typographical design of the book, he was persuaded by Fleming to contact me. To our surprise, Waugh invited both Fleming and me to his lesser club, the St James's, rather than White's.

In due course, we lunched. Fleming, logically but unwillingly a guest, also attended. Waugh sported a loud-patterned heavy grey tweed suit with baggy trousers, brolly and bowler, a rig more appropriate, I thought, for a bookie en route to Lingfield or Epsom than a literary light promenading Piccadilly. Would he have donned such a garb for an appearance at White's? Presumably, yes. He seemed to have little interest in the views of others, social or sartorial. Only his own views mattered.

Fleming proved to be a fairly sceptical onlooker during the meal. Waugh clearly had not been in the club for some time, for, after he had given the waitress our choices, she asked his name. Waugh was plainly put out. He barked 'W-A-U-G-H. Pronounced Wuff!' Fleming sought to retain an admirable impassivity with scant success. Smirks were inevitable. Putting aside this momentary setback to any host's self-esteem, we got started. Both Waugh and Fleming gradually thawed. I certainly helped the thaw by recalling that Waugh, after coming down from Oxford, had spent a couple of terms at the Byam Shaw School of Art. He clearly warmed after I mentioned that I had liked the drawings he had made for his first two novels, *Decline and Fall* and *Vile Bodies*, clearly influenced, I contended, by Jean Cocteau's unique linear draughtsmanship. This Waugh acknowledged, smiling almost benignly.

The luncheon, stiff and prickly as it was, proved successful for Fleming. The *Knox Sermons* made a handsome book and delighted Waugh, whose respect for Knox must have been one of the softer spots in his somewhat gritty and touchy persona.

There remain a few bizarre and unexpected oddments to this tale of Fleming's publishing career on behalf of Lord Kemsley which proved a prelude to his own publishing career. The first item was his lordship's acquisition of an alleged quarterly publication: *Book Handbook*. The 'quarterly' label was so casually met that, from time to time, two issues would be incorporated in one, boldly updated. This journal was a labour of love, owned and edited by one Reginald Horrox, literary advisor to Sotheby's, working from home at Bracknell in Berkshire. When the costs of publishing began to prove overmuch for his resources, he had looked around for support. Edward Shanks knew a way, or rather, a man to turn to for help: Lord Kemsley, needless to add.

Although a poet of some standing and a skilful word-wielder in his newspaper career, Shanks must have employed some especially magical phrasing in his persuasion of Kemsley to add *Book Handbook* to his private publishing outfit. By that time his lordship was heartily tired of these cheese-paring, unrewarding sidelines in publishing. Yet, despite the fact that the days of the Dropmore Press were clearly numbered, *Book Handbook* continued. The journal was soon renamed *The Book Collector* on the sage advice of Percy Muir, with John Hayward as the new editor.

Yet, in what some might see as a millionaire's ruthless petulance or foresight, Kemsley decided to end such irritating intrusions into his newspaper publishing. Without reference to the one-man editorial and unpaid advisory staff of *The Book Collector*, Kemsley sent all subscribers a cyclostyled announcement that the journal was to cease publication forthwith. He could no longer underwrite the costs of production. Following this dictatorial decision and Fleming's obvious shock and disappointment, Kemsley offered to sell *The Book Collector* to him. Fleming queried the price. £50, the owner grandiloquently quoted. Fleming paid up on the spot, well knowing that he was in a far less well-placed monetary position to underwrite the costs of production of the periodical.

Fleming, John Hayward, Percy Muir and their mutual friend, Howard Nixon, set about raising a guarantee fund to underwrite those costs. Well-known bibliophiles on both sides of the Atlantic made continued publication possible. James Shand, owner of the Shenval Press, offered to continue to print *The Book Collector* at negligibly more than cost at his Shenval Press in Hertford, and to list his London office in Soho as HQ for the publication. On this round-robin basis the journal was guaranteed continued publication. Sales soon began to increase.

The bookish pleasures of the remaining years of Fleming's life were vastly enhanced by nominal ownership of *The Book Collector*. The journal continued to be edited by John Hayward until his death in 1965 and, following Fleming's death, has been edited and owned by Nicholas Barker.

Happily, *The Book Collector* remains firmly established with an international renown among bibliophiles, librarians and scholars. Fleming's gesture can be recognised as one of the more courageous gambles of his literary career, especially as he was living through a period of considerable personal economic pressure and private anguish.

CHAPTER 22

DEBUT OF BOND

I nevitably, the ever-widening ripples of gossip and rumour relating to the supposed secrecy of the Rothermere and Fleming relationship – especially, if oddly, in the US press – were certainly percolating back to Northcliffe House, Warwick House and Kemsley House from the New York bureau. Fleming's relations vis-à-vis Kemsley were, he admitted, not what they had been. Further worries concerned Ann's health and also, even more dauntingly, his own. Ann had been in hospital in Edinburgh, rumour reliably hinting at abortion or miscarriage. Although Fleming had travelled north on an alibi that he thought would pass – golf at Gleneagles – few were convinced. Equally important, those years of his indiscriminate smoking and drinking were beginning to take their toll – alarmingly.

Although he was a fairly gifted exponent of the stiff upper lip – 'helped by the cut of his jib' as a senior one-time seagoing RN officer in Room 39 had observed – Fleming occasionally loosened up and was prepared to discuss, while we lunched, the manifold problems of his personal life. He admitted that he should have few if any financial worries for a bachelor in his mid-forties. He was well paid by Kemsley. His Hay's Mews flat was more or less a freebie. And, when deemed imperative, his mother would come to his rescue. He admitted that Goldeneye was an expensive hobby: 'The most extravagant luxury, I possess. I persuade myself it costs me £600 a year to maintain. Obviously, it costs hundreds more.'

'Why not sell? Surely Goldeneye would prove to be a goldmine of an investment?' I queried.

'Goldeneye's the only truly lasting and reliable element in my life. Thank heavens, I'll be there again within a month. The one place in which I'm able to relax and make a decision. The only place I'll be able to write – if I ever do.'

He was clearly serious and pressed on to further comments – or confessions, more accurately, perhaps. He even suggested that Silvertop should join us, saying he needed the feminine view on one or two current problems in his life. If she would join us he would be grateful indeed to hear her comments.

This threesome met the following week. Fleming still seemed somewhere near the edge of a possible breakdown, and was, for once, hesitant in both queries and answers. I wasn't unduly surprised when, almost brusquely, he introduced what was soon revealed as the major time bomb in his present jitters.

What would be a reasonable sum, he suddenly asked, for an extremely rich but not especially generous husband, yet of basically kind if somewhat detached disposition, to suggest as a pay-off to an adulterous wife of whom he was still fond but currently wishful to let go.

'As a lump sum or in instalments? An annuity, perhaps?' I queried.

'Lump sum.'

'Around a minimum of a £100,000!' I said. (Nowadays equivalent to well over a million, I learn from a student of devaluation and marital pay-offs.)

To our further surprise, Fleming blushed deeply on my suggested figure. This was certainly one of the very few occasions I had seen his invariably ruddy skin take on an appreciably ruddier hue. I surmised that my guesstimate had been some kind of bull's eye.

'What d'you think, Phoebe?' he asked, or rather demanded.

Somewhat puzzled by the way the chit-chat was going, she said, smiling: 'I leave all our real figures to Robert, especially the tricky ones. Housekeeping totals are my department.'

Fleming smiled at this dutiful dodging of the tricky line the gossip had taken.

To cover my apparent bull's eye, I hastened to add that if cuckoldry had been the only misdemeanour of the imaginary wife-figure he had introduced and that, apart from such an indulgence, she had been a worthwhile partner; I would propose doubling my suggested figure. Yet, even as I now write the words 'doubling', I realise that nowadays I would need to multiply my figures twenty or thirty times at least if a similar challenge were to come my way with a multimillionaire husband involved, even with a guilty wife.

Seeking to get away from monetary matters, I asked whether the lady in question had any other weaknesses. And wasn't the subject under discussion all supposition, anyway?

Fleming, recovering his composure, or most of it, said, smiling thinly: 'Several!' and listed a further trio. Fondness for high society. Outsize talent for extravagance on several levels. Supreme gift for belief in her stars.

'But of sterling character, no doubt?'

'Plus a mixture of mild cupidity and a lack of appreciation of other people's problems.'

'Does the other fellow, the seducer, think she's worth all this kerfuffle?' I asked, with my own thin smile.

'Probably. Or, perhaps more accurately, hopefully. Who knows? The husband has undoubtedly decided that it's worth a packet to say goodbye to her.'

'He doesn't sound quite the kindly character you seemed to suggest just now,' Silvertop said, offering her feminine view for the first time.

'He's had a good deal to put up with,' Fleming admitted, with his still-sad smile.

I was mildly puzzled by his seeming detachment now that he had recovered from my apparent accuracy over the marital pay-off. He was clearly involved in what seemed to be an oncoming turmoil. I wondered whether this situation had been manipulated by Ann and doubted whether even the toughest of men could prove any match for that tough numero. Their lives certainly seemed to be heading for a decisive move. I even wondered whether she had entrapped both men by again becoming pregnant.

A week or so later we learned that my estimated pay-off figure had been pretty accurate. Silvertop was quite impressed and said she'd bear the figure in mind if called upon for friendly advice by an acquaintance attached to a tycoon and needing quotations on marital severance pay.

'Or for yourself?'

'The subject never cropped up at the Moorgate registrar's, did it?' she said, smiling. 'And I've arranged for such a situation never to arise.'

Loud laughter.

After that Etoile revelation, Fleming was more straightforward in his references to his problems. That made matters between us simpler and more direct. He said he had been a clown: he had always had life more or less on his terms. Even his failures and mishaps had somehow had their getaway backdoors, some even tipping him into brand-new promising situations. Now, he seemed to be in the midst of near-overpowering problems, involving money, living quarters, the future. Not only that, but Kemsley, well aware of rumour, was proving rather distant, both in and out of Kemsley House. Everyday circumstance seemed to be adding up to a total guaranteed to bring a man down.

That discussion had been near the year's end.

Clearly, he had never been more possessed by a yearning for escape. Goldeneye was his only hope.

Would Ann be travelling with him?

'The whole way!' he said decisively.

Hopefully, recent worries seemed as if they would be resolved. Partly, at least, I thought.

The Rothermeres were divorced within a month of that occasion. By then, Fleming and Ann were both in Jamaica. I could only hope that Ann had managed a more-than-adequate pay-off. But how sufficient or insufficient would a pay-off need to be to cope with that talent for extravagance? Hadn't Fleming opined on more than one occasion that even her multimillionaire husband must occasionally have had shivers when the bills came in for her indulgences: from clothes to entertaining, from travel to furniture. And now she would be his own exclusive financial responsibility. I recalled one of his earlier quips concerning his lady-love: 'I think Ann lies awake on most nights recalling the items she didn't buy during the day, but will tomorrow; and Esmond probably lies awake totting up both bills, today's and tomorrow's.'

Now the totting-up would be all his own, matching another of his quips: Ann spent money like a dozen matelots ashore in Gib on a day-long jaunt.

The Flemings were married in the town hall of Port Maria, some 10 miles along the coast from Oracabessa, the banana port close to Goldeneye. Fleming was certainly stretching his usual two-month annual furlough, I thought, hoping that he hadn't overplayed what were normally his fortunate Kemsley gambles. Seemingly he was OK, although he confessed later that he had had some hideously frozen moments, knowing that he had several enemies in Gray's Inn Road, all primarily resentful of his favoured status. On his return, he learned that Kemsley had, understandably, taken a pretty poor view of the whole affair, clearly regarding the divorce and far-off marriage as akin to a guerrilla raid by an outsider on another newspaper tycoon's private property.

Awaiting his return with a fair degree of curiosity, I speculated on how long Ann would stay in what would be her new home in the gloomy Carlyle Mansions in Cheyne Walk, which Fleming, in a note from Jamaica, explained he had rented and to which he would now be moving, having returned the small house in Hay's Mews to his mother. The flat was capacious, and overlooked the Thames, but the pervasive gloom of the block offered no great homecoming after the weather they'd been enjoying in Jamaica.

To celebrate his new status and homecoming, I had presented him with an enormous, gaudily painted and gilded Royal Coat of Arms. He was delighted with the innovative touch which brought at least a gleam of gaiety to one end of the dark corridor between sitting room and bedrooms.

Somehow, I couldn't believe that Ann would be prepared to tolerate so Victorian and gloomy a house for very long, despite the fact that another move would take Fleming into his fifth home in seven post-war years.

Early visits prompted a faint belief that their new home might have its points. The subfusc ambience of the flat was picturesquely relieved by the outlook over the Thames. The rent, too, I gathered, was also quite reasonable. But there was precious little else to cheer a woman with a mind very much her own and, until recently, châtelaine of a magnificent mansion overlooking Green Park, complete with butler and staff at her immediate command.

On our first Etoile encounter after his return, Fleming touched upon the likely necessity for moving, but said the flat seemed to suit their present needs quite well. I doubted that and would have wagered that, within a year, the flat would have proved unequal to their needs and hopes.

More positively, Fleming confided that not only was he now a fully fledged married man but that during his recent spell at Goldeneye, he had at last put pen to paper, and completed a first draft of a first novel, tentatively entitled *Casino Royale*.

I applauded. 'At last! The spy story to end all spy stories.'

He grinned and said time would soon show.

He had already sent the typescript to William Plomer, who had offered to become his literary advisor and sponsor. Plomer's friendship with Fleming had derived from wartime editorial work on the *WIR*. His recruitment by Fleming had meant much to the patient, kindly, knowledgeable South African poet and novelist, who was certainly not one to forget so thoughtful and timely a favour. Fleming returned the poet's friendship. Plomer had become one of his closest and most trusted allies. He was now to find how valuable that trust truly was.

He was clearly chuffed by the completion of his first novel. He had decided to finish the script before his marriage and to that end had determinedly sat down one morning, shut himself into the rather spartan living room and set about a three-hour stint on his portable typewriter. This had been his routine every morning until *Casino Royale* was completed two months later. Once again, he said, he had much for which to thank his winter residence in Jamaica.

'How many words a day?' I asked, one scribe to another.

'Two thousand,' he said promptly, and then sprang a question that had clearly been giving him much meditation: 'Name the most compulsive name given to any hero in your real life or your wide acquaintance with novels of suspense?'

'Sherlock Holmes!' I said forthwith. I often had thought that no other name in literature had ever got anywhere near that unique christening for sheer memorability

Fleming agreed. 'Unmatchable. What about Bulldog Drummond?'

'Too obvious and too juvenile. Perfect for the world for which it was coined. *Boys' Own Paper* stuff through and through.'

'OK. What others have made their mark on your memory box?'

He seemed extremely keen on his new pastime. Fictional namedropping? I added two more names from my memory box: 'I quite like Richard Hannay, but I think that derives more from Buchan's storytelling skills than the name itself. My enduring favourite after Holmes is undoubtedly Sard Harker, John Masefield's hero in his novel of the same title. I've never seen the name supplanted for casual heroic status and memorability.'

'I haven't read the novel and the title rings no bells, but it's certainly an agreeably memorable moniker. Tell me more.'

'Sard Harker's an authentic hero figure. "Sard", I gather, is a term for a stone quartz, but Masefield's usage probably derives from "sardonic", a characteristic, no doubt, also evident in your hero. Sard is clearly depicted as a well-educated, well-endowed first mate in a windjammer in the sinister southern seas and rendered memorably by Masefield in a series of truly horrendous situations. Curious how the book's so little known. John Grierson once told me he thought the novel was a ready-made script for a Hollywood thriller, yet nobody's attempted to take it up. But why the quiz?'

'My current problem. My new novel. What about the name James Bond for a thriller hero?'

'Mildly *Boys' Own Paper*. Not in the same league as Sherlock Holmes and as hearty as Bulldog Drummond, but brief and memorable. Perhaps that's what you want. But as a label for a hero is it as brief and memorable as Sexton Blake, for instance?'

'I came across the name in Goldeneye, oddly enough. James Bond's the name of the author of a major book on the birds of the West Indies, one of my favourite books. The author's still around, I gather. I've never met him. I hope he won't mind, but I've bagged his name. James Bond will be the name of the hero of this, my first novel, anyway, and I hope, the next dozen or so.'

'But why such a schoolboy choice – compared with Sherlock Holmes, Sard Harker or Sexton Blake?' I paused. 'Why not Scad Fleming? I like those first-"s" names.'

'Very funny. "Soap-suds Harling", one day, no doubt. I wanted an ordinary yet readily memorable name for an extraordinary fellow involved in extraordinary happenings.'

'Despite his outlandish name, Sherlock Holmes got involved in some extraordinary, even preposterous happenings, most of which have remained memorable. So, too, did Sard Harker. Some horrendous.'

Fleming laughed. 'You'll soon be suggesting that I should have borrowed a name like Dunstan Curtis?'

I laughed. 'Far more memorable. I quite like it. I first thought it had a made-up fictional touch, despite its authenticity. But if ever there was a non-start name for any hero in any novel you write, Dunstan Curtis is the one. Your tale-telling genius would dry up every time you had to type the name.'

He laughed. 'What name would *you* give a brand-new, over-the-top hero?'

'I've never even thought of the possibility, but if I did I might borrow the name of a friend of yours I've never met – Hilary Bray. Unusual, memorable, easily pronounced, although those with phonetic problems might lessen his heroic stature with "Hilawy Bway".'

Fleming laughed heartily. 'I must tell Hilary that. He'd be amused. But Bond it is, and Bond it's going to stay.'

'Hero of this first and a score of future masterpieces.'

He nodded. 'I hope so, but I think I'll settle for "novel" rather than masterpiece at this stage of the game. In the meantime, I'm crossing my fingers hopefully for an OK from Plomer. I'd like to be with Cape, but William tells me the old boy has little time for thrillers. Anyway, we'll see.'

'I wish you all the outsize luck that's going the rounds.'

This wasn't a solitary discussion concerning nomenclature. 'Bond' was well and truly examined and tested on everyone he met, but there was never a chance that he would change the label. He remained resolute, especially after Cape had agreed to publish.

How triumphantly Bond's creator and christener would have welcomed the verdict by the compilers of *The Guinness Book of Film*, half a century later, that 007's self-introduction 'Bond, James Bond' in *Dr No* was voted by the public as the top oneliner in screen history.

Some three months after their marriage, Fleming announced,

over-casually, again while lunching, that Ann was expecting a child later in the summer, probably in August. I said: 'How timely.' He agreed. I added that we were also expecting our third later in the year or early in the following year, probably a third son, for since our stay in Goldeneye we had added Simon as brother to Nicholas.

What name or names did he have in mind? Not another name borrowed from another bird book? He dismissed the notion and said they hadn't yet decided. What about ourselves? Had we any preference? Another son or first daughter?

'Either. Or, better still, twins. One of each. After all, I was advised to gamble on twins before Nicholas arrived.'

'And their likely names?'

'Amanda for a girl, certainly. Caspar or Caleb for a boy. That's the shortlist. Not a bad substitute for James, any day.'

He was suddenly over-attentive. 'You couldn't possibly have Caspar,' he said too forcibly, followed less emphatically by an afterthought: 'Or Caleb for that matter.'

'Why not? I had a remote uncle I never met who had both. They've stayed in my memory ever since boyhood. Rather like Sard, a name I took to straightaway as soon as I picked up the book. I think we have a slight preference for Caspar. He'll only get one Christian name, anyway. We agree on that. Otherwise I think we'd have him Caspar Caleb for full measure.'

'I'm sure these would-be exotic names can prove an embarrassment to child *and* parent,' Fleming opined decisively, as if he were an authority on the consequences resulting from unusual christenings.

'We're not proposing Winnie the Pooh for a girl or Christopher Robin for a boy,' I assured him. 'Probably, as I said, Amanda or Caspar.'

But he was deadly serious, and went on with his lecture. 'The worth of any Christian name is its simplicity. Hence my choice of Bond. James Bond. Robert and Ian are simple enough, God knows. A simple first-rate test is: could you shout the name along a crowded beach?'

He paused and then, to my considerable surprise, pressed on with what he clearly considered as sensible advice on a basic problem: 'You've already given two sons two sensible names in Nicholas and Simon. Find another as straightforward, for sanity's sake.'

His advice teetered on the edge of nonsense. I laughed and pointed out that I had heard that my long-ago Caspar Caleb uncle had gone through an uneventful life, including a war, without any trouble on battlefields, beaches or even in brothels as far as I knew. Hence my preferences. 'And Phoebe likes both, especially Caspar,' I added for good measure.

'Give it further thought,' he growled, clearly rattled. So rattled that I began to sense something of the reason sponsoring his objection.

'As an innocent aside from Caspar, when were you last on a crowded beach? Not in Jamaica, that's for sure. On much the same basis as Delmer's snake farm, your social war-cry and holiday motto could well be: Goldeneye! Goldeneye! D'you call that as simple a name as 10 Downing Street?'

He laughed, but the volume of his hilarity fell well short of his more normal thunderclaps.

I mentioned these odd exchanges at home that weekend. We both agreed that if the Flemings were to have a son, his Christian name was already assured.

'And if she's a girl?' Phoebe asked.

'Oddly enough, that didn't crop up.'

'Ian is probably convinced it's a boy. I wonder if he'd be prepared to shout "Amanda" along his crowded beaches?'

'He's never been on a crowded beach. Not in England, anyway.'

In August, Ann gave birth to a son, duly christened Caspar Robert.

Lunching, following the birth, I duly asked after Ann's well-being, including my congratulations on the choice of names for their son. 'Especially Caspar,' I added.

He grinned in recollection. 'I was mildly bothered by your time-table and likely confusion,' he said, momentarily sheepish. 'I've always liked the name.'

'That didn't come across, although it did rather peep through your name-bashing exercise. And I doubt whether they would have met – our Caspar and your Caspar – certainly not in their schooldays. I imagine Caspar's already down for Eton.'

He laughed and skipped a reply, pressing on to say that one of the sons begotten by Augustus John, one of his mother's one-time lovers, was Caspar, adding: 'He's now a tip-top admiral.' As if the use of that commendation in this context might seem the raison d'être for his choice, Fleming finished with a repetitive defiant touch: 'Oddly enough, I've always liked the name.'

'You've made that clear now. I told Phoebe how you preferred one of those names one hears shouted so frequently on crowded beaches. Montmorency, Orlando, Wilhelmina and so forth. Even the occasional Ulrika. She was very amused.'

He grinned indulgently and admitted to having suffered what he termed 'mild qualms' on learning that Caspar was so high on our shortlist. Apologies were now forthcoming.

'Forget it. Especially the use of "mild" about your "qualms". After all, as I said, they would scarcely have stood even the remotest chance of running into each other, certainly not on the playing fields of Eton.'

'You've made that very clear.'

'Anyway, we've still got Caleb for next time around.'

'You wouldn't dare?'

'Haven't you dared Caspar?'

He grinned again.

I noted the oddity of the outburst in my journal at the time and, twenty-three years later, recorded Caspar's untimely end. I had seen him twice: a sad, good-looking teenager of considerable charm. Even at that age, he seemed to be having a rough time, outwitting his mother's ambitions for him, including returning him to Eton after he had quit of his own accord and her further insistence on getting him into New College, Oxford – a move she accomplished despite his complete lack of A levels. Although she could move many mountains when so determined, she seemed to be making no progress at all with those grandiose political yearnings she had predicted for her second son's future. Meanwhile, her earlier son by Lord O'Neill seemed to be succeeding successfully on a highly individual career in Northern Ireland, smoothly countering her fierce ambitions that he should consider his chances of becoming Prime Minister. Poor dear Ann.

Our daughter, born a few months later, was duly named Amanda, a name we'd both favoured for many years, long before we'd met. Each of us had noted the charm of the name in Coward's *Private Lives*.

CHAPTER 23

CHEZ FLEMING

W hen Caspar was about three months old, Fleming declared – in an Etoile discussion concerning his life-style – that the flat in Carlyle Mansions was proving fairly grim as a place for rearing a baby, housing a nanny and themselves. They had decided to move.

'Childhood should be spent in a house, not a flat!' he opined, with one of those definitive statements in which he specialised, whether discussing a possible feature in *The Book Collector* or the vices and virtues of a new car.

'Town or country?' I queried.

'London. Without a shred of doubt. I've no objection to a rural pied-à-terre, but I'm not the commuter type you're prepared to be.'

'I still find my Fleet Street hideaway useful but I delight in the pleasures offered by our semi-rural home. And my London trip is a once-a-week job.'

'Yes, I admit that you've worked things out quite sensibly. I think we're both metropolitan types: Ann and myself. Through and through, but now we need more space. Flats are for bachelors, old maids, those cursed with no children or their own second childhoods.'

'How many bedrooms for your next move?'

'Preferably five, Ann says.'

'Perhaps you should have swapped homes with Rothermere.'

'Ha! Ha! Very funny. All I want for myself is a couple of hundred square feet as an escape hatch with space for a typewriter.'

'But you said you can't write a novel in London. You can still spend the odd few days in Jamaica with the current flights.'

'True, but I prefer to correct novels in London.'

'I like the plurality. And you'll be sending Caspar off to boarding school in four or five years, no doubt.'

'Very funny. But I suspect it's true. He'll be off to prep school, boarding soon enough and then Eton.'

'What's the normal age for Eton entry?'

'Thirteen, fourteen.'

'Just when maturity begins to beckon.'

'Eton completes the process. Meanwhile, back to square one. I'm more concerned with finding a London house for ourselves, rather than a house at Eton for Caspar. Cheyne Walk's beginning to cramp us beyond tolerance. That's all.'

I thought I might be able to help them – almost immediately. By a timely coincidence I had heard of a compact, medium-sized period house in central London about to come on the market which might meet their needs, complex as those needs seemed. The house belonged to David Blairman, a highly successful fashion tycoon, specialising in, of all merchandise, upstage corsetry for well-heeled young women or older matrons, whose natural endowments need skilled suspension and/or suppression.

I had designed, over the years, various items of publicity for these Blairman confections, and, in the process, had also designed a copperplate script type to which I had casually given the title of one of the most expensive of these Blairman corsets. *Youthline* was my borrowed title for the type design, readily retained by the Sheffield type-foundry when releasing the letter-form. I still occasionally see and salute the type in use in determinedly discreet newspaper and magazine advertisements.

During a recent meeting, David Blairman had announced that he was proposing to retire to Brighton fairly soon and was keen to sell the Westminster lease of his Regency house in Victoria Square: 'The smallest square in London,' he opined, 'unknown to ninety-nine in any 100 Londoners, even to the hundreds hurrying to and from Victoria. An unusually quiet and charming square. Come and see for yourself.'

I went. Blairman seemed very cosily installed. Only a garage was lacking. 'Think how convenient it will be for Ann: she'll be able to drop into Buck House when in the mood,' I said to Fleming, outlining the scope of the house the following day.

'Sounds interesting. If it's still on the market I'd like to inspect.'

We arranged a viewing for the following afternoon. I went along in hopeful mood, prepared for entertainment. The Flemings were clearly delighted by the house and its modest charms, architectural and domestic. The lease seemed reasonable in price and time span. They signed up that week and moved in before the year's end, still delighted with their find. Ann had been especially keen on a circular table in the near-circular dining room and was double delighted when Blairman agreed to sell her the table and two curved sidetables ideally suited to room and purpose, less expensively, as he pointed out, than such pieces might cost in his nephew's Mount Street showroom from which they had come a decade earlier. Ann was duly grateful.

I was to visit 16 Victoria Square far more frequently than I had visited any of Fleming's previous homes, from all of which he had departed after little more than a year. He and Ann were to live in Victoria Square for the rest of *his* life. If any house rates an official blue plaque as the home of the Bond creator, 16 Victoria Square has a prime claim to be the authentic building, probably doubling with a similar plaque in Goldeneye, if such self-indulgent items are permitted in Jamaica.

From my own viewpoint, the most agreeable of spin-offs from Fleming's tenancy were the meetings devoted to the well-being of *The Book Collector*. Two or three preliminary meetings were devoted to discussions concerning the contents of each forthcoming quarterly issue. In this way, the house in Victoria Square became the HQ in the editorial production of what was soon to become the foremost international journal dealing with profounder aspects of bibliography.

From their earliest weeks of residence, the Flemings delighted in the apparent charms of their new home. Inevitably, Ann wanted to have a handsome as well as comfortable home. Above all, an ideal setting for her dinner parties. That meant new curtains, new carpets and covetable examples of antique furniture. Inevitably, this quest sponsored many visits by Ann to the showrooms of Bond Street, Mount Street and Pimlico dealers and the premier auction houses. I accompanied her on several of these trips. Fleming soon discovered that his wife's inextinguishable extravagances were speedily landing him into sizeably over-spending. Somewhat two-faced, I shared her outlook and his fears.

Despite their swift appreciation of the visual and architectural charms of the house and their decision to possess forthwith, certain spatial drawbacks were soon revealed. The house offered sharp contrasts to their respective several homesteads.

These were especially evident in the somewhat limited bedroom space, despite son and nurse being duly established on the coast. Fleming, however, somehow managed to transform a box room into a desirable study-refuge.

Other disadvantages were soon apparent. Owners and staff were inevitably frequently over-close. The vocal Mary Crickmere and her mildly aloof and sombre-mooded husband, Edgar, found Ann's somewhat dictatorial manner unhelpful.

Happily, pleasurable features were also soon evident. The near-circular dining room, complete with the one-time Blairman table, proved as comfortable and relaxing for meetings of *The Book Collector* quintet as for the dozen or so guests at Ann's frequent supper parties.

The Book Collector meetings sponsored greater pleasure for Fleming, I believe, than any of his other social centres apart from gambling and golf rendezvous, of course. He clearly enjoyed his presidential position, and the gossip engendered by his new editor, John Hayward, whose predecessor, Philip Gaskell, had returned to Cambridge academia. Percy Muir remained the irreplaceable bibliographical oracle. Even Hayward deferred when Muir spoke. They were, without doubt, among the most knowledgeable authorities in their bookish world: Muir as historian, bookseller, writer; Hayward as scholar, editor of Nonesuch Press editions of Donne and Swift and compiler of the invaluable catalogue of English Poetry. Their enthusiastic contributions were readily sparked off by a plenitude of questions from the rest of us.

How Hayward managed his professional life with a wide-ranging social life that could have made him a gossip columnist for any newspaper was beyond belief. As I watched him in his wheelchair, his body, face and voice direfully maltreated by the malady which was to kill him, I thought a VC for civilian bravery should be introduced. He would hold forth learnedly and/or scandalously concerning books, boffins and bedrooms, demonstrating that he was as well informed on the liaisons of the town as he was on the oddities of earlier and latter-day literary lions. He was an entrenched snob and vivid raconteur, especially when revealing the social discoveries and curiosities uncovered by his ceaseless party-going. Muir was the complete contrast: still the handsome, softly spoken, authoritative bibliographer, equally at home in any university library or in his bookshop in Takeley near Bishops Stortford in Hertfordshire. The remaining trio – Fleming, James Shand and myself – spoke up when our particular expertise might be involved, but we clearly preferred listening to the literary gossip of Hayward and Muir.

Yet Goldeneye undoubtedly remained the major object of domestic pleasure in Fleming's life, although he still contended that eight to ten weeks would prove the limit to his indulgence in Caribbean pleasures.

As his life with Ann grew more brittle, he discovered other pleasures at Goldeneye, additional to garden-watching and thriller writing, for by that time he had met Blanche, the partner of his dreams, possibly even more suited to those dreams than the long-ago Muriel.

We knew that we were unlikely to revisit Goldeneye. Europe had too many beaches, villages and cities worth visiting. We did, however, make two visits to New York; partly on business, and one including a trip to the Caribbean – but not to Jamaica. This diversion sponsored an unexpected bonus. My wife had revived a pre-war friendship with an American friend in Cuba and thought we could make a ten-day trip late in October 1954, taking in New York en route. Coincidentally, Fleming was in New York, involved in foreign news expansion for the *Sunday Times*. We met there and dined one evening in late October.

Learning that we were bound for Cuba on the following day, Fleming was suddenly galvanised into a combination foreign manager/ features editor, insisting that I should make a shot at interviewing Ernest Hemingway, who had just followed up his Pulitzer Prize of the previous year by his recent award of the Nobel Prize. He cabled Hemingway to say that I was en route to interview him for a 'major' feature in the *Sunday Times*. When I rang Hemingway the following morning he said my purpose verged on intrusion, but as I was so far from London he would see me that day. I hired a car, left Phoebe with her friends and made my way out to the Hemingway homestead, fairly certain that Fleming's use of 'major' had done the job.

Both Hemingways proved to be charmers. The now-reclusive legend and his delightful wife, Mary, fastidiously neat and beguiling with her tawny-toned hair, stylish blue-and-black striped blouse and *Vogue*-worthy blue slacks seemed ideally housed in their remote island home. I made no notes and just let him talk. No need for questions. And so on for a highly approved 5,000-word feature for the following Sunday's paper. Fleming was delighted by the results of his decisiveness, especially as both editor and literary editor extended their congratulations on his coup, and the outside world showed considerable interest in the feature.

We saw Fleming once more in New York but he returned to London before ourselves, his farewell highly insistent that we should keep Goldeneye on our visiting list for the following month but, no go – we now had three children awaiting our return.

In November 1956, Fleming showed himself readily responsive to a request from Alan Lennox-Boyd, Secretary of State for the Colonies and a member of the Cabinet, to extend an invitation to Anthony Eden. The PM had been advised, or virtually ordered, by his personal physician Sir Horace Evans to seek serious rest from his post-Suez political duties. How Goldeneye came to be suggested as an appropriate sanatorium-in-the-sun for so eminent, touchy and self-indulgent an invalid was something of a mystery, especially to those who had visited the house. Lennox-Boyd hadn't. Neither had Eden's wife. Nor any member of the No. 10 staff. No doubt Lady Eden, née Clarissa Churchill, had listened to Ann Fleming's chit-chat concerning the attractions of a house, which, after all, had proved a magically convenient escape hatch for Ann from the rigours of her London life as Rothermere wife and hostess. That seems the most likely surmise. Ann's disillusionment with the house and dismissal of any charms in or around Goldeneye were to surface a year or so later. What is known for certain is that Lennox-Boyd had the easiest of tasks in persuading Fleming to offer Goldeneye to the PM.

Thus the scene was set – at least in London.

The scene in Jamaica was somewhat less idyllic, we gathered. The problem was now in the hands of Sir Hugh Foot, Governor of Jamaica, who quickly found his most expedient course was to hand the manifold problems of domestic arrangements over to his wife and to give his attention to matters of Goldeneye security.

Lady Foot and her immediate aides visited Goldeneye and were somewhat shaken by the Caribbean Bauhaus qualities of what they saw, and the rigid demeanour of the staff they met. A house so sparsely furnished and with so practical and modest an attempt at interior decoration offered fairly bleak quarters for an ailing PM plus basic staff:

essentially a one-woman set-up: the round-the-year occupancy of cook-housekeeper, Violet. This set-up had proved a lively and agreeable household for Fleming's bohemian cronies invited for winter escapes and excursions, but was clearly unlikely to prove an ideal holiday refuge for the No. 10 supremo. All this apart from the need for a security network needed to transform a highly accessible seaside clifftop retreat into a semi-fortress for an international politico.

The PM's rest cure was later deemed to have been eminently successful, although one or two scribes were prepared to report on flaws in, and omissions from, the stay, but Fleming was delighted by the majority verdict of success. 'I can only wish that my stays at Enton Hall could be deemed equally successful,' he said, 'although that's probably more my fault than theirs. I return to my wayward ways immediately I leave the caring set-up. Let's hope the PM has learned to live the leisurely life.'

'Then why on earth do you visit Enton Hall?' I queried.

'I've made some of the most entertaining and enduring friendships of my life at Enton Hall. There's something about mutual, expensive fasting that links people – like shared sexual experiences on desert islands, I daresay.'

More importantly, this upstage visit by the PM sponsored a crisis-cross-domestic upheaval and security arrangements which proved the basis for the introduction of Blanche Blackwell into Fleming's life. He was to meet her when he visited Jamaica on his annual visit a month or so later. They took to each other on the spot, became instant friends and, following the briefest of delays, devoted lovers.

Inevitably, these encounters in Jamaica prompted anecdotage and discussion after Fleming's return to London. I listened avidly to his second-hand and watered-down account of the PM's visit, seeking to sort unpalatable truths from inevitable gloss. Far more beguiling was meeting Blanche Blackwell on one of her fairly frequent visits to London soon after Fleming's own return.

There are only three women of consequence who can be regarded as Fleming's mature loves, despite dozens of others with walk-on or, more accurately perhaps, lie-down parts. Those three, in order of their appearance and influence, were Muriel Wright, Ann Charteris and Blanche Blackwell – an attractive and charming trio. First and third were uncommonly sweet-natured, possessed of qualities apt to prove somewhat rare and unexpected in those of comfortable upbringing and ready expression of their own wishes and desires. Both had grown into worldly charmers, quick to laughter and readily responsive to others' needs. Ann, the flamboyantly and seemingly dominant figure of the trio, was 100 per cent different from the others: insecure, wilful, determined, arrogant and, when she deemed necessary, quite ruthless. Inevitably, Fleming married Ann, but a perceptive onlooker through the years might have thought that either of the other two would have made him a far more suitable and enduring wife, and might even have appreciably extended his lifespan.

Inevitably, the fact that I had met Blanche and found her delightful and quick to laughter prompted Fleming to discuss more openly at our Etoile encounters how his marriage was beginning to show its threadbare substance. He now clearly welcomed the chance to talk without reservations. Occasionally, he burst out: 'What the hell am I going to do about this marriage of mine?' Whatever the answer, no action followed.

I probably figure as someone akin to a Job's comforter, pointing out that there was virtually nothing he could do, for they could neither live with nor without each other. Under the same roof, they quarrelled bitterly and far too frequently and fiercely. Separated briefly by counties, or more comprehensively, countries, they had immediate need of a telephone for instant retraction of their recent home-based abuse and fresh affirmation of undying love for the future. Their letters repeated those themes. Their marriage was doomed by propinquity. He puzzled over the dismal prospect prompted by these discussions in the Etoile until days before his death. I also suspected that their physical passions, inclining towards sadism and the rest, had proved far too violent, lacking in gentleness and affection for satisfactory middle-age pairing. Above all, they were both spectacularly and egotistically selfish, determined to win any conflict that broke out between them.

Fleming could neither accept nor change the doleful and seemingly inescapable factors flawing his marriage. Like the rest of us, he was fixed in the beliefs foisted on him in earlier days. He could not, for example, give any credence to the notion that a woman can prove every whit as amusing and interesting in friendship with men as men with men. He was invincibly convinced that Englishmen are hopeless in seeking affectionate, understanding, equal-term friendships with women. The leisure interests of men, invariably in the company of their own sex, denied them the possibility of profounder interest with women. Above all other considerations, women were, for him, inferior weaker creatures, despite the fact that his wife clearly demonstrated that in every situation she was far steelier than he ever had been or could be.

Yet his belief that men were so clearly superior in all the major situations and problems of life was stiffly held. 'You may have enjoyed deep and lasting friendships with women,' he once announced to me. 'To my mind, they suggest that you're overly eccentric. Perhaps you should consult Silvertop's one-time boss.'

'Oddly enough, Strauss thinks I would be quite good for *him*,' I said. 'One of his earliest experiences was to be told by his mother that he was ugly, reason enough apparently for him to be taken from the day-school he attended and liked and sent to a boarding school he hated. He was born a Jew yet converted to Catholicism. He's also a congenital homosexual. Shall I continue with my analysis?'

Fleming laughed. 'You imply he's well beyond help.'

I continued with my contention: 'The kind of antipathy towards women with which I associate so many Englishmen isn't due to wealth, boarding schools or social privilege. I saw similar characteristics during the war in scores of sailors and marines from working-class backgrounds. My view is that although few Englishmen have an innate interest in or authentic affection for their women, most of them are utterly incapable of *demonstrative* affection or friendship towards their women, the rarest form of affection between Britain's married couples.'

'How d'you think it happened, then? This lack of demonstrative affection you rabbit on about?'

'Being cut off from Europe and our devotional slavery to sport, pubs and clubs have probably helped. And, probably, the weather.'

He grinned. 'You may have a point. Taken-for-granted affection's probably a far easier option than this demonstrative stuff you're so keen on. Taking-for-granted can be practised in silence, and is probably better suited to the northern temperament than discussing the manifold aspects of love or what shall we do tomorrow or next weekend?'

'The Fleming philosophy. Little wonder the divorce figures rise and rise. Yet you've known three special women out of your scores and any one of that trio would have willingly responded, I contend, to any demonstrations of true affection. Basically, I think you wish you could live without them once you've had your wilful way with their limbs.'

He grinned and, oddly enough, said quite casually: 'There's probably the odd touch of truth in what you say.'

CHAPTER 24

TRANSATLANTIC HEADHUNTING

Despite Fleming's somewhat dyspeptic views of various aspects of his marriage and what I gathered were occasional cataclysmic domestic outbursts, his life was speedily being changed by the pleasures vouchsafed by his expanding, even exploding, literary fame, sparked mainly by the reception of his fourth novel, *Diamonds Are Forever*. He now began his transatlantic trips on behalf of the greater glory of Bond and, incidentally, Fleming.

Halfway through a meal at the Etoile, he said in a mock-gloomy manner that he was booked to fly that night to New York on a three-day trip. He was to be interviewed on television for his views on current international spying in general, and Bond in particular.

'But you'll enjoy the whole caper,' I amended.

He shook his head. 'This kind of fame is dreadful. I've said farewell to any private life I had. I'm now prepared to cross the Atlantic merely to appear for twenty minutes on a TV programme. It's a degrading confession. Like hashish-smoking. Or getting interested in politics.'

'But this is the kind of fame you've always yearned for. Your brother's literary successes irked you no end and your expanding renown doesn't come amiss, either to your mother or yourself.'

'There may be a grain of truth in your wide-ranging analysis,' he said, grinning his agreement.

'Nothing of any authentic psychoanalytic worth,' I said. 'I just think you occasionally overdo the mordant touch, that's all. I think you're thoroughly enjoying these oddments in your rise to fame and gain.'

'You're probably right. In my own dismal way, I'm quite enjoying the oddments, as you term them. The last time I came back from New York, I took a berth on the *QM*. Across the captain's dinner table, I was introduced to a very pretty girl who said, with just the right emphasis, "*The* Ian Fleming?" I was agreeably flattered and realised that I should have got into the Bond game twenty years ago. Nevertheless, the incident was reassuring.'

'I'm sure it was. Bear up!' I said soothingly.

'I still find it fairly preposterous to be lunching here now and booked for breakfast in New York tomorrow morning. Yet it's daily fodder for some.'

'Preposterous but not repugnant, and it's heading your way.'

He laughed again. 'Well, on this trip I'm lunching with the television types but taking breakfast with Patcevitch. Any messages for him?'

'Why should I have? I scarcely know him.'

'I thought you might. He's a long-term friend of mine – and Ann's. You've met him surely?'

'Fleetingly. For a couple of minutes. I was introduced to him by Ann while he was waiting to reclaim his bonnet after a party.'

'How? Why? Where? What party?'

'Oddly enough, at a party given by your wife – then your mistress – at Warwick House.'

'Whose party?'

'That particular night, Ann was hostessing an alleged Rothermere party – undoubtedly her very own – for members of the New York Ballet Company, then performing at Covent Garden. Quite a show!

I was fortunate enough to be invited to both – performance and post-performance. Why weren't you there?'

'Not my line is the simple answer. How did Patcevitch get in on the act?'

'Presumably as a US VIP and boss of the glossy Condé Nast empire – *Vogue* and so on. Indeed, he was a highly important guest. Ann introduced us while he was waiting for his Homburg headpiece. For a few icy minutes, the cloakroom girl couldn't find it. Happily she did. But back to your trip? All Bond, no doubt.'

He nodded. 'All Bond!' he said. 'And to think that ten years ago I only flew the Atlantic once a year just to get to Jamaica. Now, just for James bloody Bond, I'll hop on a plane.'

'Poor you! The things you do for a living. But it has its admirable two-way side: working for Bond, and he for you. Best hotels and all the trimmings for free, no doubt.'

'They come with the agonies of promoting Bond rather than inventing him.'

'Does Patcevitch have anything to do with Bond?'

'Nothing. We're just keeping a long-time friendship warm, that's all.'

As our exchanges continued, I experienced an odd revival of some recent broodings of my own. If I were to mention them there and then, I decided, Fleming would probably have to be removed from the table in a fit of choking, spluttering laughter. Yet, to my own vast surprise, I heard myself saying: 'Oddly enough, I do have a kind of message for Patcevitch. Surprising, no doubt, but worth forwarding – from my viewpoint. Tell him I'll take over the British *House & Garden* glossy if the directors over there are in the mood for change, which, rumour suggests, they are.'

Fleming was clearly puzzled, possibly mildly stunned. 'What on earth are you talking about? What d'you mean by "take over"? Buy it, or what?'

I hastily sought to clarify my use of 'take over': 'I just meant to take over the running of that particular Condé Nast magazine here in London. Editorially, that is.'

A loud guffaw greeted this simple explanation. Fortunately, he was about to raise his glass, which he swiftly replaced on the table. I was relieved.

'Why should he be looking for another editor? What about the characters running the outfit? How did you hear, anyway?'

'Grapevine. The only authentic news service worth listening to. Sales down. Staff somewhat adrift. Editor bored and looking elsewhere.'

'Surely that could be gossip? Anyway, you can't be seriously interested.'

'I think I could be. Very.'

'But it's right outside your present successful career.'

'I wouldn't mind a change. I'm far more interested in mildly historic houses, furniture, decoration, period and modern, than in advertising the merits of cigarettes, films, women's bras, dresses, shoes. You may also recall that I'm architectural correspondent of the *Sunday Times*.'

By then he had begun to take my comments semi-seriously. 'You wouldn't dream of leaving that mink-lined rut you've dug for yourself in advertising. Far too profitable and you seem to enjoy your other life – designing front pages and the rest on Saturdays in Gray's Inn Road. Throwing all that away to run a dodgy glossy? You must be mad!'

'I'm as sane as I'm ever likely to be and I'd be delighted and grateful if you'd pass on my message.'

'I'll have to think about it.'

He had begun to sound as if he thought I might be engaged in some kind of leg-pulling prank he and Bryce practised on each other, and was prepared to blow the would-be prank sky high.

'I'm serious,' I said. 'I'm prepared to write to Patcevitch direct if you'll take the note with you?'

Slowly pacing out his words, he said: 'You mean – no kidding! – that you'd be prepared to throw up all your current profitable commitments to edit a chancy glossy?'

'Not necessarily *all* my current commitments, but I'd like to discuss the possibility with Patcevitch or someone near the top of things over there or over here.'

'You really mean all this? Genuine? No leg-pull?'

'Absolutely!'

'And I can tell Pat all this without some ghoulish giggling finale?'

'Absolutely!'

He shook his head disbelievingly and still unconvincingly: 'All right. I'll mention your apparent madness to Pat. Against all my convictions to the contrary, you seem dead serious, so I'll do my best to laud your virtues. It'll be good for a laugh, anyway.'

The 'Pat' of these exchanges was Iva Sergei Voidato Patcevitch, one-time cadet in the Imperial Navy Academy who had served in the Russian Navy in the final stages of the First War. In the early '20s, he had emigrated to the United States. In New York, he had met Condé Nast, the French-sounding but thoroughly Americanised magazine tycoon, owner of *Vogue, House & Garden* and a dozen other fashionable glossies. Nast had first recruited Patcevitch as his PA. Following the death of Nast, the one-time Russian naval cadet had been appointed president of the world-famous publishing house.

I was in the mood to be serious. A month or so earlier, sitting in the Piazza San Marco during a brief marital excursion, I had mentioned that I was inclined to make an off-the-record bid for the job I had mentioned to Fleming. I was well informed concerning the background to the set-up I had mentioned. I had learned via one of Fleet Street's less frenetic grapevines that Michael Middleton, editor of *House & Garden*, was restive and keen to switch to the Civic Trust, founded by Duncan Sandys when he was Minister of Housing in the mid-'50s. Sandys keenly wanted Middleton back and Middleton was just as keen to be back, seemingly preferring social endeavour to glossy journalism. Previously, he had proved a successful picture editor of *Picture Post*, but had, presumably, found editing *House & Garden* far less interesting, after his spell with the Civic Trust.

Thus, although I had vastly surprised Fleming, this was no sudden whim on my part. A long-time friend – the interior designer and decorator Olive Sullivan, decoration editor of the glossy – had sensed that Middleton was unhappy in the job and that he was keen to return to the Civic Trust and 'upper-working-class housing projects', as she had concluded her note. In the postscript, she added: 'Surely you would be interested, Robert? I think it's made for you and vice versa. Don't let it slip. Please?'

Fleming's casual reference to Patcevitch had transformed daydreaming into would-be positive action on my part.

On his part, Fleming continued with his disbelieving questioning; but, half an hour later, while we were finishing our meal, he seemed almost convinced that my words were perhaps authentic.

Parting at the top of Haymarket, although still in a mildly sceptical mood, he again sought final and positive reassurance that I was serious. He shook his head, still in a disbelieving mood. I wished him well on his trip and in his Bond endeavours. He gave me the New York telephone number of the *Sunday Times* in case I should change my mind by the following morning. I pooh-poohed such a possibility. Fleming said, 'OK!' and crossed to Haymarket. I crossed to Piccadilly. I knew only too well that he hoped for that call.

I could not restrain a smile as I wandered back to Hertford Street. My sudden suggestion had clearly seemed something of a fantasy fling to Fleming, but I had given much thought to the project during the past week and had decided that this was probably a venture well worth serious consideration. Such a highly speculative transition had been thoroughly discussed à deux at home and encouraged.

Whether I would have taken any serious steps on my own account to leave my 'mink-lined rut', as Fleming had termed my current career, for a gamble with a glossy magazine awaiting fresh editorial direction, is perhaps doubtful, but life is crowded with these 'Shall I? Shan't I?' queries. Fleming's New York trip had clarified matters.

My interest in typography and graphic design had long been shared with what was possibly an even keener interest in English domestic architecture. As architectural correspondent for the *Sunday Times*, I had written a good deal on the subject, ranging from interviews with Gio Ponti in Rome to Arne Jacobsen in Copenhagen; from Erno Goldfinger in Hampstead to Sir William Holford in Regent's Park. I had practised my own precepts on interior design and decoration in my pre-war and post-war homes. I had also been responsible for the design of the few issues of a now-forgotten glossy, *Interior*, which James Shand had, post-war, briefly taken over as printer-publisher, with Hugh Casson as editor and John Betjeman as sideline advisor. But *Interior* had had no colour pages and no sizeable publishing-house backing and became defunct. *House & Garden* could, I thought, flourish widely.

Two days later, I had proof that Fleming had put aside his suspicions and/or scepticism and acted on my behalf, for I received a cable: 'PAT INTERESTED – STOP – LONDON WILL CONTACT. IAN.'

I was telephoned the following day and interviewed within the week in the then UK headquarters of Condé Nast Publications in Golden Square. My interrogators were Harry Yoxall, chairman (a First War colonel and MC, as English as nearby Piccadilly Circus) and Reginald Williams, managing director (as American as Broadway, despite a Harrow and Cambridge background). I had first met him during my brief spell as a pre-war trainee on the *Daily Mail*, where he, too, had started.

The interview was genial and not especially lengthy. The subject of my proposed fee and expenses was raised and agreed on what might seem a mildly eccentric approach, but what I deemed a logical basis. Prior to the interview I had noted on a scrap of paper the minimum annual fee I would accept. At what seemed to me to be an appropriate moment I explained what I had done and suggested that my interviewers should record the fee Condé Nast would be prepared to pay. I had based my figure on the belief that a so-called creative director of a successful up-and-coming advertising agency would be likely to receive rather more than the editor of a glossy magazine with fairly modest and declining sales.

Both men thought my suggestion an outlandish gimmick, but, mildly amused, they agreed to the procedure. My figure was somewhat higher but not too intimidating. An annual differential of £750. The difference could doubtless be met, Yoxall said, smiling. One other matter of consequence was also settled: I would be allowed to retain my consultancy with the *Sunday Times*, thus ensuring myself a satisfactory income and fulsome working week.

Agreement reached, I left and wandered back to Hertford Street. I telephoned Fleming – by then returned from his New York trip – and told him I had accepted the job. He guffawed, saying he was clearly in the wrong job and should now set up as king-pin of a headhunting outfit.

At the Etoile, early the following week, learning that I would be retaining my contacts with the *Sunday Times*, he suggested that I should have taken up a career in politics, where six careers could always be passed off as one.

Continuing with a subject so agreeably self-supportive of further nonsense, I suggested that perhaps headhunting was his forte, after all, reminding him that he had conducted a similar working transition for a joint friend, Philip Brownrigg, then dolefully fed up with his job as editor of the *Sunday Graphic*, a Kemsley paper in decline and doomed to extinction.

'Maybe you're right,' Fleming said, amused by my quip. 'Nothing too serious. Just my own worldly wise assessments passed on to questing employers.'

'Of course,' I agreed glibly. 'How did the Brownrigg switch come about?'

Fleming had come to know Brownrigg at Eton: the son of the headmaster of Magdalen College School. After Oxford, Brownrigg had joined the Royal Berkshires as a territorial, become a captain and was awarded the DSO following the Battle of the Ardennes. Post-war he had joined the Kemsley Press and risen to his dubious editorship. Fleming introduced Brownrigg to the big shots at the vastly different Anglo-American Corporation of South Africa, the giant mining group. Within a couple of years, Brownrigg had been appointed London agent and later a director of the vast organisation in what was then Rhodesia, becoming en route the close friend and biographer of President Kaunda of Zambia.

'What were your guidelines for Brownrigg's and my own switch?'

'Mainly whether I thought either fellow would be up to the job. I thought Brownrigg, who was, I gather, a first-rate commander, needed a job requiring serious handling of men, marketing and bosses. Any further queries?'

'Shouldn't you seriously consider setting up Fleming's Fledglings as a new and sensationally successful outlet in the headhunters' league?'

'Very funny. On the serious side, I think such a business might grow too quickly too soon. The last thing I want.'

'What about women? Would you act as headhunter for them?'

'I'd have a go, but I don't think I'd be all that successful. I'm not all that interested in women's achievements in business anyway, although I'm always impressed by a woman's impressive income in any job.'

'What about a marriage guidance maestro? Aren't the same searching talents required?'

'Far from. First, one would have to interview each separately and then both together. What a prospect! No thanks!'

Well within a month, still to Fleming's astonishment and near-disbelief, I was ensconced in my new job, complete with a staff of eighteen and a trio of specialist advisors: Elizabeth David on cooking, Loelia Duchess of Westminster as discoverer of little-known beautiful houses, and Olive Sullivan on interior design and decoration.

A supposedly congratulatory note from Fleming prophesied that the glossy under its new editor would undoubtedly fulfil the dreams of all middle-class housewives aspiring for L-shaped drawing rooms decorated by Olive Sullivan; chaste dinner parties with Elizabeth

David's latest recipe for asparagus soup, followed by Robert Carrier's recipe for *coq au vin au Beaujolais* with Andre Simon's suggestions for exquisite finales. Plus, of course, Loelia's contributions documenting Somerset rectories in the William Morris manner and Mayfair boudoirs with typical John Fowler flair. And so on and on.

As the months progressed, sales began to rise, and Fleming continued to be sceptically amused to have acted as the successful intermediary in this bizarre essay in transatlantic headhunting. Above all, he was delighted, some months later, to receive Patcevitch's personal congratulations on his contribution to substantial signs of success in the venture.

The episode undoubtedly helped to confirm Fleming's belief in his skills as a manipulator of other people's destinies, and, indeed, further proof of the truth of his one-time assertion that he was prepared to help any friend, or even passing acquaintance, in such matters so long as the task could be conducted by telephone without leaving his desk at Kemsley House or his dining room in Victoria Square.

He was not without his quips, of course, following this untoward venture. The transition gave his creative streak full scope. Letters from Jamaica and elsewhere abroad invariably asked after the well-being of *Parlour & Patio*, *Attic & Allotment*, *Front Room & Backyard*, *Bedroom & Beyond*, and the state of the glossy's sales.

For my part, he had doubtingly and dubiously brought about the most interesting and zestful job of my life for well over the next three decades. Long after my sceptical sponsor's death, alas.

CHAPTER 25

OCTAGONS OF FRIENDSHIP?

Despite amorous exchanges in the letters that continued to be flown between them and continuous references to each other's flirtations and probable infidelities, the full reality of the Blanche liaison came as a bitter blow to Ann. She realised from the earliest whispers that this was no fleeting frolic but the real thing. Yet their love letters continued as if they were still devoted lovers. For them, distance was their most reliable go-between.

They had considerable scope for these epistolary exchanges, for Fleming, much against his will, was frequently abroad, not only annually in Jamaica, but also on frequent forays for first-hand research for a series, 'Thrilling Cities', for the *Sunday Times*, at the flattering behests of his latter-day editor, Denis Hamilton and literary editor, Leonard Russell.

Invariably, the Flemings were fiercely embattled until their last moments before parting. Yet, within an hour of his arrival in any thrilling city, he would be on the blower in the ever-hopeful, ever hopeless quest for confirmation of their mutual love. I once opined that if they could have been kept apart, their love letters would have put them high in the well-known Heloise and Abelard league. Fleming nodded, dolefully.

A worldly wise legal friend contends that the major reasons for marital breakdowns that come his professional way are discordant sex and finance. To these, the Flemings gave the substantial addendum of animosity. Their temperaments shattered any chance of long-term reconciliation. Both had extremely short fuses. Neither could suffer disagreement. Above all, their respective lifestyles were leagues apart and getting wider. Their only recognition of each other's worth seemed via telephone or correspondence or, possibly, when together, by their own brand of sado-masochistic sex – probably increasingly rare.

As Fleming's health declined, Ann's seemed to improve. In London he could seek superficial escape in Boodles or the Portland. She could continue with her mix of politicians, literary lights and social grandees: Waugh, Quennell, Bowra, Muggeridge, plus the most recent, most unexpected and most devout of her admirers and lovers: Hugh Gaitskell.

I met him one evening at Victoria Square, having returned from an evening meal in the Garrick. Fleming had been keen to meet Eric Strauss, the eminent psychiatrist and Silvertop's one-time boss, already mentioned on these pages. He wished to discuss some psychotic side-line looming in a new Bond episode. I invited both men to dine at the Garrick. After a long question-and-answer evening, Fleming and I returned to Victoria Square. On our entry Fleming, well plastered, wearily mumbled goodnight to myself and greetings to Gaitskell before making his way slowly upstairs to bed. He was neither very sober nor very well.

I stayed on for a while, along with Gaitskell, while Ann made a duty trip aloft to her husband. We drifted into discussing Labour's current social values, which I thought fell far short of what the party should offer a class-ridden land. Why didn't Labour nationalise all land, every acre? Why retain the House of Lords? Why continue with these titles from the past and even continue to distribute others to so many in the present? Why not hand Ulster over to Ireland? And so on.

Unlike so many politicians in a sitting room or on a platform, Gaitskell was an attentive listener, occasionally shaking his head, not in disagreement, but at the impossibility of Britain ever being able to face such explosive yet logical social changes. He asked whether I was Marxist. Not a chance, I said. Far from. I was merely asking questions I expected a Socialist to aspire to answer in an understandably logical manner. If pressed, I'd probably call myself a simple realist or a mildly leftish Tory.

He laughed. Quite heartily.

I left soon after Ann's reappearance. She, presumably, had made sure that her husband was deep into his alcoholic slumbers and I was quickly convinced that I was unwanted, for Gaitskell became a different man on Ann's re-entry, quite obviously the besotted devotee. Ann had shown me one of his virtually worshipful letters. I have occasionally speculated upon the whereabouts of those many epistles. If still existent, they must be well worth their weight in bank notes.

Musing in the taxi on my journey down to Fleet Street, I decided that Gaitskell seemed an unusually docile lover for the lively Ann to have around. But he was eminent and likely to become even more so, a prospect unquestionably attractive to Ann. Not even the most gifted crystal-gazer would have been likely to spot that only half-a-dozen years were still left to Gaitskell – even fewer than for Fleming.

Thus, within five years of their marriage, the Flemings were desperately apart: Ann preferring to remain in Victoria Square, planning and presenting her increasingly frequent dinner parties; Fleming arriving home from clubland too dim for chit-chat, even uncertain of his movements. I decided that Ann, despite the threat of Blanche, had decided that social life in London sponsored far more pleasures than the erstwhile escapes to Jamaica had ever offered. This cessation was made certain on both sides by Fleming ordaining that Caspar was no longer to come to Goldeneye, contending that his own efforts to cope with the adventures of Bond were destroyed by his five-year-old son capering around house, garden and beach.

Over one of our Etoile meals at that time, Fleming suddenly asked, yet once again, what he could do about his marriage. Sadly, I could only echo my earlier reply: that as far as I could judge, they couldn't live with each other or without each other.

His sardonic humour was still there. He said: 'I refuse to believe it's as bad as all that. Give your reasons.'

'Who knows? Deep down, I suspect that most of us are inclined to believe that pleasure and/or disaster in marriage will begin – and end – in the bedroom. Too soon and too bitterly for too many.'

'I doubt whether the average psycho would agree, but I think you have a point,' he said and then, rather to my surprise, moved on to a subject seemingly far removed from his current problems.

'D'you think home influences play a big part in our childhood?'

'Probably. Looking back, I think I was lucky. I was left to my own devices and interests. A rare experience for youngsters in most familial settings, I suspect.'

'You were fortunate,' he said. 'Mothers can prove very influential in our early days, especially if they are dotty about success in their offspring.'

His comment had recalled a quotation on the subject I'd pocketed to present to him when occasion might next arise. As now. I said: 'I was recently reading Quennell on Byron's years of fame. He makes a few relevant points about this subject. I thought they might interest you.' I took the typed oddment from my wallet.

'Myself and Byron! You must be mad! That semi-cripple, semi-poofter. Don't make me laugh!' Fleming scoffed, taking the cutting. He read seriously. 'Byron hated women because he had hated and perhaps resented his mother: he pursued them because affection and admiration never come amiss and because he himself was sufficiently feminine to find in their society – much as he despised it – a strange influence that he could not account for. Among men, his social faculties were keyed up, he was at his best.' Fleming looked up at me. 'Very funny. Byron had a point. When did Quennell write this?'

'Mid-'30s.'

'I daresay he'd write the same today.'

'Probably. Why not ask *him*?'

'What a hope! But I suppose it's remotely possible. But back to square one. What would you say caused this apparent breakdown in the Fleming set-up in the first place?'

'Ann's extravagance. Your financial worries. Her dinner parties. Your hopes for Goldeneye. Your escapes to Boodles and the Portland. Your hard drinking. Ann's sharp tongue. Your bitter tongues…'

'Christ! What a hatful.'

'We've all got our personal flaws.'

'Your own marriage doesn't seem to have so many so far. Don't your respective flaws upset each other?'

I laughed. 'If two people decide they need each other as well as want each other, things will go quite smoothly.'

'What did you need from Silvertop's psycho?'

'Her composed and gentle persona. Like most men, I'm keen on getting my own way. Pretty selfish and so forth. I was puzzled and, well, entranced by these gentler qualities.'

'You sound as if you're coughing up a few chestnuts deriving from some marital counselling handbook that's come your way.'

I laughed. 'Oddly enough, my own thoughts derive from personal reflection.'

'Perhaps the *Sunday Times* should have a weekly "Miseries of Marriage" column,' he said.

'Edited by yourself? Why not a few footnotes on peace and understanding in the family circle?'

'I'm the last man in Europe with an appropriate background for being able to cough up such footnotes.'

I smiled. He had a point.

Not all the subjects raised in our exchanges were as serious as marriage. Far from. A more light-hearted session over another meal concerned friendship. I suggested that he was apt to specialise in what I termed 'octagons of friendship': casual-seeming groups of half-a-dozen or eight, each group with more or less specialised interests: golf, money, newspapers, gambling and so on, and each group virtually self-contained.

'Good phrase. Octagons of friendships. I may well use it sometime. No copyright, I hope. Basically, I think your notion's more or less on the right lines, although I think hexagons would be more accurate. What the hell's the term of five- and seven-sided?'

'I seem to recall pentagonal and heptagonal.'

'Not bad. How would you classify these so-called octagons? Or whatever?'

'First, your city-slicker cronies. Your one-time stockbroking friends: Pitman, Bray, Dunbar and so on. I've never met one. Then your publishing group. Muir, Shand, Carter, Hayward, Harling and the occasional Plomer – more of a hexagon than octagon, I agree. There's certainly a golfing octet, although I can't name one member. Much the same with your bridge cronies, all unknown to me, although I can certainly name your US bunch: Leiter, Cuneo, Gallico, Patcevitch for starters. I'm almost persuaded that you spent quite a few early years in the New York glossy world making friends.'

'Not a chance. The Yanks are more forthcoming in friendship. You sound as if you're preparing a *Sunday Times* feature.'

'Not quite. I'm just commenting on what I'd term your emotional early life hexagon or whatever: Ivar, Brownrigg, your brother Peter and so on. Friends you had at Eton or before you were twenty. Bray may be in a couple of the groups, but your main objective seems to have been to keep the groups apart.'

He laughed. 'Maybe there's something in what you say. Actually, I think you're right. Introduce your friends to each other and you'll quickly or gradually lose 'em. That's long been my belief. They'll become friends in their own right and goodbye to earlier friendships.'

I thought these reservations and observations on the subject some-what unusual, even somewhat callow. They might also imply a certain degree of insecurity, I suggested.

He seemed inclined to agree, once again putting this down to his mother and her critical view of himself in boyhood and beyond. A complete contrast to his brother Peter's easy ride to success, he said, as if to himself. He went on to point out that I hadn't mentioned any female hexagon he might possibly have sponsored.

'You wouldn't dream of hosting half-a-dozen women all by your lonely self. In any case, the words hexagon and octagon are out of place. Your full array would probably need whatever the geometrist's word is for a fifty- or sixty-sided figure. And then some.'

He laughed. 'You didn't suggest even a quartet.'

'No go. Your friendships with women aren't anywhere as deep or long-lasting as those with men. And, according to your sexual phi-losophy, they'd probably soon be tearing each other's eyes out. One at a time is your limit.'

He nodded. 'Probably. I'm certainly not as given to the kind of friendships with women you seem to enjoy. In any case, I'm pretty sure I'm nowhere near as keen on their company as you seem to have been all your life.'

I agreed that was probably true. He went on: 'Apart from a favoured two or three, most of my relationships with women have been exclu-sively sexual, superficial and short-lived. I'm apt to find that when sex is over, everything's over.'

As he spoke, I thought of a fairly recent recollection of Ann's: a passed-on comment that Ian was a bang-bang-thank-you-ma'am performer who then got up, dressed and went home to be sure of his favourite meal – breakfast. I wondered whether Fleming had ever thought of himself along those tough lines. I doubted that he harboured such a basic view of this aspect of his life. I wasn't prepared to find out. In any case he wished to return to our main theme: his octagons of friendships. To my surprise the subject seemed to have a curiously serious interest for him.

'What induced you to work out these masculine octagons and the rest? I've never thought of my friendships in geometrical terms,' he mused.

'Just an odd thought about friendships.'

We discussed the subject for a further few minutes. Fleming concluded with the comment that he was relieved that I'd included a place for myself in one or other of his own hexagons or octagons of friendship.

I nodded. 'I've vastly enjoyed your publishing frames – and still do – but, generally speaking, I don't think I'm much of a maker of even a quartet. I quit the Garrick, the RNVR club and the senior common room of the Royal College of Art all within a month – and never regretted the deed or missed the 100 per cent masculine groups. Our sessions here are far superior to any sextet or octagon in any club.'

He was inclined to agree. 'I've almost quit dropping into Boodles. I seem to prefer the lighter touch of Scott's or here.'

'Especially with one of your exes, no doubt?'

'I don't think I've much of a record entertaining exes beyond our first half-dozen sessions. Two or three exceptions, of course.'

Exchanges switched and continued as they invariably did when concerned with the opposite sex.

Fleming concluded: 'Everything connected with sex is better discussed between acquaintances of the same sex, despite the one-sidedness likely to be demonstrated.'

'Certainly rather than likely!' was my own summing-up.

Later, reflecting at leisure on those octagons and other forms of friendships, I decided that the closest Fleming had ever come or would ever come to authentic compatibility had been with Ivar Bryce, friend from their Eton days. They shared a similar philosophy for coping with the vicissitudes of life if not death. Both were beguiled by, even though suspicious of, women. Each deprecated his dependence upon them; each suspicious of feminine intentions; each desirous of wealth without toil and/or tension. For either, a truly well-heeled wife was a partner worth possessing.

Oddly, too, both were given to fairly juvenile friendly jokes. I had recently been regaled with details concerning such a near-schoolboy prank. As each was well aware of his increasing weight, they had decided, while in New York, to lose at least 20lbs *avoirdupois* apiece before their next meeting, likely to be again in New York some three months hence. Their weights had been verified by Bryce's local medico. On returning to New York some four months later, Fleming – well pleased with his own reduction by some 10lbs – espied Bryce awaiting him, clearly much heavier. Fleming waved, delighted; the winner's perks virtually already in his wallet. Bryce had arranged that they should drive directly to their medico for verifying strip-offs. There Bryce proved an easy winner as he delivered himself of the substantial cushion he had secreted beneath his shirt prior to his journey to the rendezvous. Indeed, he was victor by almost 6lbs. A further touch of farce was added to their competitive play-offs: by the medico's confession that he was so impressed by the results achieved by both contestants that he would follow the regime Bryce had evolved for his victory.

Fleming certainly had no doubts concerning Bryce's friendship, although Ann occasionally intimated that their union was of doubtful origin, probably another tale which could be told by Eton's studies if walls could talk. She remained highly dubious of the worth of their friendship. I also thought that she was somewhat piqued by the ease with which Bryce had got himself divorced for remarriage to one of the richest women in the USA, whose first expansive gesture was to buy back the one-time Bryce family mansion with its sizeable acreage in Essex, an early marital memento of what would prove her undying love for her new husband. A gesture, alas, threadbare within five years.

Meanwhile, by the mid-'50s, Fleming's own deep self-yearnings for enrichment via Bond were beginning to show signs of burgeoning, due mainly to his determination to provide his growing public with annual offerings. *Live and Let Die* followed *Casino Royale* within a year, and was followed by *Moonraker* in 1955, *Diamonds Are Forever* in 1956 and *From Russia with Love* the following year.

Needless to say, the soaring success of Bond aroused the interest of the film moguls. A serious offer was made by Columbia. Others followed. The oddest approach was from the *Daily Express*. A bright spark there had the brilliant notion of making Bond a hero of a strip cartoon. Five years earlier, Fleming might have been enthusiastic but, thanks to a fairly inexplicable decision by one of the *Express* high-ups, the strip was summarily ended without warning. The accusing finger for the cessation was pointed at Beaverbrook himself. At the time, Fleming and Ann were both somewhat piqued by this sudden conclusive decision, leaving the adventurous strip world to Modesty Blaise. The *Express* bosses must have had serious regrets later for this seemingly inexplicable finito.

Fleming unashamedly revelled in his surprising, ever-growing fame, and made a fairly unconvincing downplay of his pleasure in this rise and rise. Ann was torn. She viewed his increasing earnings with interest but her notions of literary fame were more concerned with the likes of Connolly, Waugh, Quennell and so on. She was inclined to deprecate her husband's sensational rise to literary fame. Indeed, she readily agreed with a quip from one of these alleged friends who declared that Fleming was basically at ease 'in an armchair at Boodles, a glass of something fairly lethal at his side, lost in dreamy reflections concerning Jimmy Bond's next appalling affray or death-threat or carefree affair or unbelievable escape from an impossible situation plus any other impossible but triumphant episode that might add to the imaginative glory on the world's film screens. Salute, then, to the cinematic never-never land of the Fleming imagination and the shekels in his bank.'

Happily, by then, the Fleming legend was already too solidly welcomed for such comments to dent Bond's rise and rise, although they were apt to pique the author's own sensitivity to these quips.

CHAPTER 26

METROPOLITAN ENCOUNTERS

We continued with our luncheon encounters, weekly when possible, but occasionally quarterly and beyond, as Fleming became a rather unwilling globetrotter on behalf of two incompatibles: James Bond, and the editor of the *Sunday Times*.

Did he pick up many notions for the further adventures of Bond in these visits to alleged thrilling cities?

'Very, very rarely,' he admitted. 'The occasional glimpse of some little-known technical device. Little else.'

'Then why press on to the distant East, the Seychelles, Hong Kong and the rest with what you term a backcloth of sweat, slaves and syphilis? And all this when you suspect that your *Sunday Times* career is moving to its close?'

'Ever-hopefully, I probably try to see it as a bit of a Bond roller coaster.'

Curiously, we rarely discussed our respective careers, although Fleming's was entering a 'golden globe', as Ann described his growing rewards. *The Enormous Shadow*, a novel I had written after *The Paper Palace*, was made into a BBC television film with Denholm Elliott in the lead. Fleming was insistent that I should write a novel with a glossy magazine background. 'Surely a setting of your Hanover Square office stuffed with those ruthless, practical, sex-starved girls at the mercy of their sex-maniacal bosses has more to offer the public than any seedy, geriatric, man-run newspaper office?'

'No go. I find the glossy background an ideal setting for compiling a monthly glossy concerned with other people's homes, but no background for sex mania. Not yet, anyway.'

'No sexual dalliance available?'

'Available, but my preference for a small, select staff means hard work for the job in hand. Under-burdened staffs in newspaper offices are the cause of too many touch-ups.'

'Sounds rather holier-than-thou stuff, but probably true,' he agreed reflectively.

In moments of reflection, I doubted whether I would continue with any further novel-scribbling, despite Chatto's pressures. I was becoming too engrossed in what Fleming termed my 'glossy world of reality in which ready-made interiors were proving more interesting than evolving excruciating plots', and went on to compare my own relaxed approach to fiction with his own increasing endeavours for greater fame (or 'gory glory' in Ann's words) for Bond. He was truly set on his ways, contending that 'the best way of writing a novel is to shut oneself away in a hotel one can't really afford and write fast. One of my troubles now is that there are no hotels I can't afford,' he added.

He also had the problem of where to find a ready-made office to house himself after the conclusion of his *Sunday Times* career. That would soon occur. His ever-increasing royalties would soon make his *Sunday Times* salary 'sheer peanuts', he declared. A friend, Renne Hoare, suggested a couple of offices in Mitre Court in a small block owned by the adjacent long-established Fleet Street family banking house. The two offices needed a few decorative touches. Adrienne

Spanier, decorator and design director of Peter Jones and sister of a Parisienne friend of Fleming's, was invited to submit suggestions. Her main advice was to encourage a choice of 'a dark green, 2-inch wide, striped wallpaper'. The effect was highly suitable and readily acclaimed by Fleming. I sent a note to Adrienne, a friend of Silvertop's, congratulating her on the choice. 'I'm glad you found my suggestion suited Ian Fleming's persona,' she wrote. 'One of the aspects of my job that I like so much is to discover what I think would suit my client's taste. The psychological side fascinates me because I never want the final result to be *my* taste – although, of course, I do show them things I like – but to their taste, hopefully.' She certainly succeeded in this Mitre Court office. The comfortable but mildly sombre background suited Fleming's persona: twenty days in any single month, at least.

Into this setting, Fleming introduced a new secretary, who was to serve him well until his death: Beryl Griffie-Williams, inevitably known as Griffie. She proved the ideal support for Fleming: secretarially efficient and possessed of an authoritative and unusually understanding personality – an ideal protective shield for a boss who looked much tougher than he was.

I suggested that his Mitre Court set-up should be called James Bond Inc. or Ink. 'Quite funny,' he said, 'but I'm determined to keep my own personality to the fore as the creator of that doughty he-man.'

I thought that this was perhaps the carefree moment to suggest that rather than wait for the inevitable plagiarist who would sponsor a female Bond figure, he should jump the gun by starting a double act rather in the William Powell-Myrna Loy tradition and arrange for Bond to marry a girl with an easily remembered name. Why not a fresh set of novels and films about James and Jemima Bond, or Jimmy and Jem? They might set the literary and cinematic worlds even more blazingly alight.

'A notion fit to be dismissed on the instant, but don't tell anyone, for Christ's sake. Your bloody Jemima could make a writer of comic scripts rich overnight.'

Fleming continued to be his own press agent, determined to get both himself and his hero more widely known, using every device known to a born promoter. Although Bond had proved a slow starter, his creator was determined to keep him moving upwards in the biggest and swiftest manner. I suggested that, if he were to devote as much energy and scheming to the promotion of the alleged objectives of any political party, he would be well placed to be made a life peer or, possibly, even given an earldom. If that could be guaranteed, he said, he would say 'Snap' and switch straightaway. He already had his title ready. After the titles of his wife's two preceding partners – their lordships O'Neill and Rothermere – he was ready to rise from the commonality with the title of Lord SW1 or even Lord Victoria Square.

His major problem, apart from his marriage, was health. 'Fast declining,' he confessed. But only a few were aware of his debility. What I knew, I learned from Ann. Her husband was at farcical pains to emphasise his bounding good health, she claimed. Indeed, he seemed to revel in the wide-scale tasks for which he became involved in seeking fame for Bond. The sad irony in all this was that, as his persistence in these endeavours became increasingly successful, his physical resources steadily decreased. Apart from the annual Jamaican escape, his favourite journey was his weekend visit to one or other of the golf clubs of which he was a member. This was his ideal inclusion to weekends at the cliffside cottage overlooking the Channel at St Margaret's Bay, bought from Noël Coward. Then, too, he was always prepared to fly to New York for any chance to discuss Bond with any established Hollywood promoter.

His reactions to his meetings with the film moguls were mixed. 'If I'd been twenty years younger when I began to hit this Bond jackpot,' he ruminated, 'I'd have made very different arrangements about payments for film rights. Now, I'm merely paid in money. Being paid in leading ladies would have been an interesting innovation for a scribe in his thirties. An established routine for producers, however antique, I'm told. But they – cunning bastards – invariably get the lolly as well as the body.'

Despite his authorship of 'Thrilling Cities', Fleming admitted that he was insufficiently curious concerning any of the cities he visited. None was thrilling. All were depressing. I asked how he set about these metropolitan enquiries, pointing out that enquiries made from his Thunderbird or in some foreign tycoon's Rolls was no way to explore any town or city, thrilling or otherwise. Foot-slogging was the only logical way.

'I don't have this city wanderlust you suffer from,' he said. 'Not even in New York. I invariably find that cities are agglomerations of sweat and concrete. In any case, my so-called "thrilling city" visits are usually under the direction of a local historical, architectural or topographical pundit – or even the threadbare info of our local correspondent. Or, worst of all, a local political bigwig.'

'Then why do it? Surely you can break away? Can't you give thanks to your immediate host but say you think the best way to explore is solo?'

He was wary, 'I know your views. Towns and cities can only be truly explored by foot-slogging, preferably solo.'

That was still my view. 'As a Lowland Scot, you doubtless also recall that I cited the authentic James Bone not Bond as one of the very best with his London perambulator and Edinburgh books. That was Bone's procedure. And my own solo foot-slogging only. I'm merely trying to discover Bond's.'

He laughed. 'I suppose you think your solo wanderings around the world's biggest cities put you in a special category of explorers.'

'More or less. I've always preferred solo wanderings. I've never got around to writing a book on any of the cities I've visited. I did once compile a pre-war *London Miscellany* for Heinemann. That was quite successful, but prompted no wish on my part for a repeat. There was too little perambulation needed.'

'I suppose you'd say much the same about being dumped in some godforsaken town or city in the English provinces.'

'I'd make sure I got my full share of wandering solo. I found

Bradford and Birmingham extremely entertaining. An ideal pair of examples for any series of unthrilling cities.'

He laughed. 'Why were you there?'

'I spent six months apiece in each, trying – not all that success-fully – to learn more about the technical side of printing, of which I thought someone, terming himself a typographical designer, should be aware. Actually I found it only superficially necessary.'

'What d'you mean about *extremely* entertaining? How much did you learn about the people there?'

'Quite a bit. Certainly more than I learned about machines. On my first day in Bradford I asked the head printer for guidance. He knew the landlady of a lodging house, three minutes away, special-ising in guests from the acting and music-hall professions. Bradford rather prided itself on its evening pleasures. That settled my social life. Never a dull moment.'

'So you were tied up in the evenings. What then?'

'The head printer was a sound advisor there too. He'd heard on sound authority – his son's – that some very attractive mill girls pat-ronised the local skating rink opposite the printing house. He was right. I found them very forthcoming, to coin an appropriate term. I even became a racy performer in the rink. I also did a good deal of healthy weekend rambling in the Wharfedale hills.'

'Trying to keep up with the keep-fit mill girls, no doubt.'

'They came high on the list of Bradford's pleasures. Saying good-night to a girl living in a Bradford back-to-back demands its own technique.'

He laughed. 'What about Birmingham?'

'There I was advised – this time by a genial proofreader in the print-ing house I was frequenting – that the local library was the place for promising pick-ups. A more serious type of girl, for starters. Thaw-ing inevitably after closing time. My informant was dead right. Then, too, Birmingham is close to the Clent Hills. Ideal for weekend ram-bles. Always consult a knowledgeable local.'

'I'm reassured. I'd begun to think you thought the primary require-ment for gaining topographical expertise was to meet a local tart.'

'If all else fails, why not? I gather you're referring to my agreeable Istanbul and other memories. Why didn't you include Istanbul in your thrilling cities, by the way?'

'I was put into the care of a rich and kindly local luminary as my guide and counsellor. He knew little of the Turkish background you explored.'

'Did you ask him?'

Fleming, always ready to quiz anyone concerning his or her tech-nical interests or skills, whether railway engine driver or deep-sea diver, was, as usual, quick off the mark: 'Incidentally, did you learn much about the technical side of printing in these provincial outfits?'

'Enough. Just about. A drawback was that the printers were fas-cinated by the novel designs that designers like myself could evolve, using their own everyday raw materials: types, paper and coloured inks. They wanted to learn what one might be able to teach *them*. They were bored by their years with their machines. After I started designing covers for the typographical magazine that took your fancy, James Shand, the publisher-printer – now printing your *Book Col-lector* – begged me to keep away from his works. The designs I set them were far more interesting, demanding and rewarding than daily bread-and-butter set-ups.'

'Why not write a series on the unknown underworlds of Britain's titillating cities?' he suggested, grinning. 'I've finished with the thrill-ing ones.'

'A good title for starters.'

Yet he did find an authentic city perambulator around this time who proved a most sympathetic companion. Lunching John Betje-man at Scott's, discussing a likely feature for *House & Garden*, we were joined by Fleming, who had expressed a wish to meet the poet. They were immediately congenial companions and soon began to share visits to widen their respective interests. Fleming introduced

Betjeman to various vendors of the brass reliefs he collected; Betjeman introduced Fleming to various churches en route to or from those brass-founders and vendors. Their friendship prospered. Later, Betjeman even insisted on reviewing the next Bond novel, which he did, nobly – or was it charitably? Probably both.

Despite his thrilling cities, Fleming strenuously retained his liking for his cottage at St Margaret's Bay and was there for most of his weekends in England.

I drove down to this not-too-distant corner of Kent occasionally. On one trip, I arrived fairly early and was invited to join in some fairly boisterous farewells being staged next door by Noël Coward for some departing American visitors. After this hullabaloo, and their departure, he returned to his sitting room and said: 'Take a pew, Ann, and don't stand there being so standoffish, Mr H.'

'You've met Robert before?' Ann queried, clearly surprised.

'We met a year or so ago in Jamaica. Robert came over to Blue Harbour with Ian. When your husband plunged into the Caribbean depths, doubtless to make contact with some randy young barracuda, we sat on the balcony and destroyed a few reputations.'

Ann laughed, as usual entranced by Coward's vocabulary.

'And today you recalled his name immediately. What a memory, Noël, dear! Infallible.'

'Just the word I would have chosen,' Coward said, plainly enjoying yet another of his beguilingly immodest performances. 'An infallible memory for names. One of the very first lessons that should be instilled into any child at birth. Alas, a responsibility I shan't ever have, but there it is. As my mother told me: "Noël, darling, always remember names – from the regally eminent to the utterly contemptible. One never knows whether one or the other might prove useful one day."'

He was off, well away on another solo afternoon matinee performance. We were enthralled to sit and listen until he broke off to ask after Ann's current metropolitan hostessing involvements and when he would next see her in Victoria Square: 'That decorative annexe to the palace,' he affirmed. And so on and on.

Meanwhile, back in London, my life had become agreeably and deeply involved with glossy journalism. Fleming was a consistently enquiring reader of *House & Garden*, particularly interested in the career of his close friend Loelia Westminster, still frequently undertaking roving excursions for the magazine. I said that she would prove a success in any job that needed drive, energy and charm. Her title doubtless helped, but she was possessed of such rare energy and ebullient zest that the doors of any stately home, modernist semi or clifftop cottage opened to her. I occasionally accompanied her with her latest favourite photographer on these documentations.

Fleming was especially amused to hear of one such visit to the one-time Rothermere rural stately pile, Daylesford, in Gloucestershire, designed by Samuel Pepys Cockerell for Warren Hastings in the late eighteenth century. Fleming had stayed there for three or four Christmas gatherings in the immediate post-war years during Ann's marriage to Rothermere. He recalled that he had found the house incomparably cold and intimidating. Only adulterous sex had inveighed him there, he asserted. He had heard that Esmond had since spent vast sums in transforming the house under the direction of John Fowler.

I recalled for him how Loelia had marched into the house, sweeping past the butler, saying in tones not to be gainsaid: 'Now where does Esmond keep his drinks?' She had crossed immediately and unerringly to the relevant sideboard. Out came the drinks and tumblers. She had also arranged with Rothermere that we would be lunched there. Highly agreeable provender was speedily forthcoming and speedily despatched, for Loelia was a professional to her fingertips and the photographer was about his tasks well within the hour.

'So she really knows her stuff?' Fleming murmured, clearly amused and somewhat surprised by this first-hand report.

'She knew Fowler would have made the house into a superb showpiece and she was determined to get the first documentation.'

'I seem to recall that Ann got Fowler going on the job. Left to his own parsimonious ways, Esmond would never have spent that kind of money on Daylesford or anywhere else – not even on Warwick House. Did you explore the grounds?'

'In a brief escape from Loelia's dominatrix display, I took off for a glance at the orangery and the lake. All very touching as I wandered round and thought that Ann had sacrificed all this and Warwick House for you.'

'She got Goldeneye in exchange, but she now even spurns what she terms my "tropical bolthole". Meanwhile, her London life escalates and escalates. That's all that really matters to her,' he concluded glumly. 'She crowds almost as many guests into Victoria Square as she did into Warwick House.'

'And you wander upstairs?'

'I can't stand her parties. Less still the sight of that melon-faced Connolly holding forth. Anyway, you've been to one or two yourself. You know the scene well enough.'

'I prefer our *Book Collector* lunches and the criss-cross gossip of the owner and the editor.'

'Well said.'

He was back to familiar evocations. Those luncheons were among his favourite escapes. Neither of us was a dedicated diner-outer or host-within.

Oddly, the occasional dinner party at Send Grove rivalled the repasts at Victoria Square. Loelia invested her supper parties with rare vivacity, exercising her talent for social mixing: Malcolm Muggeridge seeking to impose his bogus leftism on all and sundry; his upper-crust friend Lady Pam Berry, daughter of the legendary F. E. Smith, the first Lord Birkenhead, easily overriding his assertions with her highly articulate right-wing convictions; John Fowler seeking to explain the sense and sensibility of his passion for English 'muddy' tones to the engrossed listeners around him…

Inevitably, I occasionally speculated on the untold differences that

Ann must have experienced between life in Warwick House and in Victoria Square, a move beyond belief for a seemingly sane woman to make. Few women can have experienced two such domestic polarities in their middle years: a vast mansion overlooking Green Park plus all necessary staff at the press of a button, and a three-bedroom Regency house in a tucked-away London square. Yet her social life seemed to burgeon rather than diminish in Victoria Square. Luncheons and dinner-cum-supper parties proliferated and she quite clearly enjoyed demonstrating her talents as a hostess in her L-shaped first-floor drawing room.

In this room I had my last meeting with Waugh. I had arrived at Victoria Square to escort Ann, having invited her to lunch in the senior common room at the Royal College of Art, of which I was then a member. Waugh had arrived half an hour before my arrival. Fleming had just returned from a trip to one of his non-thrilling cities. The house had been plunged into something of a melee by his return. Ann went upstairs to say a few solicitous words to him while he took a bath and she took her pleasure.

As Waugh seemed to be staying on, I asked whether he would care to come with Ann and I for luncheon at the RCA.

'What's the food like?' he asked without preamble.

'Quite reasonable as common room food goes. Nothing special but nothing awful.'

'And the wine?'

'With Ted Ardizzone's help, Darwin is slowly converting his ever-growing staff of professors and tutors from beer-swillers to wine-bibbers. Uphill work, but he seems to be winning. So that should be all right. But why the quiz?'

'I come to London so rarely that I have to do my best to get some decent food and drink while I'm here. I can look after the wine at home but the food is invariably awful!'

As is your connubial loyalty, I thought, but, nevertheless, found the remark quite funny. 'Why not take a chance and come with us to give the RCA chef and your own demanding appetite the benefit of your doubts?' I suggested.

He came.

In the taxi, mildly masochistic as ever, Ann said: 'Phoebe would never have left you in the bath as brusquely as I've left Ian if you'd just returned from distant places, would she, Robert?'

I murmured an evasive *humph*.

She turned to Waugh: 'And Laura would never have left you just like that, would she, Evelyn?'

Waugh gravely considered the query before pronouncing judgement. 'I once returned – admittedly somewhat unexpectedly, from Patagonia, I recall – only to learn that Laura was in the garden. I was *extremely* annoyed.'

Ann laughed guardedly; myself immoderately. Apart from a demonic gleam in his eyes, Waugh retained his magisterial mien, with the remotest glimmer of a smile. Ann, realising that he was in light-hearted mood, echoed my laughter and said how glad she was that he was coming with us to South Ken.

Waugh clearly enjoyed lunching at the college, especially after Hugh Casson joined us at the table. He was especially appreciative of Casson's quip that a literary acquaintance, an ex-pat living in the Dordogne, had recently asserted that most of the boys of sixteen or so in that part of France were unduly proud of their three especial possessions: a moustache, a mistress and a hoop.

Waugh offered another of his caustic comments after my suggestion to Ann that Ian should have vaulted from his bath and joined us here, adding: 'Isn't he now a member of the council of this very same Royal College of Art?'

'I didn't give it a thought,' she replied.

'Very rightly, too,' Waugh concurred. 'But is it true?'

'Of course it's true,' Ann said. 'Don't forget, Ian and Darwin coincided at Eton.'

'Ah, but of course,' Waugh said. 'Triumphant English factors. No matter that Ian has never bought a painting or drawing in his life. I wonder how much boyhood schooling counts in France towards being invited to accept a similar eminence in the hierarchy of l'École nationale supérieure des Beaux-Arts.'

He rattled out his quip with authoritative intonation.

'Now, now Evelyn. No venom,' Ann said, thoroughly enjoying the quip, along with Casson and I.

The meal went with a swing and Waugh was even prepared to venture his opinion that the food was 'extremely and even surprisingly pleasant' and he had thoroughly enjoyed his visit.

At a rendezvous with Fleming a couple of days later, I mentioned Waugh's obvious enjoyment of the RCA luncheon, omitting reference to his comment concerning Fleming's Council membership. I then learned – not to my great surprise – that Ann had already regaled him with the tale.

With his usual unexpected twist, Fleming thought Waugh had a point, so why not voice it?

I suggested that Waugh probably spent too much time at home in the country. He clearly needed more frequent metropolitan encounters to air his incomparable rancours.

'He hates the time he spends at Piers Court,' Fleming growled in saturnine agreement. 'He even calls the place "Stinkers". He hates the house, hates the food and, I even suspect, he hates his family.'

Recalling Waugh's remarks about his home life, I decided that the grimmer moods of both men probably derived from their domestic circumstances, from their marital links, their bibulous intakes and their steady declines from the sound health each had enjoyed in his twenties. My oddest thought was that both men would have been prepared to assert that they enjoyed the company of women, but that neither wished to have a woman on the equal terms on which they held their male friends. Odd, but very English, I decided.

CHAPTER 27

LEGAL AND LOCALE DEFEATS

The space allotted by newspapers to the personal triumphs of eminent politicians, tycoons, sportsmen and the rest rarely equals the space allotted to their disasters. As Fleming discovered.

He had to face this dreary truism in the late '50s when Bond's growing fame seemed likely to be grievously halted by what he contended was the most ignominious situation in which he had ever been involved – the serio-comic, golden-oldie, eternal triangle battle between the Indian wife of an antique British aristocrat and Fleming's mother, Mrs Eve Fleming – or Mrs Valentine Fleming, depending on mood or audience.

As I have noted earlier, Mrs Valentine Fleming was an outsize snob, and had no wish to figure in any sensational front-page matrimonial squabble. For starters, a sizeable pension from her husband's will would have been jeopardised by remarriage. Nevertheless, she had long yearned for a title, retaining the firm belief that had her banker-husband not been killed, he would have been knighted in due course. In pursuit of this elusive bauble she had become fleetingly engaged in 1951 to the 16th Marquess of Winchester but opted out after those monetary complications had been revealed to her. Yet she still coveted the title. Even after Bapsybanoo Pavry had married the marquess in the following year, Mrs Fleming retained her grip on the old boy, inviting him to her home in Nassau while Bapsy was wintering in India.

Then followed a venomous legal contest, the marchioness accusing enticement of her husband by Mrs Fleming. Two years on, the case seemed to have ended in a fairly waspish stalemate with both women assuring the judge that they would keep well apart. Then, however, Bapsy was once again accusing her adversary of venom and jealousy. She won her case but on Mrs Fleming's appeal in 1957 this decision was reversed and the appellant, surprisingly, was even given custody of the Marquess until his death. He achieved that destiny – as a centenarian – in 1962, at the Hotel Metropole in Monte Carlo. But no title had come the way of Mrs Fleming.

How Mrs Val managed her extraordinary legal triumph, nobody seemed to know. Fleming certainly didn't; neither did he want to know. Bapsy, however, might well have seemed the final realistic winner, for she lived on for some thirty years after the deaths of her husband and her rival.

For her triumphant final appearance at the law courts, following the close of this protracted and undignified squabble, Mrs Fleming had made sure that she would be photographed flanked by her two newsworthy literary sons, Peter and Ian, authors of differing but eminent renowns. Richard, the third brother, seems to have been omitted from this presentation, despite his attendance at the court. The photograph appeared throughout the press. Fleming confessed that this was the most demeaning photographic session in which he had been involved, especially as the pictures were given wide news coverage.

He sought to translate this farcical photographic side of the trial into a sick joke. 'A trio for the tabloids,' he captioned the picture, but he was clearly vastly relieved that his two-day notoriety enjoyed scant longevity against the ever-growing Bond legend.

Nevertheless, he deemed that that kind of publicity was a drawback to him in both his literary and social lives. He preferred the levities of fame. For instance, he had recently been introduced to a dozen guests at a dinner party in New York as 'creator of the most thrilling hero in the fiction of our time'.

'A trifle far-fetched,' Fleming admitted back in London, 'but guaranteed to set any writer up for his next few working days.'

This reaction, somewhat tongue-in-cheek, was at odds with a private pronouncement of his own. 'Bond's a bore,' he had suddenly affirmed as we lunched. 'The discovery's been creeping up on me for some time and now I know it's true. I don't know what I shall do with him.'

'I forecast that you'll keep him *and* the shekels and carry on investing the winnings,' I said. 'The royalties will still be rolling in for several decades. Does Ann consult your royalty returns, by the way?'

'She doesn't get a chance.'

'I shouldn't bank on it. Ann's got friends in both high, low and odd places – as you well know.'

'Only too well,' he near groaned.

Far more debilitating, even destructive, than the Bapsy case, however, was another legal tussle, which persisted posthumously for the Fleming estate. Bryce and Fleming were sued by their one-time friend Kevin McClory, contending that, in his novel *Thunderball*, Fleming had plagiarised several of McClory's original ideas. The two friends lost the case, which cost Bryce a slice of his wife's formidable fortune and Fleming an impressive slice of his accumulating wealth. More poignantly for his friends, the case undoubtedly dented his life expectancy. Within a month following the decision he had a serious heart attack during an editorial meeting at the *Sunday Times*. Fleming was no longer foreign manager of the *Sunday Times*, but, after buying the Kemsley newspapers, Thomson had taken a shine to Fleming and requested his continued presence at the paper's weekly news conferences, continuing to pay him a very civil retainer.

Following this sudden shock, Fleming was admitted to The London Clinic and, on release, convalesced, fairly unconventionally, between Brighton and France.

Returning from this dubious convalescence to a more-or-less restful daily round, he telephoned to ask whether I would take a trip with him to look over a Wiltshire house that Ann was determined they should buy. Indeed, she was already referring to the house as Sevenhampton, the name she proposed to replace the existing title: Warneford Place.

'Fairly near Faringdon and Buscot, her wartime boltholes in Oxfordshire. The locality where you first met each other,' Fleming said.

I agreed to make the trip. Our starting point was Victoria Square. I crossed from Victoria station and within five minutes was climbing into the open Thunderbird. 'But why another house?' I asked early en route. 'You've already got Goldeneye for Jamaica, Victoria Square for London, and St Margaret's Bay for golf and Noël Coward. And haven't you got some place in the wilds of Kent: the Old Palace at Backbone or some such?'

'B-E-K-E-S-B-O-U-R-N-E,' he spelled out. 'An outpost of the archbishops of Canterbury in the old days. Ann bought it and now says I did – to be near golf and Sandwich. Damn lie.'

'Is would-be Sevenhampton another old palace?'

'More or less.'

'What brought Ann down to these parts?'

'Tipped off by the Faringdon outfit. They want her as a neighbour.'

'What about your golf?'

'Finito if we get there. Somehow, I've got to scotch the whole bloody prospect.'

I laughed but he was serious. 'You found us the practical London house we needed and one we would never have found for ourselves. That's why I need you to come on this trip. Your views may dissuade

Ann from what threatens to be another disastrous encumbrance, domestically and financially, for that's what it will be.'

'Does Ann have any outstanding reason for moving on? Is Victoria Square too small for Caspar and nanny? Are they also too often in the way at St Margaret's Bay?'

'She cites those as overwhelming reasons for getting this house.'

'Perhaps she wants to see more of her husband in a cosy setting.'

'Balls! Well, let's press on and you can see and judge for yourself.'

I was persistent. 'Do you really know what kind of country house you really want, starting with the premise, of course, that you really don't need one at all with St Margaret's Bay?'

He laughed. 'That's true. Back to your old theme: Need or supply? Partner or popsy? Mistress or housewife?'

'Well, for starters, how many bedrooms d'you need?'

'I'd say five. Perhaps six. Ann wants eight minimum.'

'How many has this place got?'

'Ann's keeping pretty quiet about the size of the damn place, but I've heard a whisper it's got over thirty bedrooms, three bathrooms and only one ballroom.'

I laughed. 'Ann will like that. But will one ballroom be enough?'

'Barely! God knows what she'd do if she gets the place.'

'Is the place period or modern?'

'Period, basically. God knows when since. Dammit, you didn't ask these questions before finding us Victoria Square. Just find every drawback and disadvantage in this monstrous intrusion into my life and all will be well.'

During his visit to our home in rural Surrey, Fleming had been impressed by the eighteenth-century gothic elevations and windows and, above all, the practical comfort of the sitting rooms, study and seven bedrooms. Ann had also visited us one Sunday afternoon during the previous summer, bringing with her a close friend of Princess Margaret's, much in the news at the time. She, too, had been delighted by the house, favouring its practicality and, above all else, its secluded setting. Why then, I puzzled, did she want to take on the kind of place Fleming had outlined?

'If you can daunt her quest you'd better concentrate on Georgian or early Victorian rectories, with the emphasis on "early". Those holy practitioners knew how to provide themselves with cosy homesteads.'

'Well, get weaving then: it's a race against time. Daunt the damned woman. But why this passion for rectories?'

'A special breed of house. Comfort and convenience clearly came first for these clerics. A large entrance hall for parishioners awaiting guidance to the Holy Man, all seated on fairly comfortless chairs, doubtless to underline the expected brevity of their visit. Adequate drawing room and dining room for keeping in touch with the local gentry. Plus a fair-sized kitchen as these clerics all seem to have had outsize appetites. Plus suitable bedrooms for themselves. Plus attics for the staff.'

He laughed. 'Enough of the Pevsner–Betjeman stuff. Just destroy this place and if we must have more room, find us a rectory like your own.'

'How long have I got for dislocating Sevenhampton?'

'Damn little. About a week at the outside. Ann's blood is really up.'

'Right, I'll cry "Stop!" if I see a likely rectory en route.'

He grinned and drove on.

That journey to the west was enlivened by further discussion on a subject I had begun to find engrossing and mystifying. This seemed an opportune occasion to air the matter. I was interested to discover whether Fleming had anything to say on a subject which was beginning to prove one of the doubtless predictable but mildly incomprehensible spin-offs from the Bond adventures. This was the emergence of claimants who asserted that they had been the originals for the heroic figure of Fleming's Bond. The first was Merlin Minshall, an RNVR officer who had been involved in various hopeful but blunted undercover exercises in the Danube area in the earlier months of the war. Another was Fitzroy Maclean, who had had an adventurous war in the Middle East and, rather to Fleming's disappointment, had enjoyed considerable success with his book *Eastern Approaches*. Maclean, rather skilfully, let the rumour that he was probably the prototype for Bond grow into a persistent legend. There were others wishful to identify with the growing legend. I would have named half-a-dozen others.

Such claims were inevitable, Fleming said. He was amused by my reference to two of the foremost claimants.

'Amazing the number of characters who want to leave something akin to a legend after they snuff it. Perhaps I'd better set about fostering a notion that Bond was essentially based on a few personal heroics.'

'You'd better hire a press agent forthwith.'

'Too late. Too late,' he said. Not without a touch of regret, I thought.

Some thirty years after Fleming's death, another claimant to the Bond legend was one Patrick Job, who, in an interview with a *Daily Mirror* journalist, built up an impressive dossier identifying himself as the inspiration for Bond. I found this a somewhat improbable possibility as Job had been scarcely known to Fleming, despite his membership of 30AU. Fleming's contact with the unit was almost exclusively via Curtis. At various times I met all three men: Minshall in London, Maclean in Alexandria and Job when we were both involved in 30AU operations.

The truth, of course, was (and is) that Bond was a Fleming alter ego, rescued from the dream world of his boyhood and early manhood. Had he wanted living models for his invention he could have found them in two of his naval contemporaries: Captain Alan Hillgarth RN and Commander Wilfred Dunderdale RN. Both had been deeply involved in pre-war undercover intelligence operations of bizarre and potentially deadly order. Both had engrossing tales to tell without reference to Bond.

My broaching the subject en route had been prompted by yet another recent newspaper feature: 'Who was the prototype for James Bond?'

'Surely you're the original for Bond?' I queried, having introduced the subject.

'We all have our dreams from boyhood on,' he said. 'And one can always borrow from the more unbelievable adventures by members of 30AU, which one was constantly taking for granted.'

'True enough. Some of those should be recorded and stored in appropriate museum reference rooms.'

'Including those on the Walter Mitty level?' Fleming queried.

'Don't become dismissive. Surely you've had your own dreams of grandeur and glory?'

'Not of the Bond and/or spy-wins-all variety. What were your own dreams of glory?'

'Far from battlefields or ocean waves. In earlier days I certainly indulged in the occasional dream of having my own private press. Not much more than that. I've found my daily round quite agreeable and acceptable. Especially nowadays, and probably likely to continue into my days of alleged maturity. Anyway, have your heroic ambitions been far higher than mine?'

'There's probably a grain of truth in that,' he granted, but switched: 'What about women?'

I was also willing to switch: 'I think women are invariably prepared to be more adventurous than men, although most start life with far more financial and career obstacles than men. You could start with that stalwart Swiss girl your brother's written about.'

'Ah, Maillart. You've got a point there, for women as the more courageous, competent, clever, cool-headed sex. Now, let's forget Bond, and even women, and get back to rectories. The first requirement being to find one within a week, as I said.'

Further exchanges, mostly concerning Bond and the possibility of a new home kept us busy until our destination.

The house was near the village of Highworth, a few miles from Swindon. Fleming seemed to know the way with no call for any map-reading from myself. Within a couple of hours from London he had brought us smoothly to a large empty house with unappealing elevations and a gruesomely intimidating mud-ridden approach.

An agent awaited us.

The house, allegedly Jacobean, had seen a full measure of would-be updating through the decades. We faced a mix of elevations from early brickwork to pseudo-Georgian with round-headed windows. The main feature of the façade was an emphatic square portico, approached via a dozen steps of a somewhat woebegone *piano nobile*. Visually quite effective. Unfortunately and surprisingly, the front door did not open into a spacious entry hall, as I had expected, but straight into a sitting room as in a semi-detached suburban villa.

We went over the house fairly comprehensively. Moving around, I became increasingly depressed. The house clearly had possibilities for an eccentric multimillionaire prepared to give carte blanche to a latter-day traditionalist of the eminence of Francis Johnson or Raymond Erith, but preposterously large for a family of three plus domestic help, and certainly no home for anyone in dodgy health and still convinced that he needed to watch his pennies and his footsteps.

Fleming clearly shared my misgivings as we proceeded slowly around the interiors.

Our own rectory had needed quite substantial alterations to restore the house to its original, compact, late eighteenth-century elevations, but these were straightforward structural changes. Warneford Place was a far older, larger and infinitely more complex structure to reduce to agreeable proportions, and likely to demand far more attention and cash than Fleming would wish to provide for such a gloom-ridden scheme. Above all, I judged, he was physically incapable of managing such a project.

I made two or three sketches in a small pocketbook. These pencilled scribbles showed how I thought the house might be made visually more amenable and possibly more comfortable. Normally I enjoy sharing such carefree graphic scribbles with any friend considering such a domestic venture, but that day the experience was without the slightest entertainment value. We were finding our excursion a thoroughly downcasting exercise. Quite clearly, Fleming wished the house razed to the ground. Preferably that afternoon.

I offered him my pocketbook. 'You say you designed Goldeneye, lock, stock and guest rooms? Here's my pad. Have a go.'

But he was too disheartened to join in even that doleful challenge. I could readily read his thoughts as we went outside and sought a step-by-step circuit through the mud.

'Not your scene, surely?' I queried, fairly gently at the end, after our conventional we'll-think-about-it farewells to the agent.

'Not by a million miles or fifty rooms!' he said, feelingly. 'OK as a semi-open prison for geriatrics, but not for me. If Ann persists in her madcap scheme, I'm out. If we have to have something, I'm all for your rectory idea or something akin to a small Cotswold manor house. That's how Ann first described the place she had in mind. Not this archaeological heap. Ideally, I want nothing. Certainly not this damn pile.'

'More Swindon than Stow-on-the-Wold.'

He smiled gloomily. Merriment was far, far off.

He didn't stand a chance, of course. Ann was determined to have the house and within a week or so had paid the deposit and commissioned an Oxford-based architect to undertake the renovation. She plunged into two or three worrying years of formidable outgoings in her determination to convert this vast house into a familial home. I think that the Warneford battle was the most depressing and destructive of the many discordant episodes of their marriage. Fleming undoubtedly regarded this as the most decisive of their conflicts, the defeat of defeats.

His gloom on that return trip was virtually impenetrable. I sought to lighten the mood by offering my gratitude for a copy of his most recent Bond ventures, the sixth: *Dr No*.

'The main point to which I already know the answer is, quite simply, will you read the damn thing?' he barked.

'Already packed for next month's trip to Venice.'

'Far too glib a response!' he said, but grinned. 'Scarcely ideal reading for a trip in a gondola.'

'There's always a deckchair on the quayside.'

'Very funny!'

Having received the early copies of my two war books and post-war novels, Fleming had been quick to return the gesture from the publication of his first Bond, *Casino Royale*, in 1953. Within, scrawled across the opening fly leaf was the mocking message: 'Robert: The first of Balzache's collected works. Ian.' I received further volumes as they were published, with his words within. His last Bond book, *You Only Live Twice*, published in 1964, the year of his death, carried the injunction: 'To Robert. But not to read! From Ian.' I had expressed my annual gratitude for this build-up of a Bond library but omitted to mention that each novel was seized on arrival by one or other of our schoolboy sons.

On his part Fleming lamented that he had not received any of the splendiferous *House & Garden* publications I seemed to be editing. But would the creator of Bond and his suicidal adventures be interested in such titles as the *H&G Book of Cottages, Modern Houses, A Dictionary of Design and Decoration* and so on?

He laughed and said he'd prefer to continue with the novel-for-novel arrangement.

'Little chance!' I said, for I was beginning to find the planning and editing of these books a more entertaining task than scribbling away at fiction, especially as we had even more impressive volumes planned for the near future, including a *History of British Gardening*.

'Oh God!' he groaned. 'To think I inveigled you into publishing for glossy, garden-city Goldilocks!'

'Inveigled!' I scoffed. 'What a myth! I seem to recall I had to push you every inch of the way towards New York, Patcevitch and Condé Nast.'

'True enough,' he said. 'But my technique worked. Did I or did I not reward you with the most rewarding main line of your life's journey so far?'

I laughed. Loudly.

'My thanks and fondest wishes for the immortal Fleming–Bond set-up.'

'Better Bond–Fleming!' he said. 'In much the same way that more members of the world public have probably heard of Shylock than Shakespeare.'

'A good quip, but I doubt its truth.'

And so we pressed on to London and its manifold pleasures after our depressing trip.

I did not visit Warneford Place again. A couple of months later, in one of my fleeting visits to Victoria Square, Ann said she had something interesting to show me and produced her architect's proposed plans for the house. I suspect that she soon realised that my hopefully polite noises indicated scant enthusiasm for what she was about. Despite my abiding passion for period houses, especially those being considered for conversion to family homes by friends, Warneford Place, renamed Sevenhampton House, was, for me, a non-starter in the Country House Stakes: too enclosed in its setting; too wayward in its floor plan; too expensive to convert and maintain.

Several years later, Evelyn Waugh recorded in his diaries that he and his wife, Laura, had visited Sevenhampton House on a two-day visit in 1963, several years after my trip with Fleming. The Waughs had arrived via a cart track after dark, having taken a wrong road. The basic staff arrangements were confirmed by Ann admitting that the butler had only just beaten the Waughs in arriving and entering the house via the dining room, thus confirming the dubious nature of that direct entry to a reception room which I had deprecated those years before. 'The only means of access,' as Waugh touchingly recorded in his journal. But for the Waughs, the full totality of drawbacks of Fleming's country retreat did not appear until the following day. The discomforting and depressing ambience of the house underpinned his view that Ann had spent twice the price demanded for her Sevenhampton House compared with the prices of some far more beguiling houses advertised in *Country Life*.

I certainly agreed with Waugh's views, apart from his use of the word 'twice'. My own estimate was nearer 'four'. Fleming said that Sevenhampton House had proved the whitest of all the white elephants in his life, making Goldeneye the bargain of the century. Later, I learned from Ann that her husband's weekends in the house were always the gloomiest of all his sojourns anywhere. 'As you doubtless prophesied,' she added tartly.

Fleming, indeed, confessed that he hated the house, hated its setting, hated the journey. Above all, he hated the distance – almost 200 miles by road – from his beloved golfing club and its nearby hotel, where all his creature comforts were indulged by an understanding host and staff. Huntercombe and its course was there, of course, but the true 'weekends' he loved were denied him by this extraordinary Warneford whim so determinedly concluded by Ann. As Bryce had affirmed some years earlier, she possessed 'an inflexible will and whim of iron' when set upon a personal course.

Yet the most puzzling aspect of this Sevenhampton venture remained inexplicable. Why had Fleming offered little or no opposition to the project? He would have had sufficient data for a convincing thumbs down: size, costs, distance, lack of amenities, lack of architectural charm of any kind. The reason was, undoubtedly, his physical decline. He was in no state to conduct the warfare that would have been launched and conducted ruthlessly had he refused to buy the place. He was, quite simply, no longer even the shade of the Fleming of Room 39.

Without the slightest doubt, Sevenhampton House should have been included, along with his drinking and smoking, as among the definitive causes of Fleming's comparatively early death. No single feature of the house gave him the slightest pleasure. Looking back, I would place the Flemings' move to Sevenhampton as one of the more gruesome essays in marital sado-masochism I've encountered in this far-from-cosy world. I occasionally speculated upon the possibility that Ann wished to return to the casual grandeur of

Warwick House and thought that Sevenhampton, so near Oxford and some of her up-stage friends in their nearby mansions, might encourage the legend she seemed to be seeking so vigorously: 'Britain's most spectacular hostess.'

CHAPTER 28

FLEMINGS IN *VOGUE*

During the summer of the year I became editor of *House & Garden*, I had met Alex Liberman, Fleming's other close friend in the Condé Nast New York outfit. The first, Ivan Patcevitch, who had, so curiously, sparked off my transition to Condé Nast occasionally visited London and lunched with Fleming, Ann and myself.

Following one of those occasions when he was impatiently waiting for his Homburg at Scott's and then, having tetchily taken it from the waiter and putting it on, Ann said: 'Oh, Pat, I've just realised: you look just like Mr Exeter.' Mrs Exeter was then the highly suitable title given to the well-dressed, middle-aged, upper-crust fashion model portrayed as a regular feature figure in *Vogue*. Patcevitch was not amused. Ann was. I managed to keep a straight face.

Alex Liberman was the art editor of *Vogue* and nominal art editor of all Condé Nast European publications. He never exercised these feudal rights, being an unusually generous-spirited man and far too busy in his own diocese, for he was not only editorial editor, but also art editor, artist, sculptor, author and photographer. His annual escape was to his beloved Ischia. Returning regretfully from these visits he would spend a couple of days in London. He invariably lunched with Fleming. From my first year on I was invited to join them at Scott's.

I liked Liberman from our first meeting. He had unusual editorial tenets of which the rarest was that any authoritative editor should have sufficient graphic talent to be his own art editor and that any first-rate art editor should also be articulate with the written and spoken word and able to edit. I shared his novel views 100 per cent.

He certainly practised his own precepts. Viking, Thames & Hudson and Macmillan had recently published – simultaneously in the US, UK and Canada – his book, *The Artist in His Studio*, a comprehensive survey of the studios and working lives of the major nineteenth-century French artists. Liberman had taken the hundreds of photographs, written the thousands of words for the authoritative text and designed the weighty book and the brilliant dustwrapper.

A couple of years later, lunching with him on a visit to New York, he said: 'Well, we've been talking about Annie and Ian; why don't you write about them? Bond is such a runaway success here that the creator's private life is ready-made for a *Vogue* feature. Parks would be the ideal photographer for such a job. Agreed?'

I agreed, adding that I was pretty certain that Ann and Ian would also agree, and that Norman Parkinson would jump at the chance of such a coup.

'Good, I'll tell Diana,' he said, referring to Diana Vrieland, then the legendary editor of US *Vogue*.

Within a week of Liberman's return home, I received a follow-up note from Allene Talmey of the New York office: 'We are delighted that you are doing the article for us on Ian Fleming: his way of life, anecdotes, his guns, his hobbies, his wife etc., perhaps the food he likes, the menus he likes and so on. (Fleming has always given James Bond such enticing food to eat.)'

Dear Miss Talmey

Ian Fleming has now seen the draft of
the piece and approved about 98%. There
will, therefore, be no need to send him
a further carbon or the proof. I will
make corrections where necessary on the
proof.

I spent an hour or so with Norman
Parkinson at Fleming's house last week.
Parks tells me that he got some good shots.
He certainly put the Flemings through
the hoop.

There is one point I wanted to
mention about the piece. It probably
won't arise, but just in case. This is
a proviso that I should be consulted about
any further rights in U.S.A. And I should
wish to reserve the right to let the London
Sunday Times reprint it in England, say,
two months after you use it, if Vogue London
don't want it. You may not know but I
am fairly closely involved with the Sunday
Times here and I should like them to have
a bite at it if they wish to.

Robert Harling
EDITOR

Miss Arlene Talmey
NEW YORK OFFICE.
April 30th 1963

In this casual manner I came to write quite a lengthy piece which was published for American *Vogue* in September 1963. For the US feature, Liberman's commissioning of Norman Parkinson was a triumph. This tall, elegant, assured and exuberantly extrovert sophisticate had also bought a Caribbean retreat – in Tobago. This Caribbean connection certainly encouraged a good deal of reminiscing with Fleming following Parkinson's arrival at Victoria Square.

Thanks to many years devoted to the documentation of catwalk beauties, Parkinson excelled in unusual portraiture. His portraits of the Flemings were first-rate character studies. Fleming was shown with his nose almost sniffing the weapon he held before him – a Ruger Blackhawk: 44 Magnum, then and possibly still the most powerful handgun in the world. Ann was shown in an armchair, confirming the caption as 'dark, handsome, highly strung', but here looking supremely relaxed and upper-crust.

Beatrix Miller, editor of British *Vogue* was keen on the feature and it was published in the UK a couple of months later. She preferred to rely on some excellent photographs by Cecil Beaton and others, but the Parkinson set clearly won the day for novelty and surprise, plus the approval of the subjects, both of whom, reassuringly for the scribe, also approved the text, shown to them before publication and returned with not a single suggested alteration.

Here follows the text of that feature published in both US and UK *Vogue*. The US version was headed 'The Ian Flemings'; the British version 'The Ian Fleming Legend'. Each carried a similar sub-head stating that the piece was 'concerned with the improbably domestic background ("backdrop" in the US version) of the author of the world's most successful spy stories ("thrillers" in the US)'. Such are the subtleties of sub-editors.

Needless to add, Fleming expressed both surprise and delight on the oddity of these two leading fashion glossies becoming interested in Bond and his popsies.

Here, then, is the English version:

THE IAN FLEMING LEGEND

During the war, Ian Fleming, as personal assistant to the director of naval intelligence, fathered and was put in charge of one of those private 'armies' apparently inseparable from modern war, although Hannibal was doubtless plagued by them; Nelson, too. This unit, of which I was a member, was known generally as 30AU, more formally as Number Thirty Assault Unit, and finally, as Number Thirty Advance Unit, and was organised as a result of the direful experiences of the British in the battle for Crete, when a similar German unit captured valuable British secret material. The British, always ready to learn, however late, decided to copy this rewarding notion. Fleming maintained close control over 30AU, a necessary procedure, for members of the unit sometimes seemed to think that the war was being waged for their particular entertainment.

On one of Fleming's visits to the unit, in company with his chief, Rushbrooke, permission for 30AU to operate with American advance troops under General Patton's command was suddenly deemed necessary. Off we went. Patton was in one of his more histrionic moods. Like Garrick playing Hotspur he strode before us, explaining how he would pip the Allied Commanders to Berlin. Later, over our K rations, under an intoxicating euphrasy induced partly by Patton and partly by Calvados, when the end of the war seemed imminent, I asked Fleming what he would then do. He replied simply and grandiloquently: 'I shall write the spy story to end all spy stories.'

I thought this was a bit steep but let it go.

Nobody, of course, had better grounding for the task. Before the war he had worked as a special correspondent for Reuters and *The Times*. He had served under two directors of naval intelligence. He had taught himself to write a spare and simple prose. Above all, he knew how fictionally preposterous are the true espionage stories. Altogether, a reasonably factual springboard later for his own brand of fantasy.

But all this was long ago. Twenty years. And the James Bond books didn't start appearing until ten years later. By then he was doing a fair-sized job as foreign manager of the *Sunday Times* and other newspapers. In between he got married and that was a fair-sized job, too. As Fleming is, in spite of physical vigour and other outward appearances, a somewhat idle fellow, these, allied with his other activities, all helped to postpone the Bond saga.

He published *Casino Royale* in 1953, its successors at yearly intervals. The demand for them is apparently insatiable and worldwide.

In the course of this melodrama of success, Fleming has changed very little – physically, mentally, and all the rest. He has put on a few pounds and slowed down a few steps, but he remains what he was, a tallish man with black hair, now touched by grey, above a dark-skinned, strong-featured, deep-lined face. His eyes are blue and of a sharp and gay intensity. When moody or broody, he can look somewhat sombre and threatening but the mood soon goes. Merriment will out.

He dresses well but simply. Navy-blue suits, heavy in winter, lightweight in summer. Blue shirts, black-and-white spotted bow tie, very occasionally a striped club tie. His suits and shirts are made, his casual shoes – he eschews buttons and laces – bought off the rack. In common with most Englishmen, he hates shopping and always seems mildly intimidated by salesmen, whether in gunsmith's or shoe shops. At weekends, he exchanges these scarcely formal London clothes for a simple wardrobe of pullovers, hound-tooth tweed trousers, and leather casuals. He is no fancy dresser, but is interested in his clothes and even more interested, perhaps, in the clothes of his friends, especially when touched by any dash of eccentricity. Being a direct man by nature, he is prepared to point out these oddities. 'Why that high-buttoned Italian jacket?' he will say. 'Carrying a gun or bicycle chain?'

During his brief sojourns in winter in London, he adds a fairly exotic black-and-white check tweed overcoat to his outdoor accoutrements, but almost always carries his hat, a battered soft black felt, which, when worn in a sudden shower, is seen to be a sinister rakish headpiece that would arouse George Raft's envy.

Because the minutiae of the so-called sophisticated manner seem to preoccupy Fleming in all his books, many critics have accused him of snobbery of a fairly material order, but Fleming is incapable of the self-conscious imprisoning dedication needed for snobbery. He doubtless has his personal alleyways of snobbery (who hasn't?), but they would take a lot of unravelling and are not very obvious. In any case, leanings towards snobbery are usually attributes of those lacking in self-confidence or vitality (not always related qualities) and Fleming has an abundance of nervous vitality and is, above all, natural in his dealings with all, friends, enemies, bores and nobodies. His voice is straightforward, English, unaffected. So, too, is his laughter. So, too, is his genial disregard for other people's feelings. Scarcely the ideal equipment in any approach to snobbery.

The interest of James Bond in the subtleties of food, wines, fun, cars and the other material oddments of the high life, with which his critics make much play, are not stressed in Fleming's own existence. His breakfast is based upon good coffee and honey. The honey is Norwegian, which may sound esoteric but is not: he simply regards this Scandinavian variety as the best for his palate. His favourite midday meal in his favourite restaurant, Scott's at Piccadilly Circus, starts with a large Martini followed by a dozen Colchester oysters (which he prefers because they are the biggest and best) plus a Guinness, followed by a Scotch woodcock. On a fiendishly wintry day he will be likely to choose steak, kidney, and oyster pudding – quite a dish. He has no sweet tooth, rarely tastes cheese, and, like most heavy smokers, is no trencherman, despite the fact that his housekeeper, Mrs Crickmere, is one of the best cooks in London. Fleming is no wine drinker either. He prefers Martinis midday and, in the evening, fairly stiff potions of brandy and ginger ale or, not the drink of his forefathers, Scotch, but bourbon and water.

He has always been interested in motorcars, personally and generally. Before the war he had a deep regard for the Invicta (now no longer made) and the Le Mans Bentley models. He has been through a tidy post-war collection. At first, they were British models, and even, for one day, a Daimler, but on his wife's flick-knife remark that he looked rather like the late Queen Mary inside it, he swapped it forthwith for a racier model and has stayed racy ever since.

He has written at length about his passion for guns. This derives partly from schoolboy hangover stuff, and partly because he has enormous respect for all beautiful handmade objects, whether simple-seeming but complex steely mechanisms made to kill or enamelled golden Faberge objects made to captivate.

Part of the recondite expertise which he provides in his books and which drives his critics into apoplexy derives from his deep foraging interest in other people's offbeat jobs. He will dig relentlessly away at the professional know-how of gunsmith, wrestler, geisha girl, engine driver, deep-sea diver, croupier, matrimonial agent, tightrope walker, or steeplejack. And as almost anybody will willingly talk about his job, Fleming always gets his data.

He cannot bear to be bored. He likes companionship – on his terms. In spite of his obvious attraction to and for women, he prefers the company of men. He has an enormously juvenile sense of humour, and takes delight in bizarre tales with prosaic endings or *vice versa*, especially if the tales are of happenings to his friends.

Fleming loves his friends dearly, particularly if they make no demands upon him. A reasonable request, for he makes no demands on them, apart from a hope of entertainment, and of this he gives as good as he gets. He keeps his disparate friends away from each other and they rarely meet. He has, say, a couple of friends in each of his several worlds: golf, journalism, gambling, Boodles, publishing, finance. He spaces out his luncheons with them so that neither side is bored by too frequent a rendezvous. These meals and their pre-planning are important to him, though in general he prefers to eat alone. So, too, is the spacing-out and distance-keeping, for, although to his friends he is a warm-hearted man, he has a hard-rock reserve, a fairly formidable seam reached pretty early on in acquaintance.

Like most of us he has a yearning for affection, yet, like most Englishmen – or Scotsmen – of his kind, is ill fitted by upbringing and habit to acquire the technique of affection-getting which, after all, is basically a reflex of affection-giving. The English upper crust wants and needs affection as deeply as any other crust, but impulses towards this important emotional release are frequently stifled for them at about the age of eight when boys go away to boarding school. Affection by letter and postcard is as broken-backed as most emotions by proxy. The boys grow up, professing to hate what they so need. Hence the undertones of sadism and masochism so frequent among British males. Hence, perhaps, those passages in the Bond books which have provoked such bitter attacks.

The imprisonment of the emotions is gradually being dismantled in Britain, but it gripped Fleming's generation in steely handcuffs. Yet because emotion cannot be wholly buried in print and must out somewhere, somehow, Fleming's temper is occasionally explosively violent.

His interests are basically *mouvementés*. He was an athlete at school and in early manhood and still retains his interest in sport. He was a partner of Donald Healey, one of England's more enterprising racing-car drivers before the Second World War. He has climbed and skied and sailed, but his first love was golf and remains so. This respect for physical achievement is reflected in

his continuing capacity for hero worship. He started by hero wor-
shipping his elder brother, Peter, a scholarly explorer-reporter.
He continues to admire men who excel in games of endurance:
Cousteau, the deep-sea explorer; Bannister, the first four-minute
miler; Peter Thomson, the golfer; Heinrich Harrer, the seven-
years-in-Tibet man.

Yet he has interests far off from the sporting and strenuous life.
I met him because of his interest in the complexities of typography,
my own absorbing hobby, and I have travelled with him into one
of the more derelict purlieus of London to track down brass reliefs
of mythological gods and goddesses – he has the finest collection
of brass pictures in England. He has similarly wandered with John
Betjeman to inspect some of the lesser masterpieces of London's
ecclesiastical architecture. He formed, with the help of Percy Muir,
one of the most notable and knowledgeable of English book dealers,
a remarkable collection of books on milestones in original thought
through the great revolutionary periods from the end of the eighteenth century. His wide and unique collection includes such rarities
as first editions of Darwin's *Origin of Species*; Einstein's basic paper
on the theory of relativity; Helmholtz's monograph on the ophthal-
moscope; Lenin's 'What Is To Be Done?'.

Muir, a long-time friend, vividly remembers Fleming's succinct
instructions: 'You get the collection going. I'll buy it, book by book,
but I'm not very keen to do overmuch work on it myself.' Fleming kept to his side of the bargain without going back one whit
on his word, Muir warmly said. The collection was valued some
years ago by John Carter, the bibliographical pundit of Sotheby's,
at many thousands of pounds. He prefers the books. Another of
his side interests is his ownership of *The Book Collector*, perhaps
the world's most erudite bibliographic journal, edited by John
Hayward. Fleming has kept this magazine alive through thick and
thin, and cosseted the journal into its present valuable authority
and financial stability.

Fleming married in his early forties. This fact should not be taken to indicate either a lack of interest in women or a predilection for the celibate life. He had known many women, but had managed to elude them. As someone said: 'Ian is like a handful of seawater; he slips away through your fingers – even while you're watching.' Perhaps the girls were too undemanding, for when Fleming did marry it was only after a period of shattering personal complexities and tensions for himself and his wife, experiences which would have meant nervous breakdowns for lesser combatants.

Ann Fleming (née Charteris) was first married to Lord O'Neill (who was killed in the war in 1944), then to Lord Rothermere, from whom she was divorced in 1952. She married Fleming immediately she was free. As a simple 'esquire' he remained unperturbed following these resounding titles, but promised his wife that if he ever become ennobled he would choose as his title 'Lord SW1', the London postal district in which he lives.

Ann Fleming (known as 'Annie' to her friends) is a slim, dark, handsome, highly strung, iconoclastic creature of middle height with a fine pair of flashpoint eyes. She has something of the air of an imperious gypsy, and I have always thought that long, multi-coloured flouncing skirts would become her even more than those of more modish length. Suitably attired, she would, seated on the steps of a caravan, have made a magnificent addition to the late Augustus John's paintings of the Romany folk.

A woman of clear-cut views, Ann Fleming provokes extreme reactions as a wasp provokes panic. Her friends adore her. Others, intimidated by what they consider to be her ruthless vitality and unequivocal views on this or that, are more reserved in their response. She is certainly more interested in men than women, although she does have a few fairly close women friends, notably Lady Avon (wife of the former Sir Anthony Eden), Lady Diana Duff Cooper, and Loelia Duchess of Westminster. But her main friendships are with men, or possibly with the minds of men, and she retains a bright schoolgirl's undue respect for academic distinction of political achievement. Thus her closest friends include Somerset Maugham, novelist; Evelyn Waugh, novelist; Sir Isaiah Berlin, philosopher; Sir Maurice Bowra, classical scholar; Sir Frederick Ashton, choreographer; Cecil Beaton, artist et al.; Malcolm Muggeridge, most ruthless of commentators; Noël Coward, playwright and songbird; Randolph Churchill, controversialist; Lucian Freud, artist grandson of Sigmund; Peter Quenell, poet and historian; Cyril Connolly, critic and wit. And so on and on. The list is lengthy and formidable. All these men delight in her company, savouring the occasional sharp edge of her tongue, but, even more, her talent for provoking others to dispute.

Perhaps somewhat inevitably, with these intellectual predilections and companionships, Ann Fleming has taken a mildly dyspeptic view of her husband's runaway success with his controversial thrillers. 'These dreadful Bond books,' she has called them publicly, and there is no doubt she would swap a thousand James Bonds for one Stephen Dedalus.

The Flemings started their marriage in a large Chelsea flat overlooking the River Thames, a far cry from his discreet bachelor mews house in Mayfair and her own in one of London's largest mansions, Warwick House, Lord Rothermere's house, overlooking Green Park. The large flat, with its sometimes gay but more often melancholy outlook over the wide grey river, didn't suit Ann Fleming's mood or manner and they soon moved to a small Regency, cream-stuccoed house in London's smallest square, about 100 yards from the riding school of Buckingham Palace. The house is a particularly pleasant example of English urban architecture, probably even better adapted for living in today than when it was built.

Within, the house has a warm, welcoming, carefree air, resulting from a skilfully casual arrangement of comfortable chairs and

sofas, Regency furniture with a profusion of brass inlay, Fleming's black Wedgwood busts, multitudinous books and a highly
individual collection of pictures, including paintings by Augustus John, Lucian Freud, Victorian lesser masters and, of course,
brass pictures of flighty goddesses and martial heroes.

This doll's house has a bowed dining room that seats eight in comfort but must frequently take a willing dozen in diminished comfort,
for Ann Fleming is perhaps the most naturally gifted and successful
hostess in London, a position due chiefly to her own high vivacity
allied with a simple belief that the perfect recipe for an entertaining
evening meal is well-chosen, well-cooked food, good wines, and a
group of egomaniacal talkers with diametrically (or, even better,
diabolically) opposed philosophies. The results are noise fierce,
and memorable. Fleming is rarely present at these dinner parties
(or *gabfests*, as he terms them) which are likely to take place at the
rate of a couple a week in the season. Forewarned is forearmed, he
claims, and at the appropriate moment, he is more likely to be settled in at the Portland Club, temple of gastronomy and the game
of bridge, playing an expensive game with reasonable responsive
results, than sitting at his own dining table. Returning at midnight,
he is likely to find his wife's guests still at table, still embattled in
high-voiced political diatribe, abuse and argument. Fleming, waving not too demonstrative a greeting, proceeds upstairs to his own
room and comparative tranquillity.

Occasionally, he openly pines for a quiet little mouse of a wife
who might worshipfully await his evening arrival with carpet slip-
pers and a large Martini, but *au fond* he is another man who needs
to re-sharpen his wits from time to time and finds his wife a ready
sponsor for such an enterprise.

They are one in affection for their ten-year-old son, Caspar,
less at one perhaps, in their hopes for this young man, for Ann
Fleming believes that the highest destiny for any Englishman is
to be Prime Minister, while it is certain that Fleming would settle

for a lesser, and perhaps more permanent, career. Whatever bent the boy does eventually follow, lucre need not be his primary ambition, for he is the unknowing recipient of much of Fleming's income from the Bond books.

At this time the Flemings have completed another house in a fairly remote part of Oxfordshire. This new house has been added to the remains of a seventeenth-century house built by the side of a woodland lake of considerable bucolic charm. Here, the tale goes, Fleming will find the restful background he needs for writing his books, but others suspect that in truth he loathes the quiet sequestered life in England and prefers his present split-level life between London, various golf courses and the Caribbean.

Fleming does a good deal of his more ephemeral writing in a small office in Mitre Court, off Fleet Street, a courtway set among the chambers of barristers and the offices of journalists. There, for three or four days a week, he keeps more or less regular hours and copes with an avalanche of demands for his views of Life and Luv, revolvers and flick-knives, food and drink, travel and adventure. Here, too, he sees agents, interviewers, and a growing tribe of film men. But his books are written in Jamaica.

He bought his Jamaican property in 1946 inspired by two war-time weeks conniving with the US Office of Naval Intelligence to counter the U-boat offensive in the Caribbean. All those who have a dream house in mind yet cannot draw should take heart from Fleming's enterprise, for although he cannot draw a line, he designed his own house. And the house is the most practically and pleasant house any traveller could hope to find at a tropical journey's end.

Here, for two months every year – January and February – Fleming is at his mellow best. The transplanted Englishman becomes a genial Caribbean squire. Here his yearnings towards a more exuberant wardrobe are given scope by recourse to an occasional shirt. For the rest it is life in shorts and sandals.

To his resident Caribbean housekeeper, Violet, every word of the master's is both law and benediction. Every culinary whim must be indulged. Every possible comfort quadrupled. Here he works, with a fierce intensity, as he is one of those men who would rather work as a galley slave for two months than be a 10–6 serf for eleven. And here the Bond books are written. 'I've got this bloody man Bond halfway up a cliff and must leave him there overnight if I'm to answer your letter. Well, here goes…'

Here too, he swims for long hours above and between the reefs which ring his private beach. Once upon a recent time he was a keen underwater swimmer, but now, less adventurous, he peers at the nearer denizens, floating away the afternoon, dreaming up, for the pleasure of President and policeman, professor and popsy, yet more improbable situations for superman Bond to love in or escape from, all of which, according to rumour, will be translated into more languages than exist.

Re-reading that long-ago *Vogue* piece, which vastly amused the two subjects documented, my words seemed to offer a fairly authentic view of a pair I had come to know so well. The only omission – deliberate – was any reference to the gradual dissolution of their early passion into their tragically querulous relationship. Fleming thanked me wholeheartedly for what he termed 'the most smoothly egoistic experience for its subject(s) with, above all, not even a shadowy reference to the couple's marital problems, evasions, ambitions, dreams.'

I saw little of Fleming following the publication of the *Vogue* pieces. He was to spend his final escape to Jamaica gamely setting about writing *The Man with the Golden Gun*. On his return to London he was involved with the increasing financial problems attending his growing fame. Even more doleful was his health, which accorded a brief stay in hospital in London and nursing care in Hove. His mother was hospitalised nearby in Brighton, but Fleming was in no fit state to see her. She died in late July. Fleming returned to London and thought we should meet again.

We arranged to meet, as usual, at the Etoile the following Friday. To my surprise, he said he would be spending the weekend in Kent and visiting his favourite golfing club, St George's, as he had been promised its imminent captaincy.

But the weekend was not to prove so beneficent for Fleming et al.

CHAPTER 29

FAREWELLS TOO SOON

Following an early morning call from Ann that Friday morning, however, the plan was changed: 'Ian's not feeling 100 per cent,' she said. Would I come to Victoria Square instead? She would cancel the Etoile on our behalf.

I crossed from Victoria station to the tucked-away square. Ann let me in. 'Ian's upstairs,' she whispered. 'He really is under the weather this time.'

He was in the upper sitting room, mixing himself one of his odious-looking concoctions. He was, indeed, looking fairly groggy. Little wonder, I thought, with that intimidating mix for refreshment.

'Doctor's orders?' I asked, pointing to his glass. 'Or one of your own medicinal swigs?'

'The latter. Much against the quack's advice: "Lay off or lie down and die!"'

'What was your reply to that query?' I queried.

'I pointed out that death before thirty leaves a lot undone for most of us, but death after fifty gives anyone a reasonable break.'

'Any other philosophical gems suitable for a medico?'

'I admitted that my time was probably nearly up, but I'd passed fifty, anyway.'

'You ought to collect these gloom-ridden gems. Perfect for Christmas crackers. Anyway, how are you?'

'I'm roughly what you see. Draw your own conclusions. How's *House & Patio* doing?'

'Apparently quite well.'

'I hope they're keeping a generous eye on your monetary rewards.'

'No grumbles.'

'Isn't this your afternoon in Vogue House *and* all tomorrow in Gray's Inn Road? What a busy life you do lead. Give anyone you meet – Harry Evans, Frank Giles and so on – my salutations.'

I said I would.

'But why do you go on going to the damn place? You don't need the money. Why this dedication to *The Times*?'

'I find the whole thing an entertainment. As simple as that. I'm lucky. All my working life, frankly, is pleasurable.'

'What does Phoebe say?'

'On Saturdays she usually drives up for supper. I usually give her a choice of where. But this week she's away with the family.'

'Where d'you take her for these well-earned suppers?'

'She has a free choice for dining anywhere she wishes. A fair equation, I think. So does she. She likes the Savoy Grill Room in winter or an Italian outdoor joint in Chelsea she's recently discovered for summer evenings.'

'Very heart-warming. But the whole thing still puzzles me. Why d'you go on?'

'As I said. Sheer self-indulgence. I like working on the glossy in the week and I like working with Harry on his news pages at weekends. It really is as simple and seemingly as unbelievable as that.'

He nodded and pointed to the drinks tray on the table. 'Pour yourself whatever you want.'

'I see only lethal liquids here.'

'We've run out of our homemade lemonade as usual,' he said, with sardonic glee, as we slipped into our normal exchanges.

Ann came into the room. 'Lunch in ten minutes!' she advised and crossed to the sofa.

We began to talk about recent holidays. She had been in the Med and had experienced her first trip in a hydrofoil. 'One of those motor-boats that gets up on its crutches and goes like the wind,' she said. Had I tried one? Indeed I had. We had crossed from Ostia to Giglio earlier in the year in such a craft.

I turned to Fleming. Had he been in one?

'There's one in my last novel!' he barked. 'You have to have been in one to cite one in a novel. You've both had free copies. Duly signed by the author. Clearly neither of you has taken time off to read the damn thing!'

Neither culprit had a word in self-defence from the justified rebuke. I sought desperately to switch the subject by mentioning that my family was currently holidaying more conventionally in the Isle of Wight and that I would be joining them extremely late on the morrow, followed by Sunday and Monday off.

Not the best of conversational openings before descending, as we soon did – rather gloomily – to the dining room. Fleming's descent was decidedly hesitant. He would soon need to have a ground-floor bedroom, I decided. Certainly the stairways and spaces of Seven-hampton must present problems, unless they had given the mansion a bungalow touch.

The meal was a subdued affair. I doubted whether the room had ever accommodated so subdued a trio. Certainly no *Book Collector* luncheon or any of Ann's supper parties had engendered such gloom.

As if by threesome-consent, the meal was over quickly; far from one of those extended Etoile affairs with gossip edging farewells towards three o'clock and beyond. To add an authenticity to this speedy repast, Ann claimed that she was in a hurry. I spuriously shared her intentions, contending that I needed to get back to Vogue House to clear my desk before going off to Thomson House.

'Where are you off to?' I asked Ann in the hallway. 'Shall I grab a taxi?'

'No, no need. A brief walk. I'll tell you later. Are you game for a trek across the park?'

'Delighted.'

We left Fleming essaying an alpine climb to his bedroom. 'Forty winks before pushing off to St Margaret's Bay. Not in the same league as one of brother Peter's trans-Siberian jaunts, but quite enough for me these days. See you soon!' he called faintly.

Outside, in the square, as if staging a somewhat deliberate afterthought, Ann said she'd forgotten something. She returned to the house and reappeared after a couple of minutes with a manila-toned paper-wrapper around what was clearly a frame, corner showing.

'Sorry to have kept you waiting,' she said as we turned into Buckingham Palace Road. 'I had to go back. Rather a secret move. We had a bit of a fracas at breakfast. Fierce and fearsome. I even wondered whether Ian would consider driving down to the coast. He's now grudgingly agreed.'

She sounded excessively deflated.

'So you're off to St Margaret's Bay?'

'Caspar's there, complete with nanny,' she said. 'Otherwise I daresay we would have been en route to Sevenhampton, despite Ian's dislike of the place – as you well know.'

I thought a change of subject was needed. 'What's in the frame?' I asked as we crossed towards Green Park, taking our chance between the lines of traffic zooming around the palace.

'Ian's bought what he's been told is a Lely portrait. I'm no expert but I'm sure it's not.'

'Is it one of his admirals?'

'Did Lely paint admirals, then? This is a woman, anyway.'

'I imagine all Lely's admirals are at Greenwich. Fabulous.'

'This certainly isn't. Ian gets outwitted in these matters.'

'Is it so important to have official verification if he's happy with his bargain? Perhaps he's recalled Waugh's waggish remark and is considering setting up as a collector. Why are you so keen to verify? Where are you off to – Spink's?'

'No, there's that dealer woman in the courtyard just by Lock's the hatters.'

'But she's German. I doubt that she's an expert on English seventeenth-century portraits. Why not try Spink's or Christie's?'

'I'm not in a big-time arty mood today.'

'I've only been in the place you're aiming for a couple of times but I'd say your prospect's mildly unlikely.'

We turned from St James's Street into the courtyard and crossed to the dusty, claustrophobic salesroom-cum-showroom, crowded with frames, drawings, paintings, sketches.

Ann explained her purpose to the dealer, who was clearly rather nonplussed and far from keen to express any professional opinion when presented with Ann's problem oil. She haltingly explained that English art of that period was not her forte, although she was prepared to suggest, from the few examples she had seen of Lely's work, that this example was not one of his supreme efforts. I thought she had done extremely well in a tiresome and tricky situation. She added that she thought a specialist in that period should be consulted. Ann nodded and agreed that she would do that.

Yet I sensed that the tentative advisor had done well enough for Ann's purpose, whatever that was, for she speedily enwrapped the painting within the paper covering, gave thanks, bade farewell and walked out. No hint of payment for this welcome if halting advisory interval.

Outside, I suggested wandering round to Spink's or Christie's? Both quite handy. 'Either might well give you an authoritative on-the-spot appraisal.'

But Ann had clearly achieved her purpose. I sensed that following the matrimonial skirmish of the morning, she now had a counter-blow for the evening.

We walked slowly up St James's Street towards Piccadilly. There we parted: she, presumably, by taxi back to Victoria Square, myself towards Bond Street and Hanover Square.

I never heard the rest of the story. That was Friday. On Saturday evening I took the train to Portsmouth to cross to Ryde. I returned on the Tuesday morning after a restful, familial weekend.

I was lunching at Scott's that day with Everett Jones, more generally known as EJ, head of the advertising agency he had founded with Lord Delamere, to which I had, once upon not too distant a time, acted as a consultant design director – the title that Fleming had queried so mercilessly.

On leaving the restaurant we both – in the same split second – saw an *Evening Standard* newsbill on the corner of Piccadilly Circus: BOND AUTHOR DIES.

I was shaken, but not shocked, possibly not even surprised. Fleming had looked so near the end on the previous Friday.

'Isn't that your friend?' Everett Jones asked. I nodded. 'Were you expecting anything like that?'

'I fear I was.'

'Won't his death be a terrible loss to the world's belligerent teenagers?'

'From teens to dotage.'

EJ laughed. We crossed the circus and parted. I wandered back along Regent Street towards Hanover Square, slowly taking in this gloom-ridden finality.

My solitary brooding was halted within the hour by a telephone call from Leonard Russell, literary editor of the *Sunday Times*. What time would I be in on Friday? About four o'clock. Why? The paper was devoting a four-page section to Fleming. The main feature in the inset would be an obit. 'Harry wants you to do that. He wants a piece that would have amused Ian, he says. Something similar to the piece you wrote for *Vogue*, which I've just got up from the library and been rereading. But this time Harry wants the emphasis on Bond. About 3,000 words, but feel free. Can I rely on getting copy by Thursday morning?'

'You can!'

Here follows that piece as it was published in the *Sunday Times*: inevitably somewhat repetitious perhaps of sections in the *Vogue* piece. My apologies in advance for seeking to keep the record straight.

The heading was set in large capitals across the eight columns of the page:

AN UNWRITTEN CHAPTER IN THE LIFE OF IAN FLEMING

Where Bond began

When he was appointed, on the recommendation of Sir Maurice (later Lord Hankey), as personal assistant to the director of naval intelligence some months before the opening of the Second World War, Ian Fleming took on a curious job which, his friends decided, was highly inappropriate to his true talents and would drive him mad on several counts within a month.

For one thing, he had been trained as a soldier at Sandhurst and then decided he didn't like soldiering. So what chance did an admiral stand of making him a sailor? For another thing, his passions were land-based: fast cars, golf and looking at the sea, certainly not small boats sailing upended on the sea. Yet another snag was that the job would mean being polite to the pompous and kind to the crass, and here again, Fleming was ill equipped by character or inclination for such dedication to the state. Finally, the job was chair-borne and would demand administrative talents of a tall order, whereas it was well known to one and all that Fleming was a man of restless physical energy and hates anything in triplicate – except a large Martini.

To the surprise of many, and to the utter perplexity of his friends,

Fleming took these demands in his stride, meeting them ably and equably, no matter if, as he said, he suffered from corns on his backside from sitting in his corner chair by one of the large windows of that legendary room through which all the navy's secrets had passed in the First World War and were to pass again in the second. He also suffered fools and others bravely, if briefly, and made himself into a merciless and efficient administrator.

The job frequently irked but ceaselessly fascinated him. He thoroughly enjoyed being at the heart of the matter in that large ungracious room with its high windows and enormous centre table, dominated by trays of that day's signals, dockets, appreciations, top-secret papers, and the rest, all chaotically yet efficiently neat, the half-dozen RN captains, commanders and barristers-turned RNVR lieutenants who sifted and diagnosed the piles of imperative paper.

Fleming had developed a talent for spare and simple prose which made memo-drafting for his admiral no great chore. And he liked the men, regular RN and others, he worked with. And they liked him; his gaiety, equanimity and worldliness.

Above all, he was fortunate in working for and with someone he respected and liked: the then Rear Admiral John Godfrey, a formidable man indeed, one of the least-known yet remarkable high-ranking officers of the war, a tall, broad-shouldered, quiet voiced authoritarian. With steely eyes and the manner of a relentless advocate rather than that of a sea captain, although he was known as one of the navy's foremost navigators. Like some others of his frowning mien, the admiral could assume a demoniacal relenting smile at the end of a grilling that could make a strong man wet in the palms and weak in the bowels. But, in the admiral, Ian found a larger-than-life sized match for his own impatient, restless ways, for his new chief was as unconventional as Royal Navy admirals are, historically, apt to be. In no time at all after his appointment to a job that was often spurned as a dead end by good old sea dogs, the admiral had recruited barristers and dons, journalists and graphic designers, geologists and geographers, into naval intelligence, had given them specific jobs to do, alongside RN hydrographers and Royal Marine majors and then demanded ante-dated results.

Fleming was the admiral's link with an appalling range of activities inseparable from modern war: from the cracking of codes to the practice of deception, from the preparation of topographical documentaries on the areas we had been driven from and would return to, we hoped, to the interrogation of suspected enemy agents and the training of our own. He had to keep an eye on these multifarious aspects of naval intelligence and report frequently to his always-demanding admiral.

Somewhere along the line I came into the strange new world after sea service in the North Atlantic. Fleming shed what I then mistakenly thought were a few dry and dutiful crocodile tears over his own lack of sea service and sent me off to a job that kept me absorbed and world-travelled for most of the rest of the war – until France. Fleming was at that time, I sometimes think, his own brand-image for the later Bond. Years afterwards I suggested to him that most middle-aged men see themselves always as somewhere between twenty-eight and thirty-two. He grinned and said: 'Touché!'

Fleming, then in his early thirties, was well equipped to play the celluloid Bond as Connery was to be twenty years on. He had a sad, bony, fateful face, strong-featured and with very clear blue eyes. He was something over 6ft tall, moved easily and with purpose. He should, I thought, have been like other RNVR lieutenant commanders on the bridge of a Hunt class destroyer or an MTB. Instead, he was always sending other men to be sent off, or causing other men to be sent off, to distant places with exciting and dangerous jobs to do.

Meanwhile, with the exception of an observer's role in a warship on the Dieppe raid, he had to stay put at the admiralty, apart from journeys with Admiral Godfrey to Washington and other top-brass centres. It was galling to him, of course, but fascinating and, as someone near and dear to him once said, Fleming could suffer anything but discomfort.

He had much to do on his own responsibility, keeping detail off the admiral's overflowing plate, for at that time Hitler seemed to be winning the war, and one of the apparent wins was in Crete, late in May 1941.

In that battle, which only now is to be seen as the first of the great German over-reaching exercises, part of their intimidating initial success derived from the swift penetration of our forward HQs by an operation intelligence unit, moving with the advance fighting troops. The sole job of this unit had been to seize our ciphers, evaluation of its probable worth and/or novelty before shipping the stuff itself back to Germany for expert examination and appraisal. Although we had started late in the war, the Germans recognised us as inventive types who could learn fast. And they weren't above learning oddments from learners.

Number Thirty Assault Unit, or 30AU, was the title of the outfit that began to operate tentatively in the Middle East, working with the 8th Army and under the dual command of Quintin Riley, a pre-war polar explorer, and Dunstan Curtis, a one-time trainee for the legal life with a DSC from St Nazaire. Both were lieutenants (later commanders) RNVR and the ideal of dual command wasn't as dotty as it sounds, for the unit of ten had to split up and work in areas far apart.

The unit operated with increasing success in north Africa, Sicily and Italy, until even their lordships, slow to accept shore-based novelties in their nautical lives, began to appreciate the intelligence concerning the enemy's technical know-how that began to flow back from the unit – which, despite occasional casualties was enjoying itself. The English take to life in such units with alarming ease. An inbred island fondness for piracy and a basic dislike of discipline in large doses does make such private armies and navies popular. All wars should be fought solely with such miniature forces, as Robert Graves once suggested.

Then came preparations for Operation Overlord. The unit was brought back to England and came within Fleming's close-range orbit. I had just come back from a long and mostly solitary journey for NID in the Far East, and after I had made my report, Fleming suggested that I should join the unit: 'My cowboys and red indians' as he called them. I said yes in the split second before he could think of another solitary trip. I was in.

By now, Fleming was PA to a new DNI: Rear Admiral Rush-brooke, a tall, shy, serious-minded, academic-seeming officer, very different from Godfrey. I think that the new DNI occasionally wondered what kind of outfit he had inherited in 30AU. Certainly he saw us in training, which was more than Admiral Godfrey had been able to do. Rushbrooke came down to Littlehampton with Major-General Hollis of the Royal Marines to inspect the unit preparing for its supposed work, a far more strenuous occupation than warfare itself. Fleming was unobtrusively in the background, casting a wary and threatening eye over the brigands he had more or less created.

30AU by that time had a reasonable reputation for results only mildly tarnished by its sometimes unconventional methods of getting them. For the new and enlarged unit, the DNI, via Fleming, had introduced two wings, RN and RM, the former to gain information, the latter to do any required fighting. The Royal Marines were a curious band of young commandos, and I came to know some of them extremely well. They were merry, coura-geous, amoral, loyal, lying toughs, hugely disinclined to take no for an answer from foe or *fraulein*. Fleming always enjoyed anec-dotes concerning their wayward ways.

So D-Day came and the unit began its operations, a fierce and urgent request for advanced German weapons and know-how, particularly in U-boat construction, torpedo performance and electronic devices. Heavy casualties were suffered in the early landings, but the unit very soon began to show results, and appreciative signals from the First Sea Lord were passed on by Fleming from the admiralty.

Coincident with its main job of operational intelligence, the unit had its moments of martial glory. One RNVR officer captured 300 German officers and men and their radar station with the aid of half-a-dozen men and a genial genius for suggesting, in halting German, that the whole fortified emplacement was surrounded by far heavier guns. Another, one of the most dedicated among the officers, a US liaison appointee, entering the U-boat pens at Cherbourg in an eager search for knowledge, was shot through his open mouth. This mishap caused little damage to his face but grave damage to his reputation as a tight-lipped man of US action. But the main task, the seizure of equipment and information, went on steadily and apparently successfully.

A major headache for Fleming was the remote control of this highly mobile, individual unit which he had fondly thought would be so near to hand once back in Europe. Yet his signals were patient and long-suffering, and as the officers and men were continuously passing to and fro across the channel with captured equipment and documents, he was also able to send long and explanatory, expostulatory, occasionally explosive letters to his minions. His was a nightmare task on occasions.

He had a dozen roving splinter groups to guide and drive him mad, for all our movements were controlled in a high degree from the admiralty. He gave precise orders for what we should look for and where we might seek and find, from homing torpedoes to the results of German jet experiments.

Occasionally he came across the channel to see us, and it was one of these occasions after we had visited General Patton's HQ to ask some special favour or other, that I asked him, over road-side K rations, what he would do after the war. 'Write the spy story to end all spy stories,' he had said. I almost choked on my Spam.

Inevitably the early success of 30AU meant further enlarge-ment, and the unit was ultimately incorporated in the much larger so-called T-force under SHAEF and General Eisenhower. 30AU was never the same again. Within a month it became a bureau-cratic takeover victim.

Naturally, in its lifetime 30AU had recruited some unusual citi-zens, and some of their oddities brushed off on Bond and the rest of the Fleming *oeuvre*. There was the only man wholly without nerves I have ever known whose idea of an evening's enjoyment was to spend the night in a Jeep with a couple of marine commandos in the middle of no man's land. There was the GC, GM bomb dis-posal ace who confessed to complete ignorance of all mechanisms, proved by his helplessness when his Jeep broke down. Then the naval diver who invariably timed his reappearance from inspect-ing a sunken U-boat off Toulon so that he could be back on the dot for the Cognac his current *mademoiselle* had ready for him.

They had all brought colour (and fury) into Fleming's life and he, the most generous, least malicious, most merry yet most mel-ancholy man I ever knew, in turn brought colour (and occasional fury) into the lives of countless others.

A month after his death, a memorial service was held in St Bartholomew the Great, the twelfth-century, much restored, foundation in Smithfield. At Ann's request, I had designed an eight-page in memoriam printed by the Westerham Press. Peter Fleming read the lesson and from the organ gallery, Amaryllis rendered J. S. Bach's 'Sarabande in C Minor' on her cello. Then, following the anthem, 'Thou knowest Lord, the secret of our hearts', came a memorable farewell tribute by William Plomer to 'a man of such varied gifts and high spirits who didn't suffer fools gladly but whose appetite for life, curiosity, quick understanding and admiration of what was well done used generally to bring out the best in other people. We miss him and we shall go on missing him.'

Later, Ann asked me to suggest a format for a reprint of Plomer's address, which should certainly find a place in any anthology of farewells. I still have my copy of that sombre black cloth-bound farewell, again printed by the Westerham Press.

A decade or so later I had another lugubrious obit request. I had kept in touch with Dunstan Curtis, both in Paris and later in London. His death was sudden and unexpected. A major section of the obituary published by *The Times* on Dunstan's death came from me. I never learned who wrote the rest. At this date, I can detect no obvious joins in the sub-editor's final version, published under the matter-of-fact heading, somewhat different from Leonard Russell's gaudier heading for the Fleming obit in the *Sunday Times*.

DUNSTAN CURTIS

Wartime service and European movement

Mr Dunstan Curtis, CBE, DSC, who died on September 9 at the age of seventy-three, had a distinguished career as an RNVR officer during the Second World War, during which, among many other services, he played a notable role as commanding officer of the Motor Gun Boat from which the St Nazaire raid was directed by the naval force commander, Commander R. E. D. Ryder. After the war, Curtis was an early and devoted personality in the European Movement and was a deputy secretary-general of the Council of Europe from 1954 to 1960.

Educated at Eton and Trinity College, Oxford, Curtis, an excellent linguist, qualified as a solicitor and worked for a time as business manager and legal advisor to the French theatrical director Michel St Denis, in the latter's London enterprises, and when war broke out, joined the RNVR. He became commanding officer of an MGB with coastal forces and was involved in the landing of British agents on the coast of occupied Europe.

When the operation to destroy the great dry dock at St Nazaire was conceived, with the aim of denying it as an Atlantic base to the battleship *Tirpitz*, Commander Ryder chose Curtis to command the MGB from which Ryder was to direct the naval forces during the operation. After HMS *Cambeltown*, commanded by Lieutenant Commander Beattie, had successfully rammed the all-important lock gate with her cargo of explosive, Curtis had put his MGB alongside the Old Mole and landed the ground forces' commander, Lieutenant Colonel A. C. Newman.

After hot work ashore and when he was convinced that no further good could be achieved by their remaining alongside any longer, Ryder ordered Curtis to put to sea and make good their escape with survivors. For this part in the operation Curtis was awarded the DSC. Shortly afterwards he broadcast an account of the raid in French for the BBC.

Later in the war, Curtis was recruited by Ian Fleming, then assistant to the director of naval intelligence to command the naval wing of Number Thirty Assault Unit, an operational assault force which was highly successful in the north African and Sicilian campaign. This unit was reformed to take part in the Allied campaign in France from D-Day onwards and Curtis gained a Bar to his DSC as well as the *Croix de Guerre* from these operations and was promoted Commander.

His knowledge of German, which had been of great service during the St Nazaire raids during the last moments in which the attacking force had tried to bluff the Germans by signals that they were a friendly force returning to base, was put to its final wartime use when he accepted the surrender of the German naval base at Kiel with only a Jeepful of marines, after a spirited argument on the telephone with Grand Admiral Dönitz.

After the war he was briefly assistant press attaché at the British embassy in Paris until he was taken from there to mastermind, with others, the establishment of the Council of Europe.

From the beginnings of the council, he effectively organised the committees of the parliamentary assembly until 1954 when he became a deputy secretary-general. His administrative skills and genial personality predicted that he would become secretary-general. But by 1960 the mood within the European movement was towards ensuring for the future that the office of secretary-general should be a political appointment.

Curtis left Strasbourg to pursue other activities, but always with European association, among which was practise as a partner in a leading firm of London solicitors in its Paris office. If the 1960s increased his dismay at the slowness of progress towards European unity and unhappiness at Britain's lack of enthusiasm for the common market, he never gave up the cause, which some of his contemporaries regarded as a form of Eurofanaticism.

But British entry into the common market in 1972 and the starting up of a Conservative group in the European Parliament provided Curtis with his Indian summer. Appointed as secretary-general of the group, his experience and knowledge of the European scene, together with his administrative ability, proved invaluable. Curtis was in his element in this new venture in European politics.

He was twice married, first, to Monica Forbes, by whom he had a son and daughter, and secondly to Patricia Elton Mayo, the sociologist.

Ann lived until 1981, unhappily and convinced that the fates were determinedly against her, following the early death of her husband and then the suicide of Caspar, their son, at the age of twenty-three. She ended her days in a set in Albany. A service of thanksgiving for her life was held at St James's in Piccadilly, her rarely visited local church. I had seen a little of her in the intervening years, but kept abreast of the vagaries of her life via Mark Boxer, with whom I worked at Condé Nast during his editorship of *Tatler*. He had become a close friend of hers in that final decade or so.

The service at St James's was enriched by the choice, by Amaryllis, of the prelude, sarabande and gigue from Bach's 'Cello Suite No. 3 in C'. John Sparrow read the lesson from Isiah and Patrick Leigh-Fermor read from Cicero's *De Amicitia*. Lord Annan gave the address.

Hudson died a year or so later. I had continued to think of him as a member of the younger generation; but younger generations are apt to age rather more swiftly than their elders assume. A year or so after the war's end, he tracked me down to our mill house in Suffolk and explained, to my great surprise, that he had married, adding, rather sheepishly, that his wife was a good deal older than himself. As if in self-mitigation for such a lapse, he admitted that she had brought to their marriage 'a houseful of furniture', which had saved him a pretty packet. I saw him at odd intervals after that. His marriage broke up. He married again and became a successful rep for a wholesale confectionary outfit. From time to time, he called on us in our later home on the Surrey–Kent border. He seemed booked for a ripe old age. Then, one morning, his daughter from his first marriage telephoned to say that her father, in his mid-fifties, had died suddenly from a heart attack.

I retain warm and enduring memories of these three men and their vastly different backgrounds and personalities. Friendship with all three continued in peace until their deaths, far too soon. I also append appreciation of a warm friendship with Ann, a rare and courageous woman in this man-run world.

INDEX